My River of Sorrow

A WIDOW'S JOURNEY WITH GOD

Kristina Carson Lunde

KL Press

My River of Sorrow: A Widow's Journey with God

www.kristinalunde.com

KL Press

Cover image by Sergey Peterman/2014 Bigstock
Cover design by Erin Nausin
Book Layout ©2013 BookDesignTemplates.com

My River of Sorrow: A Widow's Journey with God/
Kristina Carson Lunde. —1st ed.
ISBN 978-0-9903013-1-8
Printed in the USA

Dedication

Dearest Claire and Bennett,

This account is my memorial stone (Joshua 4:4–7) from the deep riverbed of our sorrow. I pray that you will always remember that Daddy loved us and God carried us.

"He did this so that all the peoples of the earth might know that the hand of the Lord is powerful and so that you might always fear the Lord your God." Joshua 4:24.

All my love,

Mom

Contents

[1]

Last Supper

"I HAVEN'T FELT GOOD all day." Lee's even comment included a slight scrunch of his nose, a subtle look that I recognized as negative. Albeit subdued, the look was to Lee what a scowl would be on a dramatic person. For my understated, no-nonsense husband, this merest of expressions was one of many I had learned to decode in our almost twenty-one years together.

Our nightly routine, lamented as rare compared to current family practices, involved the four of us—Claire, Bennett, Lee, and me—sitting down at the dinner table together. Participating in our usual activity, we played the "best-worst," as we called our dinner game. Each person took a turn describing the best and worst aspects of the day. The kids had each played, and now Daddy was describing his day. I knew that he did not feel good, because he did not eat.

Turning down food was very unlike Lee, but I thought he would change his mind after he sat with us.

"I just don't feel right . . ." Lee complained softly.

"Well, you felt great this morning!" I interrupted with a big smile. The love of my life gave me a knowing grin. After close to nineteen years of marriage, the shared intimacy was a precious part of our lives together, and that morning had been an incredible time of marital connection.

Lee's eyes sparkled with acknowledgment as he went on to play our dinner game. "Okay, well other than that . . . I have been tired all day. That is my worst. My best was going bike shopping today. I think I found the bike I want to buy."

Lee and I continued our conversation about the bicycle he was considering. With our youngest child in school full time, Lee had added swimming to his daily workouts. His new goal was to buy a carbon-frame bicycle to replace his steel-frame 1980s version. I wondered if he was thinking about returning to triathlons, a sport he had stopped competing in after we had children. Earlier that day, I found the brochure Lee brought home from his bicycle shop outing. Tour de France champion Lance Armstrong was pictured on the cover, arms outstretched in victory. I had grabbed a marker and drew in a mustache to match Lee's.

"I saw what you did to Lance on the bike brochure," Lee laughed.

Our bike talk was soon interrupted by the resident clown at our table. Six-year-old Bennett had shoved frozen green beans onto his eye teeth and gleefully displayed his icy fangs. Bennett's thick, blonde hair fringed back and forth as he shook his head in attention-getting silliness. Claire joined in, laughing with her wide smile as she mimicked Bennett's side-to-side head movements. Lee and I exchanged one of our *we-really-shouldn't-laugh* looks, but then we promptly cracked up.

Frozen green beans were not some weird form of punishment; they were one of very few vegetables Bennett ate. Most kids will eat frozen peas, but not my kids. How we came upon frozen green beans is a mystery to me. It probably started when I said, "No, frozen green beans won't taste good, but you can have frozen peas." Ergo, my child likely calculated, defy Mommy and avoid the food she wants me to eat. Now, to keep the ruse going, I made a fuss, as if only a cruel mother would give him beans that were not cooked.

Often, Bennett was so funny that Lee and I had to leave the room, or our son would have had his poor manners reinforced by parental laughter. Someday I would love to compare dinnertime stories with a comedian's mother and ask her my questions. How do you avoid reinforcing lousy manners when the kid is so funny? How do these kids develop a sense of comedic timing at such a young age? What do you do when you are frustrated with your kid, but he really *is* engaging and hilarious? And what do you say at parent-teacher conferences when those comedic talents are not beneficial to classroom dynamics?!

As I always told Lee about our family dinnertimes, "This is a fifteen-year training program and we will not reap the benefits." Small consolation for the regular viewing and cleaning up of partially masticated food that occupied so much of my time and energy.

After dinner, the kids ran off to play in their rooms. As I strode toward the study where we kept our computer, Lee called after me, "I'm going to go lie down."

"Are you okay?" I turned to ask, thinking it strange that Lee had not eaten dinner.

"Yeah. I'm just tired. I have to lie down." His voice reflected his exhaustion, but his ever-bronze skin color showed no sign of pallor. Since this was his second day off after a two-day work trip, by which time he would usually be rested up, I thought he might be getting sick.

I checked on him around eight p.m. when I put the kids to bed. On the dresser next to Lee's bed, I noticed a get well card Bennett had made for him. So *that* was what had kept Bennett occupied for the hour since dinnertime.

"Did you see this?" I asked Lee.

"Yes." His voice, soft and fatigued, came out whispery, accompanied by a tired smile.

"Isn't that sweet?"

"Yes, that was nice," Lee concurred in a near whisper. He continued with a bit more volume, "Are you okay putting the kids to bed by yourself, Sweetie? I am so tired; I just want to sleep."

"Sure that's fine. Are you okay? Do you need anything?" I kissed him on the cheek as he shook his head no. "Call me if you need anything," I said as I walked out the bedroom door.

On a school night, our first and third graders went to bed by 8:30 p.m. Complimenting Bennett on his get well card, I led their usual drill of teeth brushing, pajamas, prayers, and hugs. Afterwards I went downstairs to the computer.

As a typical 1980s suburban tract home, our house had little, if any, insulation to buffer sounds between the floors and walls. So when I heard a fast run across the room above me an hour later, I knew Lee must be sick. I galloped up the stairs to help him, but he had already made it to the bathroom on his own. As he began alternately sitting on the toilet with diarrhea and then turning around to throw up into it, I tried to help him navigate. Having finally finished several of these projectile episodes, he trudged back to bed.

"What do you think this is?" Lee asked miserably. I tried to help him walk, but he would have none of it.

Thank the Lord this isn't as bad as when he had food poisoning in Cabo, I thought to myself as I recalled Lee's illness that followed our successful quest for ceviche, a marinated salad of raw seafood, in Cabo San Lucas, Mexico. Out loud, I asked him a series of questions, "What did you eat for lunch? Did you have diarrhea earlier or did this just start? Do you feel better after throwing up?"

Lee crawled back into bed, answering my questions one grunt at a time. "I feel better now. I just want to sleep."

When I snuck up later with a "puke bucket," he murmured, "Thank you, Sweetie."

"You rest," I urged him, "and call me if you need me."

I went back downstairs to the computer once more. Another hour later I was jolted from my activity when I again heard footsteps racing to the bathroom. I worriedly ran up the steps and helped Lee into the bathroom. This time he used both bucket and stool at once.

"What *is* this?" Lee moaned.

"I don't know." I responded sympathetically. "It could be food poisoning or maybe you caught the flu on your last trip."

"I feel so awful. . . ." Lee continued weakly.

"Oh Lee, I know. I wish I could do something to help you feel better." I felt Lee's forehead, but he did not feel feverish. He was weak and sweaty. All I could do was pray the cry of my heart out loud, "Dear Jesus, please heal him!"

Lee leaned his head against my thigh as I held the bucket for him. I ran my fingers through his thick brown hair, trying to keep the concern out of my voice as I tenderly whispered, "I love you, Lee."

"I love you, Sweetie," he answered in a thin, exhausted voice.

"Are you sure you're done?" I asked as Lee stood and made his way back to bed. At this point he did not want me to help him, so instead of reaching for his arm, I walked next to him, ready to grab him if he wobbled. Lee was an independent man who did not often accept help, certainly not when it was unnecessary. So I respected his determination, even as I realized that he was really sick.

Tucking Lee into bed, I began to ask more questions: "Do you have any pain? Do you feel better after throwing up? Does your arm hurt? Your jaw? Is there pressure anywhere?" As a former cardiac nurse, I automatically began asking the heart-related questions. I wondered to myself why I would ask these questions when everything seemed gastrointestinal in origin, yet I still gave him a cardiac interrogation.

"It does hurt here," Lee admitted, pointing to the center of his upper abdomen, "but it is better after throwing up."

"Do you want me to call an ambulance?" I asked. Even as the words came out, I was surprised at my question. Lee did not seem that sick.

"No, of course not," Lee answered in irritation.

"Okay, but you're going to the doctor tomorrow," I retorted, anticipating resistance.

Sure enough, Lee responded with, "We'll see."

Over the years, I had learned that in the Carson family, a "We'll see" answer meant "No, and I do not want to discuss the situation anymore." I resolved to take Lee to a doctor the next day despite the inevitable refusal.

"Can't you give me anything for this?" Lee pleaded. I found some bismuth tablets for upset stomach, noting that my giant bottle of calcium antacid tablets were already on his dresser. He must have tried those earlier.

"You really should not have anything more on that upset stomach, because it will only make you throw up again," I cautioned. "Are you having pain now?"

"It's better," Lee answered as he rolled over. "I just want to sleep."

"I'll be downstairs. Call me if you need me," I urged, knowing that it was up to me to listen and notice if Lee got up. I knew that he would not want to bother me for help.

Sometime later I walked upstairs to go to bed. Lee was not sleeping but said he did not feel like throwing up anymore.

"Are you okay?" I asked, wondering what I could do for him.

"I just can't get comfortable," he replied, twisting around in the bed and trying to get settled.

"Do you need anything?"

"No."

"Do you mind if I go to sleep?" I asked wearily.

"Go ahead. Get some rest," Lee encouraged me.

"Will you wake me if you need me?" I pleaded, knowing that he would avoid waking me even if he needed help. He was not sweating as much as earlier. Lee seemed restless, but not as miserable, ever since he had stopped vomiting.

"There's nothing you can do. Just get some sleep."

Feeling guilty, I nevertheless gave in to exhaustion and fell asleep.

[2]

Lee's Early Years

TRUE TO LEE Carson's predictable nature, he was born exactly on his due date, March 3, 1959. He was the firstborn son of Bob and Lois Carson, who met while they were in the Air Force. Both lieutenants, Lois was a nurse and Bob an engineer at Ellington Air Force Base (AFB) in Texas. In 1956, Bob finished his master's degree in electrical engineering at Northwestern University. He and Lois married that fall and started their lives together in Bob's hometown of Chicago, Illinois.

When Lee was just six months old, the family set out for California. Like many young Midwestern families of that era, they were lured out west by the irresistible combination of California weather and promising jobs. They bought a home in Fullerton, California, on a street that ended in an orange grove. It was there that Lee's sister Christine was born in late 1960.

During that decade, Dr. Benjamin Spock's *The Common Sense Book of Baby and Child Care* was a classic manual for raising children. One day, while Lois hung the wash on the backyard clothesline, toddler Lee shredded the book. She always joked that Lee's destruction of the book marked the end of Dr. Spock's influence on the Carson kids.

Many of Lee's antics as a youngster were accomplished with lightning speed. Lois once rounded the corner to see that pyromaniac toddler Lee had lit all the burners on the gas stove and stood in his cotton undershirt, mesmerized by the open flames. One Sunday morning before church, Bob opened the refrigerator door to find three half gallons of melted ice cream dripping down the shelves from the small freezer above. Lee had turned all the freezer dials down to zero. Although it challenged his parents during his early years, Lee's intrigue for playing with dials was later an advantage in his aviation career.

A little eyehook latch kept Lee locked in his room so that Lois could get some much needed quiet time while baby sister Chris was napping. Thinking Lee was safely contained in his room with the necessary lock, Lois was shocked to look out the window and see Lee running around in the backyard. Toddler Lee had climbed up furniture to reach the high window in his room, opened the window, and managed to get the screen out. All that effort—plus, he survived the four-foot leap down into the backyard.

Living eight miles from Disneyland with their tow-headed children in a suburban ranch house, the Carsons lived the all-American Dream. They were a close-knit family who enjoyed spending time together. Idyllic vacations were spent renting a motor home and driving all over the western United States. California schools were tops in the nation in the 1960s and early 70s, and Lee and Chris excelled at everything from academics to extracurricular activities.

The family was active in church and at the kids' schools. Lois was den mother to Lee's pack of Cub Scouts. She recounts tales of the wild pack of Scouts tearing around the house and yard with the family dog, an energetic boxer. Later Bob took over helping with the Boy Scouts, backpacking in the Sierras on several two-week trips and supporting Lee as he achieved the rank of Eagle Scout in 1973.

Lee's enterprising and energetic nature kept his parents on their feet. (Funny how a lot of the stories about Lee's high energy and antics were not shared with me until much later in our married life! I think my mother-in-law did not want to scare me about having active children.) One Super 8mm film shows Lee, a tow-headed whirling dervish, as he ran around in his underwear and jumped headfirst into the open front window of the Volkswagen Bug. Those were just candid scenes from home movies; he did not act up for the camera's benefit. Lee lived life to the fullest, even as a youngster.

"He was always two steps ahead of us," Lois sighed. "Lee didn't want to wear a jacket to school, so we compromised. I didn't make him wear a jacket if he wore a plain white T-shirt underneath his sport shirt."

Louis "Red" Reinhart, who lived around the corner and was later elected Fullerton mayor, once called Lois to inform her of her first grader's antics. "Lois, I don't mean to tell tales out of school, but every morning your son stops in front of my house, sits on the curb, takes off his shirt and T-shirt, stuffs the T-shirt in his lunchbox, puts his shirt back on, and walks off to school." As always, Lee applied his high energy and ability to problem solve without getting into trouble.

In high school, Lee played trumpet in the band and the church brass group, sang in the church choir, attended youth group, played water polo, and swam two-a-day team workouts during the swim season. Lee started a personal relationship with Jesus Christ on a memorable weekend youth retreat led by Pastor Steve, the assistant pastor who led the youth choir and brass group. Lee later invited Pastor Steve to give the invocation at his Eagle Scout ceremony.

Bob and Lois supported, attended, and chauffeured for all of Lee's activities. Lee's persuasive proposal for a motorcycle included the time and effort he would save his parents in chauffeuring. To Lois's consternation, Lee quit youth group, choir, and band once he had the motorcycle. Although Lee had accepted Christ in youth group, he did not continue with church youth activities; instead he focused on motorcycling and high school sports.

Long before the days of mandatory helmets, Lee would ride his motorcycle, weaving in and out of multiple lanes of Los Angeles freeway traffic. The California golden boy with long blonde hair loved to be wild and free on his motorcycle. He enjoyed riding fast and, most likely, riding more dangerously than his parents ever imagined.

Lee's favorite high school pastimes were swimming and playing water polo on the school teams. Another tanned swimmer, with similar blue eyes and chlorine-bleached hair down to his shoulders, was Lee's high school friend John. Along with the rest of the swim and water polo teams, they became close friends and spent hours hanging out together and indulging in adolescent antics.

John later told me that Lee, at age sixteen, had his life mapped out. He was going to attend the Air Force Academy to become a fighter pilot, get married, have a family, and then fly for a civilian airline. John later marveled that Lee was one of the few people who accomplished all that he had set out to do in life.

Within weeks of graduating from Fullerton's Troy High School in 1977, Lee set off for the United States Air Force Academy (USAFA). Lee's long locks were shaved off as an initiation into his new micromanaged life; every aspect of this structured orientation was designed to develop new Air Force officers. The class of 1981 was only the second USAFA class to accept women, and the first weeks of initiation in the summer of 1977 were brutal for everyone. Lee was resolute in his compliance and drive to get through Basic Cadet Training, the initial training otherwise known as Beast, followed by the freshman year. Consistent with his attitude toward other aspects of his life, Lee approached being a doolie, the USAFA nickname for freshmen, with a sense of discipline and determination, knowing that this was the path to his ultimate goal of flying.

Most aspects of cadet life were scripted and tightly controlled. For example, in response to the common practice of intimidating questions from upperclassmen, doolies memorized the daily mess hall menus and recited them by rote. "Fast, neat, average, friendly, good, good." This standardized response was scribbled onto O-96, the government form for students to rate the dining service after eating in Mitchell

Hall. One way Lee escaped the regimented lifestyle was to go running on the campus trails. He loved to pound out the miles, escape the drudgery of classwork, and soak up the mountain air as he ran the foothills above campus.

Lee's freshman USAFA squadron was XIV, nicknamed Cobra. In their sophomore year, students were transferred to different squadrons and Lee was moved to XXXI, entitled the Grim Reapers. One sophomore photo shows Lee and several friends standing beneath a shield of their squadron mascot, the Grim Reaper. The candid shot captured the fun of healthy classmates whose future was nothing but long and promising. The irony of the photo is poignant only in retrospect: innocent cadets flaunted their invincible vitality in the shadow of the Grim Reaper.

Lee graduated in June of 1981 and his family celebrated this hard-earned milestone together at the USAFA ceremony. Afterwards, Lee backpacked in Europe, a classic rite of passage for many college graduates in the 1980s. The rest of that summer was spent in Colorado, where Lee bought a 1976 BMW model 2002. He maintained the car meticulously, enjoying all the details from adjusting the valves to replacing the brakes. Lee was at his happiest with greasy hands under the hood of his car.

In August of 1981, Lee ran the Pikes Peak Marathon®, a grueling footrace that starts at 6300 feet in Manitou Springs, Colorado and ascends over 7800 feet from there. Appropriately entitled America's Ultimate Challenge®, the Pikes Peak Marathon is a feat to finish, let alone to place in. Lee placed twenty-first overall, which was fifth place in his age category as a twenty-two-year-old.

That fall Lee moved to "Willie," Williams AFB in Chandler Arizona, for the one-year undergraduate pilot training, or UPT. The newly minted second lieutenants spent classroom hours studying aviation, weather, avionics, airplane systems, and emergency procedures. They learned to fly two jets: the Cessna T-37 Tweet (the subsonic "candy bar" straight wing) and the supersonic T-38 Talon. UPT was the definitive crossroads of Air Force pilot training: pass it or wash out.

T-37 briefings were a demanding aspect of UPT. With just fifteen desks in the room, the forty students and twenty instructors crowded in for these early morning sessions of oral drills. The instructor called out a name, and the second lieutenant dutifully stood at attention and listened to the description of an emergency situation. The scenario started out with a master caution light that required action. The lieutenant had to respond appropriately, verbally recognize the master caution light, describe the subsequent course of action, and implement a procedural checklist. The instructor continued detailing the scenario as it deteriorated to red lights and abnormal indications. The lieutenant had to identify the emergency procedures and recite the bold face procedures memorized earlier. Word-for-word perfection, delivered before the room full of colleagues, was mandatory for the emergency procedures. The scenario was taken to its logical conclusion with non-emergent procedures read back and explained to the instructor. This teaching method inculcated the methodical use of procedural checklists and fostered clear thinking under pressure for these would-be pilots.

Other UPT challenges were the three similar check rides that pilot candidates received in each aircraft. The contact check ride involved flying the plane and handling emergencies under visual flight rules. During the instrument check ride, the student pilot was evaluated on instrument flight rules. The instructor had full visibility, but the student's view was obliterated using either a visor on the helmet or a curtain that covered the T-38 canopy. The third evaluation was the formation check; student pilots flew in formation with instructors. While instructors flew as number one and number three in the four-ship formation, students flew number two and number four. Part of that check ride involved one student and one instructor flying in two-ship formation to practice the maneuvers as individual elements. Later, all four aircraft joined up to fly maneuvers as a single four-ship formation.

The check rides evaluated the quality of the pilot's flight, but were graded on a pass/bust basis. If you busted more than one check ride, you washed out of pilot training. The pressure of check rides—with entire careers depending on the outcome—was palpable among students. Classmates were aware of who was going to, or returning from, a check ride. A thumbs-up upon return meant "pass." A fellow student who avoided eye contact in the hallway after a check ride had likely busted, and was met with empathetic yet respectful distance.

As hard as they worked through pilot training, the second lieutenants also played. Lee and several pilot friends joined together to buy a waterski boat. Weekends were spent waterskiing on Saguaro and Canyon Lakes, two reservoirs on the

Salt River within an hour's drive of Phoenix. Three of the waterskiing pilots, Bill, Tom, and Lee began lifelong friendships during their time at Willie. As they went on to military and civilian careers that spanned the country, they often ended up rooming together or hosting each other as extended house guests. Pilots' wives later became part of that network, so our families remained close as we stayed in touch and visited throughout the years.

While in Arizona, Lee bought a custom bicycle from Colin Laing, the renowned British bicycle frame builder who had moved to Arizona. In addition to pedaling through the outskirts of Phoenix, Lee enjoyed long hours running the open desert roads. He also found time to work on his BMW. Lee's friend and classmate Bill described one afternoon when Lee worked on the vehicle's brakes.

"I don't need to go to some mechanic. I can fix it better myself," Lee announced. Several hours later, Lee came up with greasy hands and a smile on his face. In his soft-spoken tone, he admitted, "Well, I kind of tore this other line getting the part out, but I can fix that, too."

A few hours later Lee came up to say, "I found this other thing I'm going to fix while I'm working on it."

When Lee was finally done, Bill jokingly asked, "Well, how much money do you think you saved?"

"Well, I probably didn't save anything, but I'm glad I worked on it," Lee admitted. Bill claimed that none of the other pilots asked Lee to work on their cars, not because Lee could not fix them, but because Lee's tune-ups always included extra repairs and prolonged service time.

At the end of UPT, based upon check ride results, briefing performances, and classroom scores, instructors chose one of three categories for pilots: fighter-instructor qualified (the highest ranking), fighter qualified, or multi-crew aircraft (bombers, tankers, or cargo planes.) Pilots were individually ranked as well. Top-ranking pilots received their first choice of assignments when orders (i.e., the military paperwork that details type, location, and dates of the job) were handed out. Orders for the type of aircraft and AFB were delivered by the Squadron Commander in one-on-one meetings.

UPT culminated in Assignment Night, a ceremony for pilots and their significant others. In the age before computer presentations, each new pilot was called up to the stage for a brief slide show of his/her past year at work and play. The dramatic ending was a final slide that depicted the aircraft the pilot would fly, along with a verbal announcement of the base of assignment. Ranked as fighter instructor qualified, Lee's assignment was an A-7 Corsair II in Springfield, Ohio, where he would move after completing the rest of his training. The golden California boy became a golden flyboy with a fighter assignment.

After UPT, Lee attended fighter lead-in training at Holloman AFB in Alamogordo, New Mexico. The year was 1982, and although the Air Force had female pilots, they were not allowed to fly fighters. The fighter pilot community remained exclusively male. Pilots attended class eight hours per day on non-flying days. On the three or four days per week when they flew the AT-38 Talon, classes were four hours per day. Time in the air was spent flying in formation, dropping practice bombs (blue bomb dummy units) and practicing air-to-air tactics (the basic fighter maneuvers). Pilots learned how to fight other airplanes in the air (one versus one, one versus two, and two versus one), how to move the airplane into position, and how to use the machine gun to simulate shooting down other aircraft.

In January of 1983, Lee moved to Davis Monthan AFB in Tucson, Arizona. The six month course, entitled Replacement Training Unit, taught him to fly the D and K models of the A-7. As always throughout pilot training, Lee made time to waterski, bike, run, date, and compete in marathons.

Lee received a Project Season assignment after pilot training to the 178th Tactical Fighter Group, Springfield Air National Guard Base in Springfield, Ohio. There he worked with reservists as an active-duty first lieutenant. Active-duty pilots were loaned out to National Guard units to integrate with a reserve unit and build up flying hours.

Fellow Springfield A-7 pilot Steve recalled:

> An image of the suntanned face of Lee, legal haircut, but just barely, standing in a flight suit and flight jacket, hands stuffed in the coat pockets, leaning against his BMW [model] 2002 in the 162nd FS [Fighter Squadron] parking lot, shooting the breeze with me and some unknown others. It was apparent to me in those days that Lee had a strong idea of what he wanted and where he wanted to go.

Dennis, Lee's erudite, quick-witted colleague told the story best:

> Since the late 1970s, the A-7 had been flown almost exclusively by the Air National Guard. The active duty,

however, did not have enough airplanes with which to meet the demands for the number of fighter pilots they wanted trained. So, they took guys like me out of ROTC and Lee out of the Air Force Academy, and taught us in roughly forty-eight weeks how to fly a military jet trainer aircraft. They taught us how to fly straight and level without puking, also upside down without puking, in and out of spins and loops without puking, even faster than the speed of sound and six times the force of gravity—you guessed it—without puking. And most importantly, without destroying the aircraft or anything else . . . and they let us do it all by ourselves. Boy did we think we were something special. . . .

The first Project Season pilot arrived at Springfield sometime in late 1982, well before Lee arrived in 1983. His name was Mike . . . a big, swaggering, brawling, Irishman who knew how to fly, fight, drink, chew tobacco, drop bombs, smoke, cuss, and do lots of other things. He seemed bigger than life.

Lee Carson showed up at Springfield a different young man. He was lean, tan, and athletic, a fast runner and biker, so young and handsome-looking that he was quickly given the name Kid Carson. He was smart and easygoing with a sharp wit and a relaxed, California atmosphere about him. He smiled that smile we all know so well, and everybody liked him.

By the time I arrived at Springfield in the fall of 1984, the two Project Season guys ahead of me had raised everyone's expectations. . . . Both Mike and Lee took me under their wings and taught me about the Guard. . . . I was a brand new Lieutenant, fresh from the tight-fisted grasp of the strict Father Air Force, and I was expected to address this man—[the Squadron Commander] who was almost twenty years older than me—a decorated Vietnam

F-4 fighter pilot that survived the Hanoi Hilton, and a Lt. Colonel—simply "Ed." The Ops officer was another Veteran of Vietnam—who we called John—and my real boss, another Vietnam seasoned veteran—we called him Ralph. Wow, this was nothing like the active duty!

It is amazing how quickly we can adapt to the rigors of life. Before long I had dropped my active duty posture and was turning up my collar, rolling up my sleeves and trying to walk the walk of these men that were to be my role models. Lee Carson walked that walk, and yes, he talked the talk. Our vocabulary changed from the days of college when physics and calculus and aerodynamics ruled our speech to new words and phrases learned in the skies above Ohio.

An A-7's job was to fly low and fast during wartime into enemy territory and drop bombs on targets like oil refineries, missile sites, and the like. For defending ourselves, we had missiles too, and this required us to learn to dogfight would-be aggressors. On days when we fought mock air battles, the radio was full of emotionally charged cries of, "Saber two-one, break right! Take it down! We have bandits five o'clock low! Chaff and flare!" Nothing would ever seem the same again. We swaggered a little more each day.

On the days we trained to drop bombs, we flew low and fast, very fast, over 500 miles an hour, 500 feet above the trees and cows and horses and corn of Ohio, Indiana, Kentucky, and Michigan. Ours was a big playground. We streaked through the air with our practice bombs strapped to the wings and hundreds of bullets loaded into the cannon under the nose[s] of our jets. When the time was right, when we had come within a few short miles of the target, we would yank

> back on the stick of our A-7s, subjecting our bodies to four and five times the force of gravity, to hurtle ourselves skyward. This launching skyward was done in order to see past the trees and low hills around us and then, once the target was in sight, again we pulled against the forces of nature and threw ourselves at the ground at over 500 miles an hour, putting ourselves on a collision course with dirt and rock only seconds in front of our faces. When the time was right, and when we had positioned the green, computer-generated pipper just so—over the target—we released our bomb[s] and once again pulled our 4-Gs and flew away from the ground.
>
> It was exhilarating! How could all of this not go to one's head? It went to mine. We were all changed by this. This shy Oklahoma boy came out of his shell. Lee Carson was not immune to this either, but more than anyone I have ever met that called himself a fighter pilot, Lee Carson remained who he was. You could just tell that. Day in and day out, deep down, he was who he was. He could pull on the gloves of braggadocio if needed, but they never fit him so tight.

Another Springfield pilot, Tim, reminisced about Lee as the nicest, even-keeled guy in the unit, saying, "Lee was always someone you could talk to. He had a voice of his own. While others sang the chorus of the gang, Lee had his own voice."

[3]

Tina's Early Years

UNLIKE THE CARSON predictability and stability, my upbringing was characterized by challenges and changes. My parents, John and Hannelore Biltz, met in a pizza parlor as University of Minnesota students. Ironically, they never met several years earlier while my father spent a year studying at the Freie Universität Berlin, in the German city where my mother was born and raised. My parents met, dated, and married while at the University of Minnesota. I was born in the campus hospital, located along the Mississippi River, in 1961 while my father attended medical school. Shortly after his graduation, we moved to Panama for his medical internship at Gorgas Hospital in the Canal Zone. I have no memories from that time, but my mother said she put a big sunhat on me and let me run around in diapers, which resulted in lots of sunburns.

During our move back to the United States from Panama, my parents attempted to sedate me with an antihistamine for the flight, but I had a paradoxical reaction and stayed awake. My shy mother was appalled at my outgoing nature as I greeted everyone on the plane with "Hi! Hi!"

The oft-repeated story my grandparents told was my first reaction after our move from the Panama Canal Zone. I sat in their Minneapolis kitchen, pointed to the walls, and exclaimed, "No bugs!" I guess I have my year in Panama to thank for my aversion to creepy crawlies.

My father's military career moved us many times during the next nine years. He worked as a family practitioner at Offutt AFB in Bellevue, Nebraska. My sister Rebecca was born at the Offutt AFB hospital near the Missouri River in 1963. From there we moved to Lackland AFB in San Antonio, Texas for my father's radiology residency at Wilford Hall. One of our favorite outings was the San Antonio River Walk, a scenic tourist spot that was much shorter than it is today. After my father finished a radiology residency program in San Antonio, the Air Force moved us to Europe—first to Spangdahlem AFB and later to Bitburg AFB, Germany.

I attended four different first grades and also four different fourth grades, which spanned both German and English languages. When I started school, my parents placed me in a German school so that I would learn the language. I later asked my parents if I spoke any German when I started in the German first grade. In her no-nonsense way, my mother noted, "You cried every day for about a month, but then you learned the language and you were fine."

My father resigned his Air Force commission and paid off his medical school debts after we moved back to the United States. In 1971, we welcomed a new baby brother into the family; my sister was seven and I was nine when Fredric was born. Our family stayed in Minnetonka, Minnesota with my grandparents where my father took helicopter lessons while he searched for a radiology position.

When we moved to Red Wing, a picturesque town in southeastern Minnesota, life settled in. By that time, I had repeatedly and successfully made new friends and adjusted to new schools, so moving and starting over in my fourth-grade class was still fun and exciting. Tree house clubs, Barbie dolls, neighborhood kickball, unicycles, ice skating, and sledding—lots of fun kid stuff as I grew up in this all-American town along the Mississippi River, downriver from where I was born.

In 1972, my family attended a David Wilkerson rally in Minneapolis. David Wilkerson preached God's Word and relayed the story of evangelistic outreaches to drug-addicted gang members like Nicky Cruz on the streets of New York City. Wilkerson described how the Teen Challenge organization started, as detailed in his 1962 book entitled *The Cross and the Switchblade.* I remember being in the huge arena and feeling so touched by God. I was only eleven years old, but when David Wilkerson gave the call to come to the altar for those who wanted to follow Jesus, I jumped out of my seat and ran down to the front. That was the day I started my relationship with Jesus Christ. My parents loved God and taught me about Jesus from early on, but not until that night did I make the decision to accept Him on my own, as my Savior. Little did I know then, how my personal relationship with God would get me through the upcoming trauma that our family would face.

At that time, my sister Rebecca and I were two scrawny girls of nine and eleven whose job it was to train our family dog, a Great Dane named Duchess. We practiced daily with the dog, but Duchess, with her sweet nature and huge size, was just too much dog for us to master. The night of June 13, 1973, was the final test of dog obedience school at the Red Wing National Guard Armory building. As the big sister, I was the one to put Duchess through her paces for the test. As usual, Duchess ignored my commands and instead loped around, following her own interests. Meanwhile, the other dogs obediently sat, stayed, and came when called.

I was mortified that Duchess flunked the test, and I cried as we left. As my mother drove out of the armory parking lot, I sat next to her in the family car, amazed by the colorful and peaceful sunset, and how it contrasted with my hurt feelings and tear-filled eyes. Looking out toward the Mississippi River, I decided that Duchess flunking dog training had been the worst day of my life. Little did I know how insignificant this event would seem compared with another event that had happened around that time, several hours north of us.

The next morning, sunshine streamed through our second floor bedroom window, flickering through wind-blown leaves on a typical summer morning—but nothing else seemed right. Strangely, my sister and I were awakened by my mother and aunt walking into our shared room. My aunt had never before been there to wake us up, so this was unusual, and I looked down from the top bunk hesitantly. Then we heard the words that would forever change our lives. Word content, voice tone, exact explanations, and other details are lost to me now, but Mommy told us that Daddy had died in an airplane crash the night before.

In the chaos that followed, some memories did sear my mind, like the hysterical screaming that Rebecca and I started after we heard the news. Years later, that screaming still echoed in my brain as the remembered focus of that day. In the midst of the blur of activity after my father's death, another memory was oddly clear: the endless march of hotdishes and Jell-O salads to the front door, accompanied by pitying looks from well-meaning people. Not surprisingly, I still dislike hotdishes and Jell-O salad.

Our church was packed for my father's funeral several days later. I did not shed a tear until the recessional when I noticed Donna, a classmate friend of mine. Her look of pain and pity broke through my denial to remind me of why we were there, and I finally began to weep as my family marched out of the sanctuary in single file.

The graveside ceremony was held among the scenic bluffs at the country church cemetery. My father's gravestone is inscribed with Jesus' words from John 11:25–26 (KJV). "I am the Resurrection and the Life, saith the Lord: he that believeth in me, though he were dead, yet shall he live and whosoever liveth and believeth in me shall never die." Several months before his sudden death, in the paradox that frames my parents' story of divine preparation, my father planned his funeral and chose this verse for his gravestone.

Like scattered views through a river's mist, a few disconnected memories rise from my brain, but most of that day, and even that year, is lost in my fog of grief. Doubtless this would be the case for any woman's memory of her twelfth year of life; however, my memory gaps are not just childhood gaps, but protective spaces of denial where I have not allowed the pain to come through. Fuel pump failure is what I remember hearing as the cause of the fatal airplane crash, but not much was ever discussed about the event. Ironically, I later learned that Dad had flown his small, single-seat aircraft to Lake Elmo, Minnesota, to look at a larger, family size airplane that was for sale.

My recollections of that time are numbed and fragmented, whereas my younger sister has clarity of details in her memories. Her adult perspective surprised me, because she recognized that our many overnight stays at the home of our friends Martha and Ruth were as much about children's friendships as they were about help for my mom. By inviting us overnight, Martha and Ruth's mother Linda eased my mother's parenting load as she grieved.

When asked later how she did it, my mother told me, "I don't know. You just do it." Like her mother before her, whose family had lived in rural Germany—now part of Poland—during World War I, my mother learned to face incredible challenges. She grew up in Charlottenburg, a borough that was part of West Berlin, Germany, after World War II. Their family was sustained by the American airlift of egg powder and potato flakes during the June 1948–May 1949 Berlin Blockade. What little food the city's residents received was rationed. Dry milk powder stirred up with water and a tiny bit of sugar was a rare treat for my mother's family. Resolve and determination were qualities honed in the harsh wartime environment. My mother developed these traits as a child, and they characterized her entire life.

Albeit the defining moment of my childhood, my father's death did not devastate our family. My mother raised the three of us children, dedicating her time and energy to our well-being. We were loved and watched over by an amazing God who specifically promises to care for widows and the fatherless. Living on Social Security and farmland income, we lived conservatively and did not have extras, but love was plentiful. Our church and extended family loved and cared about us. My teen years were filled with the usual developmental issues instead of grief-related problems, a testament to a mother who kept her family going after tragedy.

High school was fun and games for me. Once in a while I might study for a math test or spend time writing a paper, but I never worked very hard academically. I was often bored in class, so I talked and laughed a lot. My priority was to spend time with friends, and I really enjoyed band, track, and cheerleading. I played flute in concert and marching band; playing solos and difficult pieces was a fun challenge for me. Since our town did not have an indoor ice arena in the 1970s, even home hockey games were played out of town. Hockey cheerleading, for the two years I participated, was my way of attending all the hockey games.

I never excelled at track, but I worked hard at practice and enjoyed it. Coach D was always sweet and pleasant, trying to find at least one area where I could be competitive. She encouraged me to try hurdles, but after a week of bruising my trailing knee, I gave up. She complimented my persistence and dedication, but I knew I was too slow for the sprint events I enjoyed. While my effort and attitude contributed to team morale, it never compensated for my lack of muscle mass. Four of my friends placed second in the 4 x 220 yard relay at the 1978 Minnesota state high school girls' track and field meet, establishing a local record that was posted for over thirty years at the Red Wing high school track. In contrast, my efforts at similar length races never earned any points, so I joked that my all-state friends should donate some of their hundreds of points to me so that I could meet the requirements to earn a high school letter.

While I was in high school, my paternal grandmother, Grandma Biltz, tried to convince me to work at the nursing home where she worked part-time. She had stayed home to raise her three children for twenty years, after which she returned to the field of nursing. Grandma worked for years at the Glen Lake Sanatorium, which by the 1970s was a psychogeriatric nursing home. When my grandparents moved to Red Wing after my father died, Grandma took a part-time job at a local nursing home.

"Oh Tina, come work at the nursing home. The elderly are so much fun," Grandma cajoled.

"No way, Grandma!" I could not hide my disgust. "I would *never* work at a nursing home!" Grandma's stories of "cute" nursing home patients disgusted me, and I could not understand how she enjoyed spending time with elderly, confused people.

I certainly was not interested in a medical career. As a six-year-old, I had seen a movie about an autopsy. Terrified of the idea of operations on dead people, I vowed never to be doctor. My first exposure to the medical field was the hospital field trip in sixth grade, which my Dad had organized for our parochial school. Our first stop was the laboratory. After my tour-guide father proudly introduced me as his daughter, I became faint from the smells and had to sit out the rest of the tour.

My first job had nothing to do with the medical field, but after a year of working at the Dairy Queen, I decided to push past my initial negative reaction and try working at the nursing home. Grandma was the charge nurse on weekends, so I often worked under her supervision. I grew to love working with the elderly, and Grandma ensured that I made the most of every opportunity to learn about nursing.

"Have you ever seen a dead person?" Grandma greeted me one weekend morning when I showed up for day shift. Before I got more than a "No" out of my mouth, Grandma dragged me by the arm into the dead woman's room. As aides bathed the body, Grandma explained postmortem care and physiology to me.

After high school, I knew that I would attend college, but I was not sure what to study. Of the many schools I was interested in, St. Olaf College in Northfield, Minnesota, was the last one I visited. I distinctly remember the admissions counselor mentioning the nursing program.

"It is a highly competitive program, and the admissions process is selective. In fact, you might be too late to enroll." The admissions counselor was matter-of-fact about qualifications and deadlines, and the early acceptance date had already passed.

"You mean that I would not get into the program?" I responded incredulously, knowing that my academic and extracurricular qualifications were stellar.

"The program is tough to get into, and the selection process starts early, with the fall admissions."

Everything the admissions counselor said after that grated on me. For me, it was as if he had thrown down the gauntlet. My thoughts raced. *Oh yeah?! I can get into any program I want, and if I want to get into your nursing program next fall, I will.* Although I was not sure about nursing, I was determined to get into the program. As always, I enjoyed a good challenge.

Having met that challenge, I was accepted into the St. Olaf nursing program and started in the fall of 1979. Other than a short period during freshman year when I considered changing my major to organic chemistry, I had no other doubts that nursing was my chosen career. Whenever I mentioned nursing or how much I enjoyed my studies, Grandma would get a twinkle in her eye as she smiled and jokingly repeated my never-forgotten words, "No way, Grandma!"

The highlight of my college years was the fall study semester I spent in Vellore, India, in 1982. Ten nursing students went to Christian Medical College and Hospital in southern India where we attended class, completed a research study, and participated in hospital and community clinical rotations. We were fearless but naïve American women who toured all over southern India when not studying. Savoring every experience, we furiously scribbled our thoughts and escapades into the journals required as part of our St. Olaf college credit. The highlights of my time in India were living overseas, learning about other cultures, meeting new people, and traveling to exotic places.

For their final trip before returning to the United States, several students stayed in India, traveling from Tamil Nadu to Kashmir. Meanwhile, I traveled with five others to Nepal, where I fell in love with the mountains. Gary and Pat, American missionaries originally from Minneapolis, welcomed us to their home in Kathmandu. They sent us up to the foothills of the Himalayas where we spent one night in a small hut, the Third World equivalent of a bed and breakfast. My fondest memory is standing outside at night, with the stars seeming so incredibly close, as if mere proximity to Mount Everest set us above and beyond the rest of the world. After touring the hospital Gary had helped to engineer, I fantasized about returning to work in that picturesque community near the top of the world.

Nursing jobs were scarce in Minnesota after I graduated in 1983, so I joined the United States Air Force. My hope was to see the world, but I ended up getting sent to Ohio, a far cry from my fantasy job in the mountains of Nepal. Sarah, my roommate while in India, also signed up for the USAF, and we compared our orders with great excitement. I was assigned to Wright-Patterson AFB in Dayton, Ohio. She was going to Travis AFB in California with a follow-on assignment to Fairchild AFB near Spokane, Washington. When Sarah met her now-husband Tom and backed out of her USAF offer because of him, I naïvely asked to trade my Ohio orders for her California assignment. Although my request must have seemed humorous to the Master Sergeant, he maintained his serious and negative response to my pleas for California instead of Ohio.

The medical officers' introduction to the Air Force at Shepherd AFB, Texas consisted of pool parties, volleyball parties, dances, and long days in the classroom studying chemical and biological warfare, among other USAF officer topics. The Air Force values its medical officers, many of whom complete rigorous graduate school studies before joining the military. Nothing too strenuous was asked of us; for example, we did not have to march when it was too hot. More like a continuing-education seminar, our orientation was nothing like boot camp for the enlisted troops.

Out of our class, five of us caravaned together from Texas to our new assignments at Wright-Patterson Medical Center in Ohio. Former strangers, we were soon fast friends, optimistic about beginning our USAF careers. I was excited to work hard and learn how to be an Air Force nurse. For myself, I was determined never to end up in my mother's position, raising three kids alone without a career to fall back on. After all, my biggest fear in life was to be widowed and live on Social Security.

[4]

Courting Between Courts

KINGSGATE COURT was the hub of my home life in the mid-1980s. Arriving at Ohio's Wright-Patterson AFB in August of 1983, my two nurse colleagues and I rented a shingled, two-story townhouse in Dayton, part of a complex filled with townhouse-style dwellings and apartment buildings. As young singles, fresh out of college and new to our nursing careers, Susie, Barb, and I were thrilled to find a three-bedroom place within a few miles of the base hospital. The downstairs was wood parquet and the upstairs had lime green shag carpet, the vacuuming of which we referred to as "mowing the lawn."

To our pleasant surprise, there were many other young singles, especially USAF types, in the neighborhood. The "older" captain lived two doors down. In his early thirties, he was not very friendly. His was the new (1983), silver Honda Prelude parked on our side of the parking lot. Across the way lived a handsome first lieutenant with a new, fire-red Porsche 911 Carrera. He meticulously groomed that baby of his; he spent Saturdays scrubbing her with a toothbrush. The car was okay, but the owner was an especially nice view from our living room window. I was always cautious backing my "econobox" car out of the parking spot, for fear of crunching the guy's pride and joy.

Two or three doors down in the other direction lived Jerry, a USAF captain. With a PhD in physics, Jerry was beyond genius but a bit shy. He most likely went on to great career success at his next assignment at Los Angeles Air Station, as one of the brilliant minds who worked on Ronald Reagan's Strategic Defense Initiative. My roommates had a hard time talking with him, but I did not. Jerry's eyes would sparkle and his voice come alive when asked about his work. I tried to understand and ask relevant questions, but I could never completely comprehend the discussions. Having regularly fallen asleep in high school physics class and having not studied it since, I was not a good conversationalist when it came to the study of inanimate objects.

A neighborhood fixture of regularity, Jerry arrived home at 5:07 p.m. every night. I used to joke to my roommates, as Jerry walked out of sight up the sidewalk to the apartments next door, "Okay, it is 5:09 and Jerry is opening his apartment door. He is now picking up the newspaper and it is 5:11 p.m.," as if everything in Jerry's life was strictly scheduled. That seemed so foreign to us. In our house of three nurses, someone was always at work, someone else sleeping, and somebody else enjoying time off. We had no regular schedule. To our way of thinking, Jerry led a unique lifestyle.

Also in Jerry's building lived three USAF airmen who shared an apartment. These enlisted guys rarely slept because, in addition to working full time at the hospital, they were pursuing college degrees. They also threw big parties. Louis, an orderly, later became a surgeon. One of my roommates had a big crush on Louis, but I do not think they ever dated. I worked night shift with Johnny, a respiratory therapist, who eventually became an engineer. He was a consummate professional and a cutie, but when we went out to dinner once, I felt nothing more than sisterly respect.

My roommate Susie had a crush on Greg, a guy from the other end of the court. Greg and his roommate Rick worked at the Ohio Air National Guard unit in Springfield. Greg and Susie met up in the laundry room, but Barb and I never really met him. Barb said that she wanted to meet guys, but she preferred relaxing at home over leaving the house to socialize or work out. My famous line to her, as I was trying to get her to accompany me to the gym, pool, or somewhere: "Barb you *have* to get out! Prince Charming is *not* just going to show up at the door!" Those were the same words I would have to eat for many years after I met Lee.

Several miles away, nestled between Wright State University and the Air Force Museum section of Wright-Patterson AFB, was a brand new community of quad homes. Lee Carson lived on one of the courts there, along with other single male USAF officers who had recently purchased their first homes. These condominiums were two-story homes in a complex that included a pool and clubhouse. I later called Lee's court the "He-Man Wood Splitters Lane," because the guys would get cords of wood delivered and then spend manly hours of ax time in the driveway chopping the wood into smaller logs for their fireplaces.

One Friday night I was home alone when Rick from across the court parking lot knocked on my front door with his coworker Lee in tow. I had met Rick before, but that was my first introduction to Lee. I was surprised to find two guys at the door asking my roommates and me to go out. They had already imbibed at the Flywright Club, a bar on the engineering side of the base that we had dubbed "The Fly-by-Night." Neither of my roommates was home at the time, and I was not sure I wanted to go out with these two. As they cajoled me into calling some of my "nurse friends" to go out, I realized that I would not get rid of them until I did. So I called my coworker Chellé. Out loud I asked if she wanted to go out with us, but circling back to the kitchen with the corded phone, I whispered, "Don't come. I'm trying to get rid of them." Rick grabbed the phone, but his attempts to persuade Chellé were fruitless. However, these two pilots were nothing if not persistent, so I knew I was not going to get rid of them.

Finally, they offered to show me pictures of their recent TDY (temporary duty) to Panama. That piqued my interest, and I could not refuse the accompanying offer of a margarita. We went to Rick's apartment, and Rick realized that he did not have enough ice cubes for the drinks. I offered to get ice cubes from my place across the court. Lee jumped up and offered to walk me back.

By this time I regretted my choice to be at Rick's and wondered how I could get out of the situation. Besides, I was somewhat insulted by the insinuated need for help, so I responded, "No, that's okay. I'll be fine. I'm just walking across the street." Lee was not to be persuaded otherwise, and he followed me out the door.

"I'm just going to run," I announced. One of us made a comment about racing, and then Lee offered to give me a head start.

"I don't need a head start," I scoffed, irritated that this guy who did not even know me would insinuate that I could not run against him without a head start. So off we sprinted together, arriving at my door at a near tie. *I showed him,* I thought.

The rest of the evening went downhill from there. Lee was very quiet, while Rick made never-ending chauvinistic comments, bragging on and on about their TDY. I still remember looking across the room at Lee. Sitting in his light-blue, yellow-striped, button-down oxford shirt, he looked incredibly handsome. I was struck by a sensation that this guy was going to end up being very important to me, even more important than my last boyfriend, who had wanted to marry me. I shook off that moment of impact, telling myself that Lee must have been just as chauvinistic as Rick, only worse, because he was quiet and stuck up in addition to that. (Much later, Lee told me that he had liked my feistiness and was very impressed with me at the time.) Finally I went home, firm in my refusal of a second offer by Lee to walk me across the street.

I worked the next two days in a row. Barb worked Friday night and slept all day Saturday. She was very irritated at someone who had come by, pounding on the door. Barb never opened the door, but looked out the window to see the guy who had woken her up. Her description sounded like Lee, so I told her the story of Friday night and said not to answer the door.

Sunday evening Barb pointedly announced, "That guy came by again. I am not opening the door for him, but if you see him, you better tell him to quit waking me up!" Lee did not have my phone number or even know my last name, so he was coming by our townhouse every day.

Monday, April 2, 1984, was my day off. I was washing clothes and writing letters when, sure enough, Lee came to the door again.

"Do you want to go for a run?"

"I already ran this morning," I told him, thinking that would be the end of it. I could not help but notice that he was incredibly handsome. I simply was not interested.

"We can just go for a walk then," Lee suggested.

"I need to do my laundry," I responded coldly, walking out the door to the laundry room with my laundry basket under my arm.

"I can wait," he countered firmly as he followed me.

That was not what I meant. My irritation mounted as I decided to ignore him. I went about doing my laundry, walking back and forth to the laundry room several buildings down. Each time he followed me. When I got back to my house, I continued writing letters as I had been doing when he arrived. Lee sat patiently on the floor. After over an hour, I realized that he really was not going to leave until I agreed to go running with him.

"Okay, I'll go running with you," I groused. I headed up the stairs to change into running clothes, trying to figure out how to make him go away. It was a warm spring day, but I put on what was then known as a track suit over my running shorts. *This will be the perfect solution. These layers will make me sweat like a pig, and then I will get rid of him.*

Lee opened the door for me to get into his BMW. Now that impressed me. *What a gentleman! . . . but too bad I am not interested in dating.* I had sworn off men after a painful breakup with a serious boyfriend who had pushed marriage. After that, I dated sporadically but was not interested in starting a relationship. Happily single, I was really looking forward to spending time and energy on my new career.

Lee took me to John Bryan State Park in Yellow Springs, Ohio, which was near the Springfield Air National Guard Base where he worked. The day was full of spring promise, with blue sky and sunshine. Running the trails was a blast. Lee was fun to run with and stayed with my pace, which was likely much slower than his usual speed. I was tired, given that I had already run my five miles that morning. I soon warmed up and started sweating, but I kept my track suit on, thinking the sweat would deter Lee, thus comfortably ending the whole outing. Years later, Lee insisted that I did not want to take my sweats off and run in my shorts because I did not want him to see my butt. At that point, I was not trying to impress him; I was just trying to sweat and be done with the outing.

So after this picture-perfect, movie-like scene, we ended up at a waterwheel from an old mill. The endorphins had kicked in and I was enjoying the afternoon, so of course I said yes when he offered to cook dinner for me after our outing. A man cooking a meal for me was not something I could refuse!

Back at his condo, Lee proudly showed me around his new bachelor pad. The floor-to-ceiling river-rock fireplace was the focal point. Two semicircular couches in tan tweed fronted the fireplace. Arcing over one of the couches stood a big lamp with a brass globe shade. The black behemoth stereo system, teak Scandinavian dining room set, and mini blinds completed the modern 1980s look.

Hanging along the stairs to the loft, I noticed a portrait of Lee with a woman. Gently leaning into Lee and smiling, this woman did not share Lee's finely chiseled features or golden complexion. They both looked content and happy in the portrait. I let out a sigh of relief. *Phew! No danger here; he already has a girlfriend.* (Later I found out that the picture was of Lee and his sister Chris.)

In the galley kitchen that opened into the dining area and living room, Lee prepared his signature dish of ground beef burritos. Complete with sour cream, salad, and a beer, the dinner was a great ending to a late afternoon workout. I silently reflected on my enjoyment of the day. *This would have been a perfect date, if only I was interested in dating again.*

Whether it was later that evening or another day over the phone, I do not remember, but Lee asked me out for dinner that Friday evening. I waffled, again not sure whether I wanted to go. *He's nice enough, but I am not interested in a relationship right now.* I worked day shift that week and actually posed the question to my colleagues, mostly singles who were standing around the nurses station, of whether I should go out again with this guy if I was not interested in a relationship.

"Go for the free dinner!" my charge nurse Major Hollister encouraged. Why, I had never thought of it that way. Lee was not asking for anything more it seemed, but in my heart I recognized that Lee was pursuing more than just dinner together. He had truly impressed me so far, and I did not want to string him on. But I went with the suggestion anyway. Little did I realize that Major Hollister's words would ring true; I ended up with a veritable lifetime of free dinners.

Our second date was to Elsa's, a popular authentic Mexican restaurant tucked into an industrial area of Dayton. The chips and salsa were great, the margaritas relaxing, and the ambiance perfect for a young couple getting to know each other. My thoughts after the date were mixed. *Too bad I am not interested, because he really seems like a great guy. Plus, he is gorgeous.*

And so my thought process went all summer. *Yes, I'll go out with you . . . and hmmm, he is gorgeous.* Everything I discovered about him in terms of character and integrity only confirmed the fact that he was a great guy. My leftover college feelings of negativity toward men were peeling away as I enjoyed fun outings with Lee all summer. Finally I got to the point where I realized that, if I was interested in a relationship with a guy, Lee would be exactly my type. Duh.

We continued dating, but never expressed our feelings to each other. He was open about his career plans; he wanted his next career move to be a remote assignment to Korea. Remote assignments lasted a year and did not include family. I assumed this was Lee's way of telling me that his future did not include me, so I was not to get my hopes up. That was fine with me, because I was enjoying my new career. I, too, had career goals, but I was thinking about flight nursing and heading in the opposite direction—to Europe. We continued dating, never discussing what our relationship meant or where it was going. I was content with what we had and how much we enjoyed our time together.

Lee's career was progressing well. As an Air Force first lieutenant fighter pilot with the Springfield Air National Guard unit, Lee flew A-7s. His version of his job: "I like to fly upside down and drop bombs." Lee worked with a close-knit squadron of guard employees who trained locally in Ohio and Indiana, with occasional deployments to Michigan, Panama, Canada, and England for peacetime maneuvers.

During this assignment, Lee was focused on pursuing his Master of Business Administration (MBA) at Wright State University. He began taking classes when he moved to Ohio and graduated right before he PCSed (the militarily coined verb of the acronym for permanent change of station).

One impressive aspect of Lee's personality was his self-discipline. He worked full time and took two classes per semester. He regularly studied, read, met in project groups, and wrote papers to complete his MBA requirements. During this time, he was also training for, and competing in, triathlons. He would squeeze at least one—sometimes two—hour-plus workouts into his day. Sometimes that meant biking to work or nighttime runs in the typical pouring Dayton rain. I was incredulous at how Lee could fit so much into his day. He was a master of efficiency, studying as he cooked dinner and fitting a workout into, or on the way to, his workday. He would make sandwiches of mustard, meat, and cheese on wheat bread for the entire week and freeze them. Cutting the sandwiches in half was too time-consuming, so Lee froze them whole, knowing they would thaw completely by lunch time. As with the rest of his life, only what was necessary needed to be done. Everything about his life ran like clockwork, and he managed to do well in all things he pursued.

When I came into Lee's life and became aware of his schedule, I was surprised to see how he prioritized time with me while keeping up with his other responsibilities. He never made me feel like I was second place. We began exercising together. I was not nearly as fast or as strong as he was when it came to runs, swims, and bike rides, but he never made me feel as if I were holding him back in his workouts. We swam together, but at different speeds, in the pool. We biked the hills south of Fairborn, the Mad River Recreation Trail, and the Great Miami River Recreational Trail through the city of Dayton. The John Bryan State Park trails were a favorite for running, followed by a trip to Young's Jersey Dairy for ice cream. Lee and I covered a lot of territory together as we worked out and got to know each other.

The Ironman competition in Hawaii was less than seven years old at that time, and triathlon events were starting all over the country. Most triathlons Lee competed in were not the full Ironman distances; they were usually half the length of the original event. Lee, while intense about his training schedule, was low-key about competitions. I was stunned to see that he was fifth out of the water in Shelby, Ohio, at the first triathlon where I watched him compete. I had no idea that he was so talented, because he never let on that he was competitive among hundreds of athletes. Lee did not place at these triathlons, but as an amateur athlete, he finished well. As always, Lee's modest and unassuming nature led me to underestimate his incredible talents and abilities.

During that time, my nursing career was progressing well. As a staff nurse, I transferred from the telemetry floor to the intensive care unit, which involved certifications, classes, and on-the-job training. The patient care was challenging and rewarding; my peers were dedicated and hardworking; and my career was absorbing and satisfying. The early and mid-1980s brought new scientific knowledge that we applied to patient care: immune system concepts, new disease entities like AIDS, and associated pharmaceutical treatments. Balloon pumps, venous oxygen catheters, and sophisticated ventilators were just a few of the new medical technologies and procedures we implemented. Precious patients and their families kept the technology from being routine or aimless. The nurses and technicians enjoyed reaching out to hurting patients and their stressed families. I loved what I did!

Two charge nurses submitted my name for hospital and base awards. As a candidate for these awards, I faced a series of boards, starting at the hospital with medical officers. Candidates presented themselves in dress blues for the award boards, careful to meet every Air Force standard for dress and appearance. The USAF uniform and appearance had to be impeccable: uniform pressed, award ribbons in place, and shoes shined. After winning awards at the medical-center level, I moved onto the base-wide, officer award boards, where panels of high-ranking officers graded my uniform and noted my answers to their questions about being an Air Force officer.

As a female, I was not required to have short hair. Regulations dictated that hair be styled or cut above the bottom edge of the collar, so I usually kept my below-shoulder-length hair pinned up with several combs or a big 1980s barrette. Right before one of my nerve-wracking interviews in front of a senior officer panel, I reached up to fix my hair. Something did not feel right about my twist hairstyle, but I took a deep breath and went in to face the board. Having survived detailed questions about the Air Force chain of command, leadership, current events, and how my education had prepared me for my current job, I walked out the door in relief—only to find one of my hair combs lying on the floor in the hallway. In 1985, I was awarded runner-up Company Grade Officer of the Year for Wright-Patterson Air Force Base. I later joked that it was my hairdo fallout that bumped me down to runner-up.

My nurse friends dated engineers, technicians, and doctors. Engineers in the Wright-Patterson AFB master's program were prized for their academic aptitude, stability, and "date-ability." On the other hand, my female peers considered fighter pilots to be brave and exciting, but not necessarily prime candidates for long-term relationships. Some fighter pilots had reputations as womanizers, not intellectuals. I confess that I succumbed to the stereotypes and peer pressure. When coworkers asked what my boyfriend did, I would say, "He is a first lieutenant." When pressed for details, I would add, "He is a first lieutenant with the Guard." I didn't want people to think I was dating a handsome, empty-headed womanizer.

Lee was far from that, as were his colleagues. I learned to dismiss the fighter pilot stereotypes as Lee and I socialized with each other's coworkers. His fellow pilots were dedicated and hardworking; several were decorated Vietnam veterans who had flown combat sorties. My admiration for this cadre of pilots grew as I got to know them. Lee and I supported each other in our career endeavors and enjoyed attending squadron activities and hospital functions together. Everyone recognized us as a couple, assuming that we would end up marrying, as many of our friends did during the three years we spent at Wright-Patt. Whereas friends thought we would be next to become engaged, I still believed Lee's declaration that he would pursue a remote assignment after his time in Ohio.

Lee and I had fallen in love, but we did not discuss the future. After dating for about a year, I decided that it was Lee or nothing for me. If it did not work out for the two of us, I would continue my career in the Air Force. I kept praying that if God did not want us together, He should take Lee out of my life, because I was getting too attached.

God seemed to answer my prayer when I found opportunities for other activities besides dating. In my spare time, I enjoyed attending Patterson Park Church, where my friend Meta attended. She was my first nurse preceptor at the hospital, and she had introduced me to the church a few months before I met Lee. Nestled into an established neighborhood of brick homes in Dayton, Ohio, this church taught the truths of Jesus from the Bible. I got involved in the women's Bible study and grew in God's Word, pursuits that I had neglected for years.

When Lee and I first met, we talked about being Christians and needing to grow in our faith, so I invited him to church. He soon started attending Patterson Park Church regularly with me. We confessed to each other that we had not followed God wholeheartedly in recent years. In our discussions, we realized that spurring each other on to grow in God was a big part of our relationship. Later, we realized that Lee was the answer to my mom's prayers, and I was the answer to his mom's prayers.

As our relationship progressed, we helped each other in practical as well as spiritual matters. In 1985, as had always been my method of operation, I shamelessly got my boyfriend to fill out my tax forms. Lee did more than fill out my forms, he helped me with tax planning. He encouraged me to start investing in mutual funds, starting with $25 a month from my paycheck. Lee's forte was financial analysis and planning, a talent he used personally and applied with his MBA studies, but never pursued as a career. Lee taught me the power of compound interest, and I introduced him to tithing. He had never tithed before, and it went against his savings bent, but he learned how God magnifies what we give when it is dedicated to Him. Once Lee started tithing, he never looked back, and tithing became a staunch principle upon which our finances were based.

[5]

Captains Carson

ALL WAS WELL in my world as I cruised down Ohio Interstate 675 enjoying the bright blue sky and singing along with the radio on September 10, 1985. My day off had finally come, and I was going to enjoy some shopping at the mall. That heady feeling of freedom soon vanished when I was gripped by the sudden impression to get off the freeway.

The way God communicates with me is not audible, nor is it earth shattering. Like a nagging sense of what I need to do, God's directions to me are noticeable, but not always logical to my puny earthly mind. In my heart, for reasons unknown to me, I knew that God wanted me to turn off instead of continuing on the highway. Knowing better than to ignore God's gentle prodding, I exited the freeway at the next opportunity. Finding myself near Lee's townhouse, I drove in that direction. Realizing that Lee was at work, not at home, I passed his street, and I began to ask God where I was supposed to go. Moments later, I noticed steam rising from the hood of my econobox. I pulled over at the side of the road and parked the car.

"Thank you, God, for getting me off the freeway!" I exclaimed, grateful that my car had broken down at a convenient local site instead of on the freeway. Long before the days of cellular technology, this incident had me searching for the nearest pay phone. I did not have a key to Lee's place, but I was close to the Wright-Patterson Area B base entrance. Only five miles from my house, I could either find a pay phone on base or just walk home. In civilian clothes with my military identification in my purse, I left my vehicle locked and parked at the roadside, and I walked to the base gate for Area B.

Just after I passed the guard shack on foot, a car pulled up next to me and a uniformed enlisted man asked if I needed a ride. I noticed that the military vehicle was marked with the Springfield Guard unit logo. Never having hitched a ride before—not that I was actually hitchhiking this time—I decided that getting into a marked USAF vehicle with a uniformed sergeant would be safe.

"Can I give you a ride somewhere?" the gentleman asked.

"My car just overheated down the road, so I thought I would cut across base to walk home."

"Where do you need to go?"

"If you can give me a ride across base, that'd be great."

"Sure."

Knowing that the Springfield Air National Guard Base was twenty-five miles away, I started a conversation out of curiosity. "What brings you here from Springfield?"

"I'm bringing samples to the lab."

"Do they have a lab here? What kind of samples?" This area of the base housed the National Museum of the United States Air Force and not much else, so I wondered what kind of samples he'd be delivering to this particular area.

"I have to bring these samples in from Springfield."

"Don't you need to take them to the hospital?" I wondered why he was on this area of the base, when the hospital was across Colonel Glenn Highway.

"No, these go to another lab. We lost a jet and I have to bring the samples in here."

The words hit me hard. I wondered if I had heard him right. My mind raced. Losing a jet meant a crash. A jet going down meant that a pilot had either ejected or died in the crash. Panic swelled up in me as I remembered that Lee had been scheduled to fly that day.

In a tremulous voice, I asked "Was it an A-7?"

"Yes."

"Did the pilot make it?"

The sergeant replied quietly. "No."

"Was it Lee Carson?" I practically screamed, knowing that—just as I did not want it to be Lee—I did not want *any* pilot to have gone down. I thought I must have heard him incorrectly. He could not possibly be from *the* Springfield guard unit, with *those* A-7 jets, and the pilots I knew, my Lee being one of them.

"It was Mike," he answered gently.

"Mike?!" I shrieked, remembering Mike's antics at Lee's recent pool party. If anyone could be called the life of the party, Mike was it. And now? This could not be true. He was so full of life; this could not have happened.

"Yes, it was Mike."

The shock of the statement would not fully sink in until later. I made it home, but did not know who or where to call. I thought it best to wait for Lee to contact me, since the squadron phone lines would be in use for emergency notifications. Lee finally called me at six p.m. to relay news of the tragic loss. His two friends and coworkers had been flying the A-7 in two-ship formation.

The surviving pilot described the incident:

> The day Mike died was a beautiful fall day in early September. We were flying a mission to Indian Town Gap, a gunnery range near Harrisburg, Pennsylvania. We thought it might be one of the ranges we would be assigned to fly to during our upcoming inspection, and we wanted to scope it out and get to know its targets. I was flying on Mike's wing that day as number two. We had each dropped about six practice bombs and as such were near the end of the training, and our scores were not as good as we would have liked. The range official was sitting in a truck and using binoculars to score the hits. After Mike's last pass he popped his aircraft a little higher and turned, apparently to see my bomb drop and attempt to triangulate from the target, my bomb hit, and the score given to us by the ranger. The sun was directly overhead and cast no shadows long enough to create the depth perception for a good view of the terrain, which was a series of rolling, shallow valleys. I watched as Mike flew into one of the ridges and his aircraft exploded.

Mike's auburn-haired wife and skydiving companion was my first contact with a military widow. She honored her husband by her regal bearing and composure amidst his grieving colleagues. During the days following the tragedy, the squadron members mourned together at Mike's house.

In the midst of this sorrowful gathering, I pulled Lee aside to accost him with my emotional declaration, "If that's what it means to marry an Air Force pilot I will never marry you!" That was the first and only time that the "M-word"—marriage—was ever mentioned between us in our year and a half of dating. As for my outburst, Lee gave no response, nor did he ever mention the "M-word" to me before he proposed.

I was again filled with the fears of my childhood: abandonment, death, and trauma. My father had died at thirty-five in a civilian plane crash. I was eleven at the time, and it became my biggest fear in life: to be a widow. I was not going to marry a pilot, let alone a fighter pilot, and potentially place myself in the same situation my mom ended up in, widowed and raising children on her own.

Even so, I enjoyed Lee's company, pushing my fears aside as we spent more and more time together. One of the road races that Lee and I ran together that year was the Minster Ohio Oktoberfest on October 6, 1985. "Carb-loading" was the prevailing 1980s training tactic of eating a high-carbohydrate meal the night before competing in a race. When Lee suggested we go to a new Italian restaurant on Saturday night before the race to load up on carbs, I tried to talk him out of it.

"Why do we have to go to such a fancy place? I'll just make spaghetti at my house," I offered.

"Let's just try this new place," Lee urged.

"What's the big deal about carb-loading? We don't have to go somewhere expensive. Where is this place anyway? You've never mentioned it before."

"It's in the south part of Dayton. Let's try it."

"Is it really dressy?"

"Statues and fountains. It'll be nice."

I groaned. Cherub statues and fountains did not adorn our usual restaurants; we preferred good ethnic cuisine over elegant atmosphere. I could not understand why he suddenly wanted to go to an expensive restaurant when all we were looking for was pasta. When I kept insisting that I could cook dinner at my place, he finally relented. After a homemade, economical spaghetti dinner, we sat on the couch together.

A strange look settled onto his face and he suddenly spoke seriously. "You know how well we get along? I want us to stay together; we get along so well." As he pulled out a ring box and opened it, he added, "Will you marry me?"

It was all so quick—none of that romantic, down-on-the-knees stuff—that I was in shock. My immediate response was, "No—really?!" as my mind recalled the many talks of him taking a remote assignment. I really wondered if he was serious. We had never mentioned—let alone discussed—marriage or even staying together for the long term. He reiterated his intent as I quizzically looked back and forth from the diamond ring to his face. "I want us to be together," he repeated in all earnestness.

"Of course," I sighed as the realization hit me that he was indeed proposing. From that day on, Lee ribbed me that I ruined my own engagement dinner. In my insistence on staying home to cook spaghetti, I had talked him out of a fancy Italian restaurant meal. So much for the ambiance of statues and fountains.

After the exciting events of the night before, I did not run a record pace at the 10K race the next day, but I felt as if I were flying. I remember looking at my race results under my maiden name and getting goose bumps with the realization that soon my last name would be Carson.

Walking into work soon after our engagement, I looked up to see "Biltz bites the dust" scrawled in huge letters across the picture windows at the nurses' station. My coworkers—nurses, doctors, and medical technicians—were mostly in their twenties. Showers, weddings, and births were frequent events that distracted us from the critically ill patients on our telemetry floor. We enjoyed seeing each other through these major life changes, and my coworkers were excited for me to be next at the altar.

The Air Force deadline for requesting a joint-spouse assignment was six months prior to the permanent change of station (PCS), and the couple had to be married before requesting a move together. Lee was due to PCS in May of 1986, so we had less than five months to get married. Since we were marrying so quickly, I wondered if people would think I was pregnant instead of working toward a USAF joint-spouse PCS.

March 22, 1986, dawned a crisp, sunny wedding day, free of the nasty, unpredictable Dayton weather that I had assumed would occur at that time of year. In the flurry of dressing at the chapel, I was shocked when my nose suddenly began to bleed, dripping crimson down the length of my traditional wedding gown.

"Get her over to the sink!"

"Ahhhhh! She's bleeding onto her dress!"

"Cold water! Cold water!" Shouts of panic and instruction ensued as everyone in the bride's room voiced their input on the "crisis."

"It's just a little blood," I chided in a relaxed tone. "I'll get it out with cold water. I'm so glad I didn't buy the lace gown." I was relieved at my choice of a silky polyester fabric, because the blood washed right out. I shook my head in horror at what my bloody nose would have done to the lace sheath I had originally wanted to wear.

"I can't believe how calm you are," my mother said softly in a surprised tone.

"Mom, that's me. I am calm in emergencies, because I have to be when I'm at work. It's just the everyday stuff that gets to me." As I explained my response, I was surprised to recognize that aspect of my character.

Lee and I were married at Chapel One, Wright-Patt's picturesque chapel next to the golf course. I was thrilled to see how handsome Lee looked as he walked up to me that day all decked out in his mess dress, the formal USAF uniform that he and all the groomsmen wore. We began our wedding day together posing for photographs outside, the Ohio weather unusually sunny and warm for March. Sadly, we never did get to see those outdoor photographs, since our photographer lost that entire roll of film. Yet we kept each other laughing that day, and for decades afterwards, by singing "Chapel of Love," a 1964 hit song by the Dixie Cups.

Our wedding was small but significant. We had flown Pastor Roberson and his wife from New York to Dayton for the event. Pastor Roberson had been there for so many milestones in my life: my Dad's death, his funeral, and my confirmation, as well as fun times with my sister and the Roberson girls. The Robersons were like my second parents, and Pastor's sermon was like a fatherly talk to me.

The reception was at the Wright-Patterson Officers' Club. We hired a harpist who played during our sit-down dinner. The wedding was elegant and so small that we were able to get a group picture of everyone.

Several weeks later, Lee held up a sheaf of paperwork as he walked into the townhouse. "I got my orders!" he announced with his characteristic controlled enthusiasm, taking a seat on my swivel armchair.

Lacking Lee's self-control, I ran over and jumped onto his lap, spinning the chair with both of us in it. "Where? Where to?!" I demanded.

"Just a minute," Lee interrupted to calm me down. He slowed the twirling chair to a stop as he held up the paperwork.

"Wait!" I urged, with something more in mind. "I want to make the promise to you that Ruth did. Wherever these orders send you, I want you to know that where you go, I will go and where you lodge I will lodge." These were the words the widow Ruth promised to her widowed mother-in-law Naomi in the biblical book of Ruth, but I thought they were appropriate to promise to my love as we started our lives out together.

"Nellis AFB!" Lee said excitedly.

"Where's that?" I asked, noting that Nellis had not been on our list of requests for joint-spouse assignments.

"It's in Las Vegas."

"Las Vegas, Nevada?! Yuck. I've never wanted to go there," I exclaimed with my usual first thought out of my mouth. Las Vegas was one place where I had never had a desire to go. To me it seemed to be a gambling pit of hedonism.

"Oh, Sweetie, it's out west. We don't have to gamble. We'll be busy backpacking and skiing. I'll introduce you to the Sierras. It's so beautiful out there. And the weather is so much better than here." Lee soon won me over with promises of adventures out in the wilds of the western United States. He was so ready to leave the dreary weather of Dayton. As a Southern California boy, he really could not tolerate many days without the sun. Although he loved his job and enjoyed his colleagues, he was ready for a change of climate.

"What will you be flying out there?" I wondered, not remembering anything about Nellis but the Red Flag exercises, which involved many types of fighter jets.

"Nellis is a TAC base. I'll be flying the A-7," Lee told me. [Tactical Air Command was the Air Force division that commanded fighter jets.]

"But I thought they didn't have any A-7s on active duty anymore," I responded with a puzzled look.

"This is the last active duty base with A-7s," Lee answered. This was not much information to go on, but the squadron and the mission were classified, so I never did learn much more than that.

The Air Force's idea of moving two married officers together is not the same as two young lovers might hope for.

As always, the needs of the Air Force come first. Lee left at the end of May for Squadron Officer's School in Alabama, an eight-week-long professional military education course. Some people live together before they are married; we did not even live together after we were married. I took my clothes over to Lee's place after our honeymoon, but then moved back in with my roommate Barb when Lee left several weeks later. Susie had already had a permanent change of duty station by this time.

Parting with Lee as a young newlywed was one of the most painful things I had done in my adult life. I remember crying as he loaded his bike onto the roof rack of his BMW. Stoic as always, Lee had what I imagined were tears in his eyes, but his impermeable exterior belied any emotional release. Clouds drizzled rain as he drove away. I ran back into my townhouse crying. Indulging in my pity party, I played the 1984 record album *Against All Odds* on my stereo and sobbed to the title song. Phil Collins' lyrics about leaving without a trace were tear-provoking, but I had no idea how much pain Lee's absence would yet bring.

The next months were punctuated by several reunions. I flew down to Montgomery AFB for a quick weekend and stayed with Lee in his concrete-block dorm room. As he told me about Squadron Officer School (SOS), how they played sports in the sweltering weather and completed group projects on history and ancient war lords, I was determined to avoid attending my own SOS in residence. Instead, I continued the SOS correspondence course, which I completed before leaving for Nellis AFB four months later.

In between visits with Lee, I worked in the coronary care unit at Wright-Patterson AFB Medical Center. I spent many a long night shift in front of the cardiac monitor bay at the nurses' station, listening to the ever-present beeping monitors as I pined away for my Captain Carson.

From SOS, Lee went to Safety School at March AFB in California where he learned how to investigate aviation mishaps and crashes. Long before the days of email, cell phones, and cheap long distance telephone service, we communicated by phone every couple of days during the long separations. We saw each other every six weeks, but that first year of marriage was marked by seven months of living in different states.

After he left for Tucson, I flew out to see Lee at his parents' home in Fullerton, California. We had another passionate reunion with a weekend trip to Catalina. The scenic island, so unlike any other American place in the lower forty-eight states, is almost tropical in appearance, yet only twenty-six miles from the Los Angeles shore. In the town of Avalon, we walked out onto the pier past the casino building to scuba dive in the underwater marine preserve at Casino Point. Giant goldfish, as I called the orange garibaldi, swooshed in and out of huge kelp forests. I was happy to swim among the garibaldi and undulating kelp stalks, but Lee had a more aggressive goal.

Lee motioned for me to follow him for the second part of our planned dive, exploring an old sailboat wreck. He began his descent down to the wreckage. We had planned to start at one end of the boat, submerged at sixty-five feet, and follow the edge of the boat, but not pursue it all the way to the wreck's maximum depth of ninety-five feet. As I followed Lee's course down to the wreck, I began to fall too quickly. I panicked and my goggles filled with tears. Although I soon recovered physically and was able to control my rate of descent, I was too freaked out emotionally to continue the dive, so I headed toward the surface. Lee was patient and understanding, even though I cut our wreck dive short because of my panic at the uncontrolled descent.

As always with our vacations, the constant togetherness was precious to us. We did not tire of each other's company. Just as we did on our honeymoon in the Bahamas, we ate, slept, dove, biked, and ran together in blissful unity. The weekend was idyllic, and even years later, Lee would sing his version of "26 Miles (Santa Catalina)," a pop song from 1958, to coax a smile out of me.

I finally PCSed from Wright-Patt, leaving my roommate Barb behind. The intensive care unit had been so busy that we had a column at the end of the schedule for how many days off we were owed. In the civilian world, staff gets paid for overtime; in the military, you work when they need you. I remember my days-off column stood at ten, meaning that I was owed ten eight-hour days that I had worked extra; that overtime would never be paid back. Saying goodbye to my friends was hard, one of the most difficult aspects of being in the military. On the other hand, I was glad to leave my hardworking and understaffed unit behind.

I drove in my brand new 1986 Volkswagen Jetta to Kansas City, where Lee flew in to meet me. He arrived before I did and had champagne cooling in an ice bucket at the hotel. We toasted to starting our married life together—finally! From

Kansas City, Lee joined me for the drive out west. During that trip, we talked, sang, laughed, and savored our uninterrupted time together. I mimicked Bruce Hornsby's piano solo on the dashboard every time the 1986 hit "The Way It Is" played on the radio. Lee chuckled at my antics, and we laughingly remembered the "air piano" when we later attended a Bruce Hornsby and the Range concert in Las Vegas.

At one point on the trip, I was stunned with the memory of a prophecy spoken over me more than a decade earlier. When I was in middle school, a prophet and evangelist named Jack Hines visited my hometown and led revival meetings. He had even prophesied over me, that I would be holding hands with a man sitting on fleece. Here I was, traveling with my new husband as we sat on fleece car seat covers, held hands, and ventured into our new life together. I knew this was God's fulfillment of that prophecy. I was where God wanted me to be. Lee and I were so in love with each other, and life was perfect.

[6]

Captains Carson, Continued

A CHILDLIKE WONDER gripped me as we drove down I-15 out of the mountains from the Arizona corner into Las Vegas at night. City lights glistened in the distance as we progressed from the dark, barren desert into the bustling, ever-lit city. Lost in thought, I considered it a new beginning. *This is where our life together really starts—where we can finally live together.*

In addition to flying the A-7, Lee's job was safety officer with the 4450th Tactical Fighter Group at Nellis AFB. I soon learned the expectations of the Air Force spouse when the job is classified: don't ask, because he's not going to tell. I discovered that when Lee clammed up, I was not supposed to ask questions. I had a top secret security clearance, but that meant nothing outside of my duty area. I was an outsider to the flight line; and as such, I would never receive even a hint of Lee's covert Air Force responsibilities. The USAF fighter pilot lives and dies by the code he adheres to. Lee honored the secrets with which he was entrusted. To this day, I do not know exactly what Lee did at Nellis or how the aging A-7s related to any of the base operations. My job was to support him, not to ask questions that were none of my business.

From Nellis, Lee had several deployments with his squadron. Some deployments were classified, and I did not know where he went. One of those lasted two weeks. During that time, as an obstetrics nurse at the Nellis AFB hospital, I coached a woman in labor. Her husband, in the same squadron as Lee, was on the same deployment. I felt sad that she could not share this momentous event with her husband, and I was determined to help her through labor to the baby's birth. My twelve-hour shift extended even longer when my patient delivered around shift change.

The two of us thought that our husbands' squadron might have deployed to the Far East, but we did not know for sure. Following military protocol for such situations, I called the Red Cross to give them the details of the new baby for transmission to the woman's husband. I dutifully reported her husband's name, rank, and social security number, followed by the details of his new baby. Hanging up the phone, I shook my head at the question of whether that essential information would make it to the husband accurately. Like the old telephone game, I envisioned the news changing with each person contacted, until the message came out completely different on the receiving end; perhaps the new daddy would hear that he had a small boy, when his wife had in fact given birth to a big, healthy girl.

Although Lee was deployed more than I would have liked, we enjoyed many activities while he was home. In 1987, Lee's ten-year high school reunion was a gala banquet hosted at a Disneyland hotel in Anaheim California. Across the room all I saw was a sea of real estate developers: up-and-coming moguls with similar yellow silk power ties and glamorous women in their little black dresses. I set off to find someone of depth and substance to talk to.

Wading through the sea of stylish clones, I started a conversation with a classmate of Lee's who did not wear a power tie. This gentleman may have been one of the least heralded successes, yet his story relayed much hard work and effort. In labored speech, he exclaimed, "I going to college!" Likely in special education during his high school years in the mid-1970s, this man was proudly taking on a huge challenge to further his education. After congratulating him on his new venture, I made my way across the room to find someone else for interesting conversation.

With his long hair and lack of suit or tie, the guy looked out of place in this crowd. The top half of his hair had dark roots that extended down to chin level, and the hair beyond his shoulders was white blond, giving him a rock-star look. We struck up a conversation and, to my surprise, I learned quickly that his brother had dated Lee's sister. I enjoyed his stories of his brother and Lee's sister Chris far more than the real estate talk of other attendees.

Two years later, Lee and I attended my ten-year high school reunion. What a contrast between the Southern California and small-town Minnesota reunions! For the same price as Lee's banquet dinner at the upscale Anaheim hotel, my reunion included a banquet, awards, presentations, and even a pig roast the next day, not to mention down-to-earth people who were hanging out with their kids and talking with everyone. We had a fun weekend, which Lee begrudgingly admitted. He did not usually enjoy spending vacation time in Minnesota, but he always had fun hanging out with my friends.

However, vacations were few and work kept us busy. As a nurse at Nellis AFB hospital, I worked the obstetrics floor for a year. Monitoring women in labor, caring for moms and babies during delivery, demonstrating baby care, working the nursery, and teaching prenatal classes were not my areas of career interest. Like any other job I had ever held, I applied myself and worked hard to become competent in those areas of nursing, but my heart was not in this job. Coming from the high-tech world of critical care, I felt helpless when a baby crashed in-utero and we could not access the infant to intervene. Coaching women through such pain and agony only enforced my resolve not to have children.

In January of 1988, the Chief Nurse offered me the chance to be interim charge nurse of the emergency room (ER), and I was thrilled. I was a junior captain and young for the job, but management gave me the opportunity until they found a higher ranking officer to fill the position. I loved the broad spectrum of challenges brought on by the variety of co-workers, patients, diseases, and equipment in that setting.

During my first month on the job, we performed infant resuscitations in the ER and nursery three Fridays in a row, an unusual frequency for our small hospital. I can still see the strawberry-blond eyelashes and opaque skin of a precious little SIDS (sudden infant death syndrome) baby brought in by ambulance on one of those difficult Fridays. Dealing with the pain of those grieving families was gut-wrenching. Along with the families of those patients, my ER staff needed support and debriefing to cope with the traumatic scenarios.

Several other incidents challenged my novice management skills during my interim position in the ER. On January 28, 1988, our ER received a radio transmission about two United States Navy FA-18 Hornet jets crashing in the California desert. The ER technician hurriedly handed the emergency radio call over to me to deal with a stressed flight surgeon on the other end. We conferred by radio about transferring the pilots to Nellis. Sadly, one pilot had not survived his jet's crash, whereas the other pilot had ejected safely. Any flight mishap necessitated a thorough investigation, a process I knew about from Lee, who—as a safety officer—had investigated two USAF crashes. One decision needed to be clarified—and quickly: whether the surviving pilot and the deceased pilot's remains would be transferred to us or to a civilian facility.

Some of these decisions were "way above my pay grade," as the military expression declares, so in the midst of my radio conversation, I had the ER techs repeatedly page my "higher ups." None of my superiors responded to their pagers, the communications state-of-the-art devices of 1988. The on-call flight surgeon and other commanders were involved with the Red Flag exercise, whose headquarters was a concrete bunker impenetrable to beeper transmissions. I made decision after decision, awaiting input from my senior officers but recognizing the immediacy of the actions required. The crash had occurred far beyond our Nellis ambulance coverage range, so we had to involve civilian emergency response vehicles. At one point, I was relaying coordinates from radio to telephone, knowing that calling a civilian ambulance to a secured range was a security breach. My gestures and verbal requests directed to my team of techs accelerated as they unsuccessfully paged an increasing list of senior officers for me.

One notable conversation from that stressful day was a discussion with the x-ray technician about how to deal with the incoming casualties. Bringing in the deceased fighter pilot would necessitate a prescribed set of full body x-rays to aid in the investigation, similar to what the injured fighter pilot would receive. We talked about the process and how to honor and respect the body of the deceased pilot. Our conversation included military respect and professional empathy. I spoke as a nurse manager and patient advocate, but my role did not extend to the widow left behind at a California naval air station. She would face the official blue car in her driveway, with Navy officials notifying her of her beloved's death in the tragedy. Since the pilot's widow did not live near Nellis AFB, that notification was out of my professional jurisdiction, and it was nothing I wanted to face on a personal level.

Only a few months later on May 4, 1988, my management skills would be challenged once again. This regional emergency involved a massive explosion of ammonium perchlorate stores, used in solid-propellant rocket boosters at the Pacific Engineering Company of Nevada in Henderson, Nevada, just twenty-five miles from Nellis. One of our ER emergency technicians happened to be on the phone with his wife, who was in their Henderson home as the plant exploded. She thought it was a bomb or a burglar breaking into her home. From the ER phone, her husband heard breaking glass and screams from his wife. As we began learning of the circumstances of the explosion, my ER tech insisted on making the twenty minute drive home, despite our admonitions that the roads to his house would likely be blocked off during the emergency. As a manager, I knew that I should keep this excellent ER technician with the superior suturing skills for the potential casualties we might admit as a result of the incident. As a wife, I recognized the look of love and concern on his face, and I knew he needed to get to his sweetheart as soon as possible.

Although twenty-five miles away the apparent ground zero, we could see the mushroom cloud from the ambulance pad outside the ER doors. At the time, we had no idea what had caused the blast. Several ER workers who were also Henderson residents realized that the location was close to the Kidd & Co. marshmallow factory, so in the midst of the fears of bomb and nuclear explosions, we shared hilarious jokes about exploding marshmallows. Although we prepared to fully implement our hospital disaster plan, no casualties came to our ER that day.

Not every day in the ER was that intense, but it was hard work. The best part about my ER job was getting weekends off for the first time in my career. Both captains in rank, Lee and I had military careers that were progressing well. We worked hard, but the two of us also played hard. Lee and I took advantage of every weekend to backpack, camp, bike, ski, and tour the West. We traveled and played during our free time, with the agreement that having children was not in our plans during the first five years of our marriage.

This turned out to be a good plan, as our next joint-spouse assignment request did not transpire as smoothly as the first. Lee had requested to fly F-16s in Germany. My position as a captain was junior enough to work at any of the hospitals on the bases he requested. When my orders came through before his, I was stunned to see that I was scheduled to PCS to Cannon AFB in New Mexico. Not only that, but I was to work obstetrics, which was decidedly not my area of interest. Lee had not yet received orders but thought he would be assigned somewhere in Europe. With hearts willing to serve God in Europe, we had prayed for God to give us assignments, but when the paperwork came, we did not like God's answer to our prayers.

I initiated a discussion with my lieutenant colonel nursing supervisor and the hospital chief nurse Colonel Perry, two of my USAF nurse role models. They tried to convince me that this would be a good career move, no matter where my husband ended up. I was flabbergasted at the thought of living separately from my husband, but I had to hide my shock in front of these two career officers, who had likely sacrificed much for their nursing and military achievements. I do not know what shocked me more—the orders or my superiors' encouragement to have a long-distance marriage for the sake of my USAF career. I stifled my urge to yell, "No way!" and flee the room as I listened to their admonishments to make career a priority. Back at home, Lee and I did not need much discussion to agree that our marriage and living together was a priority over career success. To the surprise of both of our superiors, Lee and I turned down our USAF orders and submitted our paperwork to get out of the Air Force.

"Carson, you're too damn smart. Get the hell out of here," Colonel Perry ordered in her salty, straight-talking manner. Albeit a bit rough, her parting compliment was one of my most treasured evaluations, because I held her in such high regard as an Air Force officer, nurse, and mentor. I left her office determined to become more like her as a nurse and leader, even though I was moving into the civilian world.

Lee and I both left the Air Force in November of 1989. He began a civilian career with American Airlines and started training in Dallas. When asked to compare the military and civilian careers, Lee liked to respond, "I no longer fly fast, upside down, or drop bombs." Meanwhile, I went to Minnesota to live at my childhood home, until Lee was assigned to a hub and we knew where we were going to move.

The next years were filled with changes and challenges, with the two of us building our careers and enjoying time together when not at work. We made two cross-country moves along with one shorter-distance move before we settled down. Initially based out of Chicago, Lee started on the DC-10 as a flight engineer. His seat placement on the aircaft was affectionately known as "the only sideways-facing seat that doesn't flush." Lee used to say that his most important responsibility was the temperature controls for the cargo hold, or the "doggie death switch." After the move to the San Francisco crew base, Lee became a first officer on the MD-80, a DC-9-based airliner.

In the midst of all the moves, I earned a Master of Science degree and worked in varied settings: as a critical care nurse in Chicago and San Francisco, a medical-device researcher at a Silicon Valley start-up company, and on a university faculty as a nursing instructor. Lee and I traveled on yearly trips to ski, scuba dive, and backpack. When we reached the agreed-upon five-year mark in our marriage, we decided that we were having too much fun to have kids yet—so we agreed to wait another five years.

In 1996, after ten years of fun and cross-country moves as a couple, Lee and I became pregnant, bought our first house, and settled in San Jose, California, to raise a family. Our daughter Claire was born in 1996; Bennett came along in 1998. The first ten years had been wonderful as a twosome, but God helped the two of us change our attitudes and lifestyle to focus on these incredible children. One of the biggest changes for us was when I quit my job to be at home full-time. I had been teaching nursing at San Jose State University in a rewarding position that I really enjoyed. It was a difficult adjustment to put my career on hold, but we believed that God's priority for us was time spent with our children.

While it was more challenging after having children, eating nutritious meals and exercising regularly remained a lifestyle for the two of us. We attempted to get our children to eat healthy. The homemade baby food was an easy sell, but as many parents experience, picky toddlers posed a nutritional challenge. My exercise schedule geared down to kids' outings in the stroller. Lee continued his intense workouts, sometimes taking the kids in the baby jogger on his runs through nearby Alum Rock Park.

Lee took vitamin E and fish-oil capsules, years before they were recommended as heart-healthy options, along with a regular-strength aspirin every couple of days. Unlike the kids and me, Lee usually turned down chocolate and rarely ate dessert. Although Lee loved sausage and bacon, I refused to buy such unhealthy food, so he would order sausage or bacon for breakfast whenever we vacationed. Other than that, he always made healthy food choices and encouraged our kids to enjoy the same.

I teased Lee about being "Golden Boy," a nickname he hated. I called him that because, in my opinion, things came to him so easily. He would protest and point out that his hard work earned him his position. My counterpoint was usually a silly example like the post office. When he went to our local Berryessa Post Office, he never had to stand in line. No matter when I timed it, a trip to the same post office always meant lines for me, even before they opened. So I always sent Lee when I could, calling him "Golden Boy," and jokingly asking if they always cleared the post office out ahead of time—just for him.

I was not the only one to recognize Lee's charmed life. In 1997, Troy High School's class of 1977 celebrated their twenty-year high school reunion. Lee's friend and master of ceremonies Randy asked, "Lee Carson where have you been? On some island where you don't age?!"

As always, people remarked on Lee's youthful appearance. His tanned skin and perfect complexion gave him a baby-faced look. When questioned how he managed to look so young, Lee always answered, "Clean living."

Once out of the Air Force, Lee grew a "temporary" mustache, but later he kept it, hoping that facial hair would age him to credibility. He was annoyed by people who questioned, "Are you old enough to fly this plane?"

At age thirty-seven, Lee had to prove his identification once while buying a bottle of wine. The clerk questioned Lee's age and was stunned to see the driver's license. "1959?! 1959?!" the clerk repeated incredulously, as he realized that the cutoff year he was carding for was 1975.

Whether he looked the part or not, by the year 2000, Lee had the seniority to upgrade to MD-80 captain, which would have resulted in a significant pay raise but less flexibility in terms of scheduling. He chose to forgo the money and career progression in order to spend more time with his family. As a senior first officer, Lee was able to bid and hold the highly desirable schedules that minimized his layovers. His bidding priority was to get turnarounds, the single-day trips which meant he was home at night after the twelve- to fourteen-hour days. One of his usual routes from the San Jose International Airport was the "Nerd Bird" back and forth to Austin, Texas. Lee described it as a commuter route between the high-tech cities; passengers pulled out their laptops almost in unison once the plane was airborne. Passengers on these flights were quiet and orderly; they worked the whole flight. If Lee left for the 5:30 a.m. sign-in, he could be home just in time to put the kids to bed at night.

Our two kids loved their time with Daddy. Claire was quite the Daddy's girl; her bright blue eyes and wide smile always inspired a big grin on her father's face. Lee usually played with Claire in the backyard; our neighbor Donna said that she did not know who squealed louder, Lee or Claire. If Lee left for work while Bennett was awake, the bereft boy would lunge at the closed door and throw a tantrum. Bennett expressed his frustration physically, his toddler face a bright red contrast to his white-blonde hair, as he pounded on the door in protest of Daddy's departure.

"I kept two kids alive today, and that is all I got done," was a typical line I would growl at Lee when he walked in the door after his long work day. I was usually exhausted and discouraged, having barely survived another day with two energetic, strong-willed children. As much as I read my Bible, prayed, and relied on God for help, the mothering role was overwhelming for me.

Our kids loved it when Daddy was home to put them to bed at night. In contrast to my "get-the-kids-to-bed-quickly" routine, Lee would savor and prolong the evening ritual. The bedtime reading lasted much longer with Daddy than with Mommy! The three of them spent extended times reading, praying, cuddling, and giggling together. One of their favorite games was "Daddy Sandwich." Lee would pretend to build big sandwiches on their tummies, tickling them with pantomimes of layer upon layer of sandwich ingredients while they squealed. How thankful I was that Lee relished the bedtime routine and that he took over at this time of day to make it fun for our kids.

In 2003, I entered a writing contest for the most romantic husband. I entitled my entry "The Non-Romantic's Lapse."

> My husband, a romantic?! No, I would never associate that adjective with the man I know and love. Not given to flowers, extra words, or any semblance of fluff, Lee lived on the serious side of life when I met him. After seventeen years of marriage, my husband is still a straight-talking, no-fuss, no-frills kind of guy. Lee does not take time to smell the roses, literally or figuratively, so I am the gardener of the family. When I was seven months pregnant with our second child, I bought hyacinth and iris bulbs with dreams of colorful flowers in the front yard. My forty-pound pregnancy weight gain and a wild toddler made gardening difficult, so the flower bulbs were relegated to the back of the garage. Or so I thought.
>
> What a joy it was to bring our baby boy home from the hospital. As I sat nursing him in the living room, I looked out the window and saw hyacinth and iris blooms! My husband had planted the bulbs to surprise me. (Just do not tell him that it was a romantic gesture!)

True to Lee's engineering nature, he planted the bulbs in a straight line with identical spacing between plants. To me, it was the perfect example of how he did something loving for me and expressed it in his way, a precise, linear formation much different from the patchy clusters of flowers I had envisioned.

That same year I wrote one of my cheesy, rhyming poems for Lee's forty-fourth birthday:

> To my husband, I love you
> Please know that it's true.
> I am actually still
> Quite crazy about you.

Off into the sunset we rode
Just seventeen years ago.
Who would have "knowed"
We'd have two wild ones in tow?

Blame the children—
Yes, that's what we'll do,
They reduce us to blitherin'
Idiots—but, hey, who knew?!

Once we have been given
Some time to just rest
Our sanity will return
We'll be back to our best.

I love you, my dear
Happy number forty-four
You get better each year
Here's to many more!!

No masterpiece of poetry or grammar, the poem served as a connection point between two very busy parents who were still in love after all the years. Lee's time off was spent with the kids; both of us volunteered at our church and at their school. I volunteered in the classroom and with the Parent Teacher Association, while Lee drove for field trips and volunteered for special events, like painting tables and digging trenches for electrical wiring to the portable classrooms. Our days were full and busy, two imperfect people in an imperfect marriage doing our best to raise our children.

[7]

Divine Preparation

IN AUGUST OF 2004 after a Bible study on Hezekiah, God impressed upon my heart the words from Isaiah 38:1, "Put your house in order." I thought about that but did not have any idea what it meant. My sense of time seemed to move faster than usual, as if I were on a treadmill and my life ran past me the minute my foot hit the track. At one point, I started thinking that I was going to die and even planned my own funeral service. Rather than ruminate in fear, I decided to obey, even if I did not understand what lay ahead. What I did was catch up on paperwork, organize photos, add to my children's baby books, write in my journal, and sort through boxes.

I even coerced Lee to venture out to the garage for his boxes. "I can't believe all your boxes of stuff!" I said as I pulled his boxes out of the garage cabinets.

"But it's put away," Lee said matter-of-factly as he stood in the doorway, not wanting to participate.

"Yeah, have you sorted through it lately? What a waste to keep it without looking through the stuff. Have you even gone through this box of high school stuff?!" My voice was raised in frustration as I realized that he preferred shuffling boxes around to sorting them.

"It's my *stuff*," Lee emphasized in sentimental attachment to the boxed items.

"Mr. Packrat! Let's go through it together." I grabbed his arm and pulled him into the garage.

"No, it's fine. I might need that stuff someday," he announced in opposition to my idea.

"You will *not!* Do you even remember what you have in here?!"

"My school stuff, like it says on the box."

"Come on. Let's go through this together."

"Not now," he dismissed, turning back toward the door into the house.

"Come on! We need to go through this crap. Okay, what is this?"

"I don't know."

"You don't even know what you *have* in here. This is a book of poetry from middle school. Did you write poetry?" My eyes rolled in irritation at the amount of stuff he had saved, but part of me considered that I might unearth fascinating new information about my husband.

"No."

"Do you know any of the classmates who wrote these poems?"

"No."

"Then why did you save it?!" More eye rolling on my part.

"I don't know." A shrug of his shoulders revealed Lee's continued disinterest.

"Look—here's some blank notepaper. Is this from junior high?" My voice pitched upward along with my level of frustration.

"Maybe just from high school . . ."

"I can't believe you keep this *crap* and we have to move these boxes of nothing every time. I always sort through my boxes. Have you *never* sorted through this stuff?!" Incredulous at the thought of all of our cross-country moves, I tried not to lose my temper.

"Nope." He said it slowly, in a drawling manner, his eyes twinkling as he chuckled at the collision between my minimalistic nature and his save-everything-in-case-I-need-it mentality.

Looking at his face, I realized that he had simply ignored these boxes for over twenty years. I reminded him of how we had carried boxes through the garage in Las Vegas, into the apartment in Chicago, up the winding staircase in San Francisco, across the sidewalk to the San Jose townhouse, and then into the garage of this San Jose home.

"You are *such* a packrat!" My irritation soon gave way to laughter.

"Yup," he smiled back at me.

"Okay, I'll help you, but you know this drives me *nuts!*"

"Yup." His ability not to get drawn into conflict when I was trying to pick a fight with him never ceased to amaze me. He was so patient, as he indulged my need to sort through the boxes. We laughed at the ridiculous items that had been packed up for so long: pens, pencils, blank paper, folders, etc. He was willing to part with non-essential items but had no desire to clean it out himself.

"See, we're down to just one box now. Doesn't that feel better?" I challenged.

"No." Lee's reply was honest but it frustrated me.

"Well, I feel better. Now did I make you get rid of anything you weren't ready to part with?" My hope was that he would recognize that sorting stuff and purging the excess would motivate him to clean out more frequently than every twenty years.

"No."

"See? We even kept those prom pictures with your old girlfriends." I really tried to respect Lee's stuff, but I was still in the clean-up mode.

"I don't care if you get rid of those."

"No, those are your high school memories—you need to keep those. Besides, this picture of you in the plaid, bell-bottom pants is hilarious! Someday the kids will love this."

"Okay. I'm going inside now," Lee replied in relief, quickly turning to the door.

"Look, Lee," I persisted, "I'm putting a new label on the box. See? It says 'Sorted under duress August 2004.'" I meant the comment as a joking reminder of how I forced my favorite saver to face his clutter. Little could I have imagined the pain that sorting through his things would bring in the near future.

The fall of 2004 brought other aspects of our lives together in preparation for what was to come. Whereas I had taught Bible study for teenaged girls the year before, this year I told our church youth pastor Kim that I wanted to teach but did not feel that I was supposed to. Kim said that she did not have a group for me, which was unusual, since she often needed teachers in fall. My schedule was cleared in several other ways; strangely, I was not very busy. I was trying to be content with a quieter pace to my life. For the first time in our marriage, Lee was not scheduling our next vacation. I thought that unusual, since he always planned ahead to where we would travel next.

At over 120,000 miles, my car was reliable and in great shape thanks to Lee's continued maintenance. I remember walking into the garage and seeing Lee smile at me from the back end of our ten-year-old Mitsubishi station wagon. Lee's blue-green eyes matched the old green flight suit he wore to work on the car. His hands covered in grease, Lee was in his element solving mechanical problems. The flight suit, or "bag," as the Air Force pilots affectionately called the flying uniform, had been relegated to garage coveralls. Unlike pilots who saved their bags as trophies of a USAF career, Lee had found a practical use for his uniform.

"I fixed the antenna, Sweetie. Now you should be able to get better K-LOVE reception." Lee grinned, knowing that K-LOVE radio station reception was essential to maintaining my sanity in a car full of kids. Nothing was more endearing to me than my favorite grease monkey displaying such an act of love for me.

The list of what Lee did to repair and maintain my car that December was incredible: brakes, tires, antenna, and more. When he asked me to help bleed the brakes, I remember asking him in exasperation, "Does this have to be done now?

Can't it wait until after Christmas?!" I was busy with holiday preparations and irritated to be called out to the garage.

"I need to get this done for you," Lee answered in typical seriousness of tone that settled the question and left no room for argument. I groused at how my priorities had to be dropped so that he could get his tasks done. I pumped the brakes hard in irritation as I thought of all that I had to get done before Christmas. Christmas cards, baking, putting the tree up, shopping for gifts—I did it all. Little did I realize that Lee was on God's timetable, working on what God was prompting him to do, not what I thought he should do. Finishing the car repairs turned out to be one of Lee's last provisions for his family.

One of my comments that December seems eerie in retrospect. "Lee, I am eating so much. I just crave protein, and I'm even gaining weight."

"Do you think it's your thyroid again?" Lee knew my history of postpartum thyroid problems, which was the last time my appetite and weight were unstable.

"No. I don't know what the deal is. I've gained almost five pounds."

"If you're eating healthy, you must need it," Lee reassured me. Within weeks, those extra pounds would be crucial to my survival.

On Sunday, January 2, 2005, I had a sense of urgency about cleaning up the Christmas decorations.

"Why are you in such a hurry?" Lee asked, "You don't have to do it all today." I was not usually in a big rush to pack up but, that year, taking down our Christmas tree and decorations seemed strangely important.

"I don't know why, but I just have to get it done today." I worked steadily after we got home from church. The only Christmas item that I did not put away, the basket of cards, would remain on the counter until the next September.

Another aspect of preparation was my reading list. For some reason, I was interested in reading all the widow books from our church library during 2004: Elisabeth Elliot, Gracia Burnham, C.S. Lewis, and Evelyn Husband. I read other great books, like Luis Palau's biography, but somehow I gravitated toward "widow lit," as I now call the genre. I was especially interested in Evelyn Husband's book, *High Calling: The Courageous Life and Faith of Space Shuttle* Columbia *Commander Rick Husband* (2003). Evelyn told the story of her husband Rick, who died along with his crew when the shuttle exploded February 1, 2003 upon reentry into Earth's atmosphere. The book was popular; it was checked out every time I looked for it in the church library. On one of Lee's last Sundays at church, I was again looking for Evelyn's memoir.

"Emily, I'm never going to get a chance to read that book! It's always checked out. I should just buy it." In addition to being my neighbor and friend, Emily was our church librarian; her daughters were two of our favorite babysitters.

"Oh, the book is on display in the foyer. If you wait a few minutes, Susie is bringing it back up to the library, and you can check it out."

One of the aspects that we loved about this church was the library, with its great selection of children's books, tapes, and videos. We had left North Valley Christian Fellowship in 2002, not for any doctrinal differences or conflict, but because we believed that God was directing us toward another church, Christ Community Church of Milpitas (CCCM). With the benefit of hindsight, I realize that God plugged us into a larger church that had the resources we would soon need. At the time it was a tough change, but we obeyed God's leading.

Looking around the library to size up what my kids might be getting into, I wondered if Lee and the kids would be patient enough to wait for me to get the book.

"We can wait," Lee offered, pulling cherub-faced Bennett out of the library closet where he was snooping through bags and boxes.

"No, it's okay," I said impatiently. "Let's just go."

"She'll be here any minute with the book," Emily said in her ever-encouraging tone.

"Okay, I'll wait." I sighed contentedly as I noticed Claire, who leaned forward with her thick brunette hair covering her face, intent on reading one of the many books she had checked out.

Had we not waited in the library that day, I would not have read the book before Lee died. Divine preparation or bizarre coincidence? I believe it was guidance from the loving hand of God. I am grateful, but I cannot explain how God could prepare me for something so horrific.

[8]

My Nightmare

QUICK FOOTSTEPS to the bathroom awakened me on that January night. I sprang out of bed to follow Lee. As he sat down, I grabbed the puke bucket, anticipating what I thought was another episode of vomiting and diarrhea. I had no idea that what followed would change us forever.

The commode room in our master bathroom was tiny. It barely had room for a door, let alone space for me to stand by Lee in support. He sat on the toilet and—as close by as possible, I held the bucket, ready for him to vomit. Whereas the toilet tank lid usually made a porcelain-on-porcelain grating sound when moved, a sound that normally echoed through the high-ceilinged bedroom, this time there was no sound as Lee leaned back against the toilet tank. Slowly, gently, and quietly, Lee closed his eyes and slumped backward. The only sound I heard was a horse-like snorting as Lee's exhalation passed through his loosely closed lips.

Dropping the bucket, the wife in me thought, *Oh Sweetheart, you are so exhausted that you fell asleep on the toilet.*

The moment was eerily peaceful; the significance of Lee's last breath took a few moments to comprehend.

Then the nurse brain in me kicked in. "Lee, Lee!" I shook him. Trying to watch for respirations and check for a carotid pulse was impossible with him sitting back on the toilet. Hooking my arms underneath Lee's armpits, I dragged all 170 pounds of him out of the tiny powder room and onto the bathroom floor.

Autopilot took over. Establish unresponsiveness. Head tilt. Look, listen, and feel four seconds for respirations. Two deep breaths. Check for carotid pulse. Follow the ribcage up to verify position. Begin chest compressions.

"One and two and three and . . ." I counted in that familiar rhythm. I had done this many times as a nurse, both in and outside of the hospital setting. As a critical care nurse, my steady, efficient, take-charge nature kicked in, just as it always had in an emergency. Twenty-two years of nursing, CPR certification, ACLS (advanced cardiac life support) certification, a master of science in critical care nursing—what I had trained for and learned from experience, I applied to the nightmare of my life.

The circumstances may vary, but the resuscitation sequence is an automatic response, even when applied to an unfamiliar situation. Just as the fighter pilot evades enemy fire in a new conflict using practiced methods, and the surgeon negotiates an ill-defined, invasive tumor with familiar precision technique, so the nurse applies standard emergency procedures to any resuscitation. Routine methods are applied to a new scenario with the experience and skill borne of much practice. Muscle memory, professionalism, and precision are honed in a career developed with continual training. The application is instinctual and routine, even though the challenge is new and different.

Time slowed down and my wife brain screamed at me. *This is Lee you are doing CPR on!* My nurse brain pushed the panic back and kept up the count. "Nine and ten and . . ."

Lee's ashen gray color in the fluorescent light of the bathroom registered in my nurse brain. *He is gone,* my gut told me. I knew it deeply and certainly, just as I had recognized that coloring on many other patients when they were dead or dying. *He is dead. He cannot be resuscitated at this point.* The nurse in me knew that this was the end of Lee's life.

My wife brain clamored as I continued CPR. *Come on Lee! It's okay. We'll make it. Wheelchair . . . a long rehab . . . no matter what . . . we can do it!*

After four cycles of CPR, I stopped to run for the bedroom phone. I grabbed the cordless phone from the headboard shelf on our bed, dialed 911, and ran back to Lee. Cradling the phone between my neck and shoulder, I resumed chest compressions.

Living in earthquake country, we had always kept one phone with a cord. Two months prior, Lee had replaced the cord phone with a cordless in our bedroom. God's provision was in place, I later realized when that detail crossed my consciousness.

As if to question whether this was truly happening, a bizarre thought crossed my mind. *I have never done CPR while holding a phone before.*

Giving my name and address over the phone, I pleaded for an ambulance. As if in slow motion, the dispatcher began reading from his guidelines. "Compress the chest one to one-and-a-half inches . . ."

One to one-and-a-half inches—no way! I wanted to scream. *On a healthy swimmer with a big chest wall and a distance runner's heart, compress two-and-a-half to three inches.* Something in me told me to just let it go; it was not my responsibility to teach this dispatcher. So I ignored the dispatcher with his incorrect CPR instructions, and I continued with an intensity that belied the professional distance my head tried to maintain.

Soon the dispatcher interrupted my rhythm, "Ma'am. Ma'am! You need to stop CPR and go answer the door. The paramedics are there."

Tearing myself away from Lee, I flew down the stairs and threw open the front door. No one was there, so I ran onto the driveway in my pajamas, flailing my arms at the fire truck that sped past my house and down the street. I gave up on flagging the emergency vehicle down and headed back into the house to my first priority—Lee. I would do CPR until they got there, but I was not going to chase them down the street. Lee needed me more.

Several minutes later, after what seemed to me like hours, I heard the paramedics coming in the front door, calling out.

"Up here! Upstairs!" I yelled.

The firefighters rushed up the stairs and into the bedroom, with the monitor and other supplies strapped to a gurney. Kneeling down, one of the paramedics moved the equipment off the gurney. He began to apply the electrode patches to Lee's chest and to set up the heart monitor. I wanted to grab the patches and cables out of the guy's hands;

he was moving much too slowly for me. My thoughts were impatient. *Hurry up!*

At that point, one of the firefighters gently pulled me out of the room and into the hallway. I resisted him, saying "What's his rhythm? Do you have anything?" as I focused on the monitor. Time to run the code, intubate, get the IV (intravenous line) in, give meds. Instinct tried to take over in this emergency.

Pulling away from Lee was one of the hardest tasks I have ever had to do. I have never left a code in progress. The nurse brain in me was looking for the rhythm, thinking about the possibility of defibrillation, anticipating what meds would be administered, and considering the myriad things that needed to be accomplished during resuscitation.

"I need to ask you some questions." The firefighter was gentle and kind with me, but I fixed my gaze back toward the bedroom door. As I strained to listen, all I could see was the sole of a fire-fighter's boot.

"PEA," I overheard.

My nurse brain remained engaged, as I went down the list of possible causes of pulseless electrical activity, or PEA. "Hypovolemia? No, he was not dehydrated. Hypothermia? No. Pulmonary embolus? No, his breathing was peaceful. Cardiac tamponade—do you think that's what it could be?" I desperately questioned the firefighter with the list of possible causes of PEA. Continuing to mentally process the medical emergency, my gaze fixated on the firefighter's boot sole. The trauma of that moment seared the emergency and the boot sole together in my subconscious mind. The two unrelated elements merged as one conjoined memory, as I would realize later.

"I need you to answer some questions right now, ma'am," The man said with a soft but insistent voice. I answered the questions, all the while focused on what was happening around the corner.

The paramedics talked about taking Lee to the closest hospital. I panicked, remembering the recently published study that cited our neighborhood hospital as having the highest cardiac mortality rate in Silicon Valley. I asked, or more likely demanded, that Lee be taken to El Camino Hospital instead, where the cardiac mortality rate was the lowest in the valley. Despite numerous recent management changes, El Camino Hospital in Mountain View was known for its skilled physicians and high-quality nursing care, characteristics that I had observed firsthand as a clinical nursing instructor working there. But the paramedics refused my request, instead insisting that Lee be transported to the nearest hospital, and not to El Camino.

My distress eased when one of the medics reminded me that the local hospital had recently merged with the downtown trauma center. To my relief he explained that, since the merger, trauma surgeons were on call at the local hospital. Whereas I had been prepared to lie down in front of the ambulance if Lee was sent to the closest hospital, the medic's soft-spoken words reassured me, and I was content with their choice for my husband.

Turning back to the firefighter in the hallway, I was disheartened by his question, "Is there someone you can call for help?"

I wracked my brain as I stammered, "I don't have any family here." The panic began to rise in me as I tried to think of someone who could come over in the middle of the night.

"There must be a friend you could call," the firefighter urged gently.

Kelly—yes, she'll be there for me. A dear friend from church, Kelly and I had been involved together in a co-operative preschool with her son and my daughter. She knew my kids well, and she would be someone they would trust. She was the first of many people I would awaken with phone calls during that long night.

Kelly came over quickly, her familiar six-foot frame and model looks reminding me of our longstanding friendship and the calm, organized efficiency she brought to any situation. I also called our pastor, Jim Tirone, to drive to the hospital with me.

Soon after Kelly arrived, my sleepy eight-year-old, her long, straggly locks of hair wispy across the fading freckles of her pale face, appeared at her bedroom door. Claire stood there, just across the upstairs landing from where Lee was being worked on in our master bathroom.

Trying to shoo Claire back into her room, I accepted her admonishment, "Mom! You let strangers into the house!"

"Yes, Claire," I said weakly. "They are strangers, but I needed to call for help. I have to get Daddy to the hospital but I can't do it by myself. You go back to sleep."

Kelly and I followed Claire into her room. I explained that I was going to go to the hospital with Daddy and that Kelly would stay with her. I hugged her and assured her that I would later tell her what had happened. Content with that explanation, Claire allowed me to tuck her into bed. Bennett was still asleep, so I did not wake him. I knew he would be fine if he woke up and found Kelly there.

While I was in Claire's room, the paramedics came out of my bedroom and headed down the stairs with Lee on the gurney. When I followed the procession, the firefighter who had interviewed me mentioned that some detectives would be coming to speak with me. He then introduced me to one of the detectives, a tall gentleman standing in my kitchen. I was thus transferred from the medical team to the law enforcement team, and a barrage of questions followed: name, address, course of events, dinner menu, contents of fridge—and on and on.

"What did he eat? What did you eat? Did you eat what he did? Who did the dishes?" The detective's questions were relentless. Lee's vomiting and diarrhea were reviewed yet again, but my mind spun incoherently. I held out open palms in exasperation and cast a bewildered glance across the room at Kelly.

Lee usually did a "leftover sweep" through the fridge after he worked out, eating whatever he found. *How do I explain that?! That was my husband, the food scrounger.* Still thinking it was food poisoning, I wracked my brain, trying to remember when I had first made the beef biscuits we had eaten for dinner. *Monday? Tuesday? Let's see. Today is Thursday. Two days on ground beef; it would not have spoiled in that time.* Then I remembered; Lee had not eaten dinner.

"I don't know," I said weakly.

"Well, may I see it?" the detective asked.

I pulled the food out of the fridge. Broccoli casserole does not smell good when it is fresh out of the oven, much less as leftovers. I pulled the lid off the casserole and grimaced at the smell.

"Is that what he ate?" the detective asked.

"I'm not sure," I answered.

I wanted to scream. *I cannot remember! I do feed him well! This just smells bad, but I do cook good food.* I was defending myself against a wave of something that was threatening to sweep me under, but I did not know what I was fighting against. All I could think of was getting to the hospital to be with Lee.

"We'll have to get a sample of that," the detective nodded to his assistant, who was standing by with sample vials.

My head was swirling. *What is going on? Where is Lee?!* Time was standing still. I did not know what was happening, but I needed to be with Lee. From the corner of my eye, I could see the assistant taping off my kitchen with the yellow "Police Line—Do Not Cross" tape.

"Did he smoke? Did he take any recreational drugs?" The questions went on and on. In retrospect, I can understand the reason for the questions. As a nurse in the 1980s, I had cared for many healthy young men without cardiac histories who suffered cocaine-induced heart attacks. Professionally, the questions made sense, but personally, I was insulted. *How could they even think that Lee would take drugs? How could they consider that I would murder him?! They were the ones who were slow in hooking Lee up to the monitor patches and resuming CPR,* I criticized angrily in my mind.

I drew myself up to face the tall detective. "No. He didn't do drugs. He was a runner. He ran six-minute miles on the trails in Alum Rock Park. He worked out every day." Inside I was screaming. *Yeah, and he could whip your butt on the trail, you big lug!* I wanted to launch into a tirade of how this could never happen to my strong, invincible, athletic husband.

Instead, I firmly said, "I have to go to the hospital."

"Do you want to change into clothes?" the firefighter standing nearby gently asked me.

"Oh. Yeah." Looking down, I realized that I was still in pajamas. So much of that night was a blur, a blur that became my reality for long afterwards.

By the time I changed into street clothes, Pastor Jim had arrived. We prayed as Jim drove me the three miles to the local hospital in the light rain.

I remember saying, "It's bad." In my heart of hearts, I knew what had happened and that Lee was gone. On some level, my brain was protecting me from the shock.

"Wow. I've never seen the emergency room so empty," Pastor Jim said in surprise.

"Yeah, you don't know how hard God had to work to clear it out to make room for Lee!" I quipped, my sense of humor blasting through the chaos of my mind. Lee did not even wait at the post office, let alone in the ER.

The attendant at the desk asked us to step into a room that they unlocked for us.

"This is not a good sign," I said to Jim, who questioned my fatalistic tone. "He's gone," I said in subdued resignation.

How long we sat together in that room, I do not know. By the clock, the time was after 12:30 a.m. on Friday, about an hour after paramedics had arrived at my house. For me, time no longer framed a reference; I was suspended in a surreal world. I felt removed, as if I were an observer in a drama.

The emergency room doctor and a nurse entered the room. Dr. K calmly sat down in the chair next to mine. I do not remember her exact words as she confirmed the finality of Lee's death, but her calm, professional demeanor soothed me. I had participated in such a setting so many times before, but on the other side of the healthcare equation—as a nurse. Never had I been the recipient of that harsh proclamation: news that validates the reality of death and confirms the deepest fears of your life. My thoughts swirled. *I am supposed to be the one delivering the bad news, not receiving it.*

"Did you ever get a rhythm?" My tone was pleading, as if a clue existed that would rewind this nightmare.

"No, we never did." Dr. K replied calmly.

"Didn't they have PEA in the field?"

"Yes, that's what they reported, but we had nothing." Dr. K patiently waited for me to verbalize my thoughts.

"What could it be? Hypothermia—no. Hypovolemia—no. PE [pulmonary embolus]—no, it didn't seem respiratory." I wracked my addled brain as I reviewed the differential diagnosis for PEA. Dr. K nodded and allowed me to continue my barrage.

"Do you think it was cardiac tamponade?!" I asked with an incredulous tone.

"Yes, I think it was a massive heart attack."

"How can this happen?!" I wailed. I wanted to list my husband's healthy lifestyle habits and lack of risk factors, as if that would pull me out of this nightmare. *He just could not have had a heart attack. That's for fat, unhealthy people who do not take care of themselves. Not Lee. Not my Lee!* My mind screamed. *This does not happen to healthy people like Lee!* My thoughts followed a line of reasoning that would haunt me for months afterwards.

Dr. K acknowledged that she did not know the cause. She patiently delineated everything that the team did for Lee from the time he arrived in the emergency department.

"Shock him?" I questioned.

"Yes, many times, but we never got a rhythm."

"Meds?"

"Yes, Epinephrine, Lidocaine, and I even tried the bicarb, although it isn't on the protocol. We did everything." Dr. K endured my persistent grilling with detailed answers to my questions.

"That's okay, bicarb will eventually show up on the algorithms again," I said. It was a feeble joke based on the American Heart Association's reciprocating changes to the ACLS algorithms. As I slumped down into the chair shaking my head, I asked what I should have done.

"There is nothing you could have done. You did everything you could do." Dr. K repeated those words to me over and over again. I will never forget her calm tone and compassionate professionalism as she reassured me that I had done everything possible, and that nothing would have helped Lee.

In the next weeks and months, I replayed the nightmare over and over in my mind, flogging myself into guilt-wracked frenzies. Dr. K's words became a mantra of Gilead balm for me, "There is nothing you could have done. You did everything you could do."

I'm not sure if it was the doctor or I who brought up the subject of an autopsy. My nurse brain said "Death after hospital admission of less than twenty-four hours is an automatic coroner's case." Somehow again the nurse brain shoved the wife brain to the side so that a protective numbness could envelop me. Dr. K agreed with me that an autopsy would help answer the questions.

"Are you ready to see him?" Dr. K asked.

The irony of her words tore at my thoughts. *That was another line that used to be mine.*

Pastor Jim and I followed the nurse and doctor around the corner. The ER nurses had laid Lee out in the cast room. He was neat and clean, lying on the gurney with clean sheets over him. His arms were outside the blankets, as I used to do for postmortem care, and they had even combed his hair. *Great nursing care,* I thought, as I recognized that they gave us the cast room so that I could take my time saying goodbye.

"I know it's just his body and that he is in heaven, not really here," I said to Pastor Jim. I was sure of what I believed, that Lee's soul was already in heaven, but not sure that this was truly happening. The surreal progression of events made me feel as if I were participating in the death of somebody else's loved one, as I had so many times as a nurse. My brain was distancing me, as if I were an actor in a bizarre play, not a participant in reality. Pastor Jim then left to give me time alone with Lee.

Ha! I thought as I looked at Lee. *That's just how I like your thick, brown hair—combed straight back—but you never liked it that way. Guess I get to see your hair the way I like it for the last time.*

Memories flooded my mind, memories of Lee getting out of the pool and finger combing his thick hair back. Doing that left his hair slightly wavy, instead of straight, as it was when he combed it. His unchangeable 1970s military hairstyle was a right part with the hair combed to the left. "It works for me," was his staunch answer whenever I begged him to change his hairstyle.

Each decade I tried. "You would look so good with it combed back . . . spiked up . . . shaved on the sides. . . ." Whatever the current hairstyle, I tried to convince him that his thick hair would look great with the change. Throughout the 1980s, 1990s, and the 2000s, Lee refused, saying he liked his hair the way it was. The 1970s military style, slightly grown out in the back, remained. I saw Lee's hair the way I really liked it only at the beach or pool. What a great parting gift those nurses gave me; they combed Lee's hair the way I preferred it.

I sobbed. I rocked back and forth. I remembered. My mind raced across countless memories of my past, while cocooning me from the present reality with the numbness of shock and grief. I cried. I reminisced. I wailed even more.

How do you know when you are done saying goodbye?! The answer to that question is never a conscious process. I am now at peace that I said what I needed to say, touched what I needed to touch, and observed what I needed to see before I left Lee's soul-departed body in that cast room.

When I opened the door to find Pastor Jim in the hallway, he asked, "Do you want to take his ring?"

Hey, that's my line! How many times had I weighed the family's grief and goodbyes versus removing the jewelry before the bodily fluids shifted and the ring could not be pulled off? That was my job as a nurse. But at this moment I was the shocked one with that vacant look, stunned beyond reality as I staggered through the nightmare of my loved one's death.

From this reverie, I was shocked into reality when one of the detectives ran up to me with a plastic medication vial and demanded, "We found this in the medicine cabinet. Did your husband take it?"

A thought painfully coursed through me. *Yes, Lee is my husband, but now he is gone.* Shoving this reality aside, I looked at the medicine vial and responded, "Yes, that's the Tylenol #3 left over from his surgery last March. That will give you the day of his surgery and the doctor's name. Our kids are old enough now that we can keep meds away from them in the medicine cabinet." I felt like I was defending myself from accusations of child neglect. Instead, as I later realized, they were looking for suicidal and homicidal causes of death.

Lee had undergone hernia surgery the previous March. As a forty-five-year-old, Lee was given a thorough preoperative workup with electrocardiogram, chest x-ray, and laboratory work. He was pronounced healthy and the surgery was uneventful. Lee had not taken all the pain medicine after his hernia repair, so it sat unused and forgotten in the medicine cabinet. When the detective at our house had asked me questions about the surgery and doctor, I had not remembered the details. All I could focus on was that Lee had been pronounced very healthy by all preoperative reports, as was his usual state of being.

The coroner pulled me aside to ask me more questions, many of which were the same ones the detective had asked earlier. I was so focused on the idea of food poisoning and how Lee could die of that, that I kept muttering my "how" and "why" questions aloud.

A few signatures later, I was back outside in the drizzle with Pastor Jim. We drove the short ride home to face the seventh of January, 2005, as the long nightmare continued.

[9]

Horrific Night

BY THE TIME Jim and I returned from the hospital, the detectives were gone, having left behind several specimen bottles and the yellow plastic tape of a police line stretched across my kitchen. Kelly was waiting for us, but thankfully the kids were asleep. Jim went to pick up his wife Sue, while Kelly filled me in on what had happened while we were gone.

"Several detectives came in and looked around," Kelly began. "Then they wanted to wake the kids up."

"Wake the kids up?! Why?" I demanded angrily.

"The detectives told me they wanted to question them. I asked if it was really necessary, but they said they needed to talk with the children."

"Oh, no. . . ." My first thought was to protect the kids from the horror of the past night. "And look at all the footprints they left!" My initial fear of traumatizing the kids was oddly sidetracked to a housekeeping complaint when I saw muddy boot prints on the beige carpet.

"I told them I didn't want them to wake the kids up. I insisted that I would wake them. Then I pointed to the young female detective and told them I wanted her to question the kids." Kelly stayed on track while my mind failed to fully grasp the situation.

I was grateful to God that He had chosen someone like Kelly to advocate for my kids. I was relieved to know that whatever had happened, I trusted that Kelly loved my kids and looked out for their safety.

"Thank you." It seemed like such a minimalistic expression of the deep gratitude that I was feeling.

"Yeah, she was probably the most junior detective, but I figured she would be gentle with the kids and wouldn't scare them."

"So they really woke the kids up to ask questions?"

"No, I woke them up. We started with Bennett. I went in his room and told him that someone special was here to meet him. I said she was a policewoman in uniform and she wanted to ask him some questions."

"Did it scare him?"

"No. He was excited to meet a policewoman. He woke up right away and announced, 'Happy New Year!'"

"What did she ask him?"

"She asked if his Mommy and Daddy ever fought."

"No! I can't believe they asked that. What did he say?"

"It was so innocent. He looked confident, shook his head and answered, 'No, my Mommy and Daddy aren't divorced!'"

"Good. Serves them right, waking my kids up in the middle of the night." I was comforted by the fact that my son had no memories of us fighting and that he was secure in his parents' relationship, yet anger burned beneath the surface. "That makes me so mad. Did they wake up Claire too?"

"I don't think she ever slept. I told her the policewoman wanted to talk with her. When the detective asked when Claire had last seen her dad, Claire said it was when she looked out the window and he had tubes out of his mouth."

My heart ached for the pain of what my sweet girl had witnessed. "I thought she was asleep, but she must have seen the paramedics take him out."

"Yes, she was awake when everything happened."

"But I thought she was in her room the whole time." I drifted off in numbness. I did not want to think about Claire seeing Daddy on a gurney, attached to a monitor with a tube down his throat and CPR in progress, under the red glow of flashing emergency lights.

"She must have stayed awake and watched him being loaded into the ambulance. Claire sat downstairs with me later on the couch, wide awake and animated. She asked questions about the police car and about the officers' training. The detective asked both kids what they had eaten for dinner and what their Daddy had for dinner." At that point Kelly just held onto my hands and prayed for me as we sat on the couch.

When Jim and Sue came back at 3:30 a.m., Kelly left for the night, and I began a long series of phone calls. The first incoming call was from the organ donation team at the University of California, San Francisco Medical Center. This was my graduate school alma mater, and I had worked in the hospital for over two years. Once again I recognized the irony that I had previously been on the other end of organ donation conversations with family members; this time it was me. The forty-five minute conversation involved constant questioning, asking me about Lee's exposure to everything from bird flu and drugs to prostitutes and dialysis. I mentally drifted off to thoughts of Lee as the series of questions progressed.

"Had he been overseas in the last year?" the organ donation nurse asked.

I answered the question, but then became lost in the sudden realization that Lee and I would never travel again. Question after question I answered, as memories of overseas travels crisscrossed the awareness that my travels with him were over. In my work as a critical care nurse, I had cared for both organ donors as well as transplant recipients. I was in favor of donating anything and everything that could possibly help someone else. Lee and I had both filled out the organ donor designation on our California driver's licenses.

I knew that most of Lee's organs would not be eligible for donation, since they were not preserved after his death and during the subsequent autopsy. When the organ donor nurse asked about each component that could be donated, I went into deeper shock and pain. I answered yes to every aspect, even as I drifted off in thought about each part mentioned: smooth, tanned skin; the rope-like blood vessels on his arms; steel blue eye color; and the tendons along his chiseled, runner's legs. So many incredible aspects of Lee that I knew in intimate detail; they were suddenly and completely gone from this world. The nurse clarified with me that the eligibility of organs to be donated depended upon the autopsy reports, but I needed to give permission for everything in advance. They would notify me what and when the tissues or organs were donated, if that indeed occurred.

With that draining conversation, I had completed the last of my hospital responsibilities. Next I turned my attention to the phone calls I had to make to notify our families. My first call was to Lee's parents.

"Hi Dad. Sorry to wake you. Please get Mom on the line. I have to tell you both something." Somehow I managed to break the earth-shattering news to my precious in-laws that their son was dead. Their shock and disbelief was likely a lot more than the few stunned questions they asked, but all I could do was get through a brief recitation of the story, one that would be repeated many times over.

Then I called my parents. My stepfather picked up the receiver. "Hi Samuel. Please get Mom on the line. I have to tell you something."

"Hi," Mom said sleepily as she joined Samuel on the phone line.

"This is the phone call you never wanted to get," I began. Then I relayed the horrendous news that Lee had died.

Shaken, Mom screamed before she gathered her wits and gently pressed, "What happened?"

So it went with multiple phone calls to family in those early morning hours. I woke parents and siblings up, had couples both listen on the phone, and told them the unbelievable news. The numbness and shock of early grief cocooned me from reality as I accomplished this horrendous task. I did the notifications by rote, dealing with the emergency calmly and efficiently in the most thorough way possible, considering that Lee's cause of death was not yet established. Thankfully, I was unaware of the myriad preparations that followed my phone calls as friends and relatives mobilized toward our house from Minnesota, New York, and throughout California.

The next job was the most miserable thing I have ever done. Up until this horror, the worst event in my life was hearing that my father had died in a plane crash when I was eleven years old. How I was told about the event, and the subsequent screaming and wailing my sister and I responded with, were nightmares etched into the most traumatized area of my brain.

Just that Thursday morning before Lee died, I had finished Evelyn Husband's book. I was so impressed by how Evelyn told her children that their father, Captain Rick Husband, had died in the Space Shuttle *Columbia* catastrophe (Husband, 2003, pp. 172–8). I remembered being profoundly impacted with the account of how she had dealt with everything that first week. Whereas my memories of being told that my dad had died in a plane crash were horrifically painful, I had resolved to do it like Evelyn had done if, God forbid, that should happen to me. When I read the book, finishing it the day before Lee died, I knew that, *if it ever happens to me, this is how I want to handle it.* Evelyn's words were God's provision for how I was able to survive initially. In fact, those first few days, I systematically imitated everything I had learned from Evelyn in her book.

Sue, Jim, and I talked on and on during that interminable night—what in actuality was only one night seemed like a year's length of agony and horror. As I made those difficult phone calls, I felt uplifted by Jim and Sue's silent prayer support. One of the things I mentioned to Sue was the screaming and wailing that I feared in response to telling my kids that their father had died. The horror of revisiting my childhood terror, and instilling that same terror in my children, was too much for me to handle.

"It won't happen," Sue said with a calm firmness. "I'm going to pray that it won't happen this time." Sue's deep, quiet faith comforted me. I felt sustained by her faith, even as I felt that I had no faith or strength at all.

I agonized over how to tell the kids, but then I remembered. *I will do it just as Evelyn did: hold them, remind them that we need to trust God, and pray with them* (Husband, 2003, pp. 172–3). With that conviction, God's peace just enveloped me, and God held my childhood nightmare at bay. After what seemed like hours, my little six-and-a-half-year-old Bennett came downstairs in his royal blue, solar-system-patterned pajamas, slowing his gait as he rounded the corner. Sensing that something was amiss when he saw people he did not know, he approached me quickly and, when I stretched my arms out to him, curled up in my lap.

"Bennett, I have some bad news to tell you." I held the sprawling six-year-old in my lap and tightly wrapped my arms around him. When he looked at me with fearful blue eyes accenting his precious freckled face, I continued, "Daddy died last night."

Bennett began sobbing and we both clung to each other as we cried softly. There was no screaming or wailing. "I took Daddy to the hospital last night after he was so sick. He died at the hospital, and the doctor examined him closely and said there was nothing we could do."

"Are you going to get me a new daddy?" Bennett asked hopefully.

The question would have ripped my heart out, had I not read Evelyn Husband's account just two days earlier. Following her guide (Husband, 2003, p. 217), I recognized that the question came from a wounded six-year-old soul and I remained composed.

"No Bennett, I'm not ready to get you a new daddy, but I promise you that I will be obedient to God."

I then introduced Jim and Sue as Pastor and Mrs. Tirone, friends of Mommy and Daddy's who were here to help us. In the classic way that kids move in and out of grief, Bennett was soon playing Lincoln Logs on the floor with Jim.

I looked at Sue in amazement and almost in disbelief and exclaimed, "He didn't scream!"

"I knew he wouldn't," Sue affirmed calmly, "and I will pray that Claire won't either."

Because I chose not to wake the kids up, I did not have to decide whether to tell them together or separately. About an hour after my early riser was up, Claire came down the stairs. She looked at Jim and Sue uncertainly, and when I introduced her, she cited, "That's the man from the driveway." That comment confirmed the fact that Claire had indeed watched the events of the evening, from Lee's departure to the first moments of our church's support; she had not been asleep as I first thought.

"Claire, please come here. I have some bad news to tell you." I motioned with my arms and my eight-year-old came over, suspending her usual feisty, don't-touch-me-I-am-a-big-girl attitude to curl her tall, lanky body into my lap. There was a solemnity to the moment and she knew it.

"Claire, Daddy went to the hospital last night and he died." We wrapped our arms around each other, both crying softly, as I buried my face in her thick, Daddy-like, brown hair for comfort. Again, Sue's prayers had been answered. In the lack of screaming and wailing, God was at work healing pieces of my own childhood trauma.

"Are you going to remarry?" Claire asked me shortly thereafter.

Stunned by the question, but again reassured by Evelyn Husband's experience of similar questions (2003, p. 217), I responded, "I don't know, Sweetie, but I am going to be obedient to God."

The remainder of the day became a blur in my mind. Maryanne, my former small group leader and mentor, came in the morning to relieve Jim and Sue. Later in the day, other friends and family began to arrive.

After a five-hour drive from southern California, my sister Rebecca and her husband arrived later that morning. One of her heartbreaking memories of shared grief that day was with Bennett. He lay on the floor, his blue pajamas curled into a tight ball of pain. Rebecca lowered herself to the ground, wrapped her comforting arms around him, and cried with him. Holding onto Bennett in mutual pain, she heard him softly say, "This is the worst day of my life."

I remember sitting on the couch, with Pastors Doug Buron and Dan Griffiths from our previous church, North Valley Christian Fellowship, sitting across from me. Their presence was such a security to me. For years, Lee and I had volunteered as youth shepherds with our youth pastor Doug. Pastor Dan was an amazing man of God who had taught us so much from God's Word during our nine years at that incredible church. Years afterward, I would find notes in my Bible and remember Pastor Dan's teachings.

So much of what happened immediately after Lee died was lost to my conscious memory; but I do remember the security and comfort that I felt in having my church family there for me, whether visitors came from our former church or the new one we had attended for the previous two years. My family also arrived, arrangements and airport rides coordinated by helpful friends. By evening, the house was full and I was enveloped in a cocoon of people who loved and cared for me.

The next five days were a manic, adrenaline-fueled exercise in survival as we prepared for the funeral and welcomed out-of-town guests. Our house became the command-and-control center, although everything seemed chaotic and out of control. I remember the doorbell ringing repeatedly as food and flowers were delivered.

God's provision was powerfully evident. At one point, my Mom stood in the kitchen and asked, "What are we going to feed everyone?" Within minutes, Kathy, a mom from Bennett's classroom, delivered a huge plate of sandwiches.

Rebecca forced me to drink fluids and had to remind me to go to the bathroom. I was numb and in shock, even to the point of ignoring basic bodily functions. At one point, I was stunned to realize that I was going to the bathroom only once a day. I must be dehydrated, I thought, but then I realized that most of my fluids were leaving my body as tears. My sister tried to comfort me with the thought that the longest night of my life was finally over.

In the five days before the memorial service, I slept only several hours. The nights were long, and I cried out to God and even argued with Him. One long night I argued with God over Matthew 11:29–30: "Take my yoke upon you and learn from me, for I am gentle and humble in heart, and you will find rest for your souls. For my yoke is easy and my burden is light."

I silently screamed the verse back at God. *God this yoke isn't easy and this burden isn't light!* I did not intend it as blasphemy. I was taking God at His Word, something I had always been taught to do.

God has never spoken to me audibly, but He used the Bible verses to address my complaint. *What yoke are you carrying? What burden do you have?*

How am I supposed to raise these kids on my own?! I can't do this by myself! Perhaps I was not shouting aloud, but my mind was screaming out in rage and anguish.

You aren't doing this on your own. I love them more than you do. God's heart for my children spoke to the core of my being.

I know that you love them more than I do, but how can I care for them? I assailed my loving God with questions. The agony of the event writhed within me as I grappled with the loss of my parenting partner.

They are asleep. You don't have to do anything for them right now. God's impression on my heart relayed the obvious truth to me.

Okay. I don't have to deal with the kids right now, but how can I get through my life without Lee?! I fumed inwardly.

That is the rest of your life. What is your burden now? God gently prompted me to think clearly.

How can I live alone once the kids are gone? The abandonment and aloneness terrified me.

But that is years down the road. What is your burden right now? God's challenge strangely quieted my worried heart.

Okay. Okay. I tried to narrow down what I needed to do right then and right there in that moment. *I guess all I have to do right now is rest,* I conceded as I let God take on the yoke of my future and my new role in it. My panic subsided as I once again recognized who God was and how His Word held true even in the midst of my chaos.

[10]

Lee's Memorial Service

THE DAYS AND NIGHTS between Lee's death and memorial service passed as another blur. We were inundated with bouquet after bouquet of flowers, until every surface in our living room—the coffee table, end tables, fireplace mantel, and shelves—overflowed with baskets and vases. The fragrance of flowers, which I had previously enjoyed, became associated with the emotional pain of that time. Relatives and friends descended on the house. The phone rang endlessly. I was overwhelmed—the people, the flowers, the commotion—all of it magnified the agony of losing Lee.

One of the fears that I knew I needed to conquer was using my bathroom again. On the afternoon after Lee died, I pleaded with my dear friend, "Jamie, come with me to go to the bathroom." Jamie and I had fast become friends when, several years earlier on our children's first day of school, my Claire and her Kenny set off and left us together outside the kindergarten classroom door.

"Okay," Jamie said cautiously, wanting to help me in any way, but wondering how much help I actually needed with basic functions.

"No, Jamie, it's nothing weird, really. I just need someone to go into that bathroom with me for the first time."

Jamie followed me upstairs and held my hand as I took tentative steps through my bedroom and toward the commode room. "Please, just stand there. You don't have to help me. I just have to face my fears of using this bathroom again," I appealed, my voice cracking. Jamie's eyes pooled with tears as she realized what had transpired in that very same room only the night before.

"Jamie, this is just one of those things I have to face. If I don't face this fear, I will never use this bathroom again." Shaky and terrified, I faced the toilet where the horrific scene had started less than twenty-four hours earlier. Breathing resolutely, I knew I had to confront this fear in order to go on with my life. This was how I began to formulate my strategy of facing my post-traumatic stress triggers. I would repeat the sequence numerous times in the upcoming months and years: face the agonizing reminders with as much support as I could find, breathe deeply, ignore the physical symptoms, and push through the emotional pain.

Through it all, one of the most precious gifts I received was the labor of love provided by two amazing women, Jamie and my sister Rebecca. They cleaned the CPR scene, scrubbing away blood, diarrhea, vomit and even boot prints. Somehow the boot prints of the firefighters tormented me; they were mocking reminders of the futility of the resuscitation attempts. The combination of the rainy night and big firefighter boots made for multiple scuff marks on the walls as they bent over to perform CPR. More prints tracked across the carpet. The image of the boot sole I had seen from around the corner as they worked on Lee, and my associated feelings of desperation, had imprinted on my mind. The mere sight of the sole of a firefighter's boot could bring the trauma back to the forefront. While Jamie and Rebecca cleaned up the memories of that night in the physical sense, they also helped remove the emotional reminders.

That Sunday, my parents-in-law, sister-in-law, sister, and her husband accompanied me to the funeral home to make decisions. We sat around a conference table for a laboriously slow presentation of options. I felt numb and dazed; my mind vacillated from listening intently to denying the painful reality that we were disposing of Lee's earthly body. The mortician seemed to drone on for hours. I just wanted to leave the place because it was so full of death.

The funeral manager's entire persona was geared to smoothing out the difficult process; he spoke slowly and deliberately. "Now, I have to go through some of these questions before cremation," he voiced gently. I wanted Lee to be cremated, but was not sure how his parents would react. To my relief, they supported cremation instead of burial. That question settled, the mortician began to ask about false teeth, prostheses, and anything else that would need to be removed before cremation.

"I'm sorry to have to go through all these questions. I think I know the answer to this question, but did Lee have a pacemaker or implanted device?"

"No, he was a self-starter." Lee's mother Lois quipped. The Carsons all smiled discreetly, while my side of the family burst out laughing in a welcome release from the sadness of the occasion.

Later that night Lee's sister Chris and I talked about our perfectionism and how we should learn to let things go.

"Yeah, you are such a perfectionist," my sister Rebecca cracked. "That's why your sweatshirt is on backwards!" I looked down at my shirtfront to confirm what she said and realized that I had been wearing it that way all day, the neckline in front sitting high and uncomfortable with the obvious lump of the tag at the center. Through all that time, I had not noticed, nor had anyone mentioned to me, that I was not properly dressed.

But a backwards sweatshirt was just the beginning of much more significant difficulties. During the initial sleepless nights after Lee's death, I was consumed by thoughts of the memorial service. *How do I honor my husband? How do I pay tribute to the love of my life?* The idea of closure was not something my conscious mind would be able conceive of for months yet, but I knew that the memorial service was an important aspect of clarifying those tormenting days since Lee's death. I prayed about the service, knowing that it would be pivotal in others' lives, as well as my own. God began to stir in my heart the idea of speaking at the memorial service.

My first response was to argue with God. *No way, God. I can't do that! I am exhausted.* Yet He nudged me gently.

God, with all that I have been through, I shouldn't have to stand up there and talk, I whined to the Creator of the universe. He then reminded me that He would be my strength to stand in front of everyone.

But God, I have two pastors doing the service. They are two totally different types of pastors, and that should be enough! My thoughts turned to the pair of pastors I had asked to speak. Pastor Doug was the youth pastor from North Valley Christian Fellowship, our previous church. In his college days at San Jose State University, Doug had been one of the long-haired, barefoot, 1970s Jesus People. He preached from the gut and kept the focus on Jesus. Always in blue jeans, Doug spoke in a bold, aggressive style; his heart was for youth to know Christ.

And then there was Pastor Jim, the assistant pastor at our new church, CCCM. Lee and I enjoyed Jim's Bible teaching for the academic depth and challenge. Jim, dressed in a conservative suit with every hair in place, formally wielded God's Word in convincing detail to passionate Christians as well as academic skeptics. I imagined the contrast of these beloved pastors and how they would impact our crowd of family and friends.

Why should I speak?! These two are the professionals. They know how to speak on Your behalf and touch lives. How can I speak after all that I have been through? I can't do this. God impressed upon me the necessity of honoring Lee as my husband. As I whined and cried out to God the rest of that night, He convinced me that it was His strength that would get me through. Thought by thought, God gave me the outline of what I was to say. I knew that I had to speak at the memorial service, and I knew that it would be one of the hardest things I would ever do for Lee.

As I prepared for the memorial service, I was struck by the solemnity of the event. I mentally compared that day to my wedding. The significance of the event, the gathering of family and friends from afar, the desire to be with Lee, the focus on our partnership, the impact on my life, the change in my future—so many things eerily paralleled my wedding day. And yet, there was a crucial fact that I pushed out of my mind: this event marked the ceremonial end of my marriage. The idea of closure did not register in my protected level of consciousness, but in retrospect, the deep drive I had to fulfill this obligation to my marriage was, in fact, a desire to achieve closure.

My hairdresser Kristi styled my hair that day. The only other time in my life I had ever had my hair done for an event was on my wedding day. I had tremors all day, and sometimes Kristi had to stop combing and styling, waiting until my tremors finished. My arms shook uncontrollably and at times my teeth chattered, but occasionally I felt God's peace pour through me, and I stopped shaking.

"Look," I said as my body finally calmed, "someone is praying for me." I felt cradled by a loving God who responded to the outpouring of prayers on my behalf. Even Kristi marveled at how completely the tremors calmed and how I was able to rest at intervals during the hairstyling session.

Given my pale skin, I rarely wore black and never had a black dress as a wardrobe basic. During my thrift shop forays the previous fall, however, I had purchased two black dresses for some unknown reason—again, divine preparation.

While I was dressing for the service, my sister took charge of getting my kids ready. My sister, who is not used to forcing uncooperative kids to dress up, became a bit frustrated by the challenge. At one point, I wondered why they were suddenly quiet and compliant. I turned to see Claire and Bennett sitting on my bed devouring my sister's bribe: an entire box of See's chocolates, one of my Christmas gifts from my in-laws. Rebecca had accomplished the impossible in talking tomboy Claire into wearing a dress, a feat likely accomplished with the chocolate bribe. Normally, I would have been appalled, but at that point I just shook my head. *Whatever it takes.* I continued to dress for the service, savoring the rare chance to take my time getting ready without dealing with kids.

Arriving at the church later, we were ushered into a side room and then taken to the front pew. The church entryway was decorated with memorabilia from phases of Lee's life: childhood, Air Force (including helmet and pilot's uniform), and American Airlines. I knew that I could not face those tables and stay composed, so I avoided the lobby. I was also relieved to avoid facing people before the service.

Although I realized that family and friends would attend the service, I did not realize just how big a reunion the memorial would be. People from every aspect of Lee's forty-five years of life, every jet, every workplace, and almost every part of the country he had lived in, came together to pay their last respects. East Coast, West Coast, Arizona, Alaska, as well as all the places we had lived together: Chicago, Las Vegas, Ohio, and San Francisco. Guys from our wedding party, USAF friends, college buddies, old roommates, high school classmates, swim team members, and former coworkers flew in. Two rows of blue uniforms honored Lee from the San

Francisco American Airlines crew base: pilots, flight attendants, and gate agents. Muslims, Hindus, Jews, and Christians came for the church service. Friends filed in from every aspect of our lives: our old church, our new church, the neighborhood, and the kids' school. The sanctuary overflowed with memories and relationships. Emotionally, I could not savor the reunion or look specifically into the crowd, but even short glances at individual people brought back memories of the life Lee and I had shared together.

Whereas a funeral service has the body in a casket at the front of the church, a memorial service does not. Lee was cremated; no urn or casket was at the altar. We believed that his soul was in heaven and his body was merely the remaining shell. A beribboned flower spray at the altar was the only indication that we were honoring a deceased loved one.

My family and friends coordinated the memorial service, taking into account my requests for specific songs and people I wanted to be involved in the service. I was demanding in my wishes, but my family indulged me. I was so intent in honoring Lee that I insisted on certain details. I wanted the Janet Paschal song "Another Soldier's Coming Home" to honor Lee's military service and draw the parallel to his earthly service to God. Chris Rice's "Untitled Hymn (Come to Jesus)" reflected our past joys and provided a way to release Lee to God, especially the last verse "Fly to Jesus." The classic hymns "It Is Well with My Soul" and "Blessed Assurance" were anthems to reassure me that my children and I would go on with God's help. Lee's mother requested "Amazing Grace," a family favorite. I wanted the memorial service to reflect both who Lee was and the God he had served in his lifetime. To that end, I made my requests known to the helpful family and church staff who skillfully arranged every detail.

Pastor Jim began the service, "Jesus said, 'I am the resurrection and the life. He that believeth in me though he were dead, yet shall he live. And whosoever liveth and believeth in me shall never die.' Let us pray."

Those were Jesus' words to Martha and Mary at the death of their brother Lazarus, from John 11:25 (KJV). The same words are carved into my father's tombstone. They represent the legacy of my family's belief in Christ's life and resurrection, despite earthly death. This Bible passage now applied to my husband's sudden death.

I listened as Pastor Jim continued with a short biography of Lee, starting with our participation in the CCCM membership class. In the fall of 2002, we first met Pastor Jim when he taught the class. He spoke of Lee's attendance, despite an erratic work schedule, and how Lee was very engaged and perceptive during discussions. Lee's written homework was an unusual source of faith statements to use in his memorial service, Pastor Jim noted, as he read the questions from the membership class homework followed by Lee's answers:

> Q: When did you first decide to commit your life to Jesus Christ?
>
> A: In 1973, on a high school youth group retreat.
>
> Q: How has your understanding of God changed since your commitment to Jesus?

A: I have a better understanding of sin, God's holiness, and my need of a Savior. Following Jesus helps me see people differently, not to hold on to things too tightly, and to see this world for what it is—a way station, not the end.

Q: What does your commitment to Christ mean to you now and for the future?

A: Jesus is the reason for my being here: to know Him and to make Him known.

Q: Why would you like to join the church?

A: As a public statement of my devotion to Christ, membership in a local body is essential.

Q: What is the job of the individual member of the church?

A: To minister to others and bring the lost to Christ using the gifts and talents each Christian receives from God.

Q: How has the Silicon Valley lifestyle affected your ability to worship God? What can you do about it?

A: I don't think it's negatively affected that. We as a family have made a real effort not to be overcommitted.

Q: What is worship to you?

A: Worship is a celebration of God. Worship helps to remind us of God's significance.

Q: What part does worship play in a balanced love of God?

A: Worship is a passionate romance with God where the knowledge of God and commitment to Him are foundational.

Q: What about the Lord's Supper, or communion?

A: In communion, we remember the costly sacrifice Jesus made for us. It is a demonstration of the unmerited love Jesus showed to us and for us. And it looks forward to the second return of Jesus. And it helps to build unity in the fellowship of His church.

Lee and Tina's faith is based on the Bible as the truth of God revealed for all of us. And in that scripture, the Bible says, "To be absent from the body is to be present with the Lord." Tina specifically said that she wanted her friends and family to know that she and Lee have always had that faith and belief, and that she has the confidence that as a Christ follower, Lee has been with Jesus from the instant he was no longer with us.

Although prepared to speak, I had left myself an escape in case I changed my mind. After looking for my nod, Pastor Jim realized that I was ready to speak as planned and called me up to the podium. Lee's friend Bill, from USAFA and pilot training, gave me his arm and escorted me up the few stairs onto the platform. I unlinked my elbow from Bill's, and he turned back for the pew.

I was alone at the podium facing the crowded sanctuary of people who loved Lee. And then I spoke.

First of all, thank you. Thank you so much for all of you who came from all of the paths of our lives, from Lee's neighbors as a child to his buddies at the academy, to the Troy High School swim and polo team—water polo team, to the military pilots and commercial pilots, his esteemed colleagues at American Airlines: thank you so much for coming. Thank you for being here with us. We want to honor Lee. We're here, and I appreciate so much that you are a part of that. On behalf of his entire family, thank you so much.

I want to read this quote from Rick Husband who was the commander of the space shuttle *Columbia,* which we lost last [sic] February in 2003: "Faith does not give us the power to change things. It gives us the ability to cope with the tough things that come our way" (Husband, 2003, p. 1).

So, twenty-one years ago, I had a roommate who was a couch potato. Her name was Barb and I was always saying, "Barb, come on! Let's go to the gym. Come on, Barb, let's go to the pool. Come on Barb, let's go to the Flywright Club. Prince Charming is not going to show up at the door. Let's go."

Well, Rick K brought my Prince Charming to the door. That's how I met Lee—a neighbor guy brought him over. And our first date, back in 1984, was going running. And that was something we loved to do together. We're not the types that sit around, and we love to run together.

I realized anyway that the running we did was like a metaphor for our lives together. Even at my prime, I couldn't keep up with Lee. So we'd start out together running and he'd run on ahead. I would huff and puff, and huff and puff. I knew he was in the distance, even if I didn't see him. I could always count on him. He'd circle around and come back. And I'm not a marathoner. He'd always come back and give me a hard time, "How come you always speed up when I come next to you?"

It's because when I could run with Lee, I could run fast and I would get energized. And I was there. And then he'd run up on ahead and I would poop out. I would be huffing and puffing and slowing down. And this I know is a

> metaphor for our lives together. Because I know . . . with him, I was running, I was strong.
>
> That man brought me to more things than I ever thought I could do with my life. He didn't push me, but he came alongside me, and he encouraged me, and I accomplished more than I ever thought I would. And now, he's gone ahead and I don't see him. I am huffing and I'm puffing and I am slowing down, but I know where he is. He is with his Creator, our King of Kings and Sovereign Lord of Lords. I know that I will be with him again one day. It's going to be hard and I know.
>
> You know, I lost the love of my life. He was the captain of my heart. I stand here in front of you. And I'm shaky, but I am standing on the promises of God my Savior. My challenge to you today is this: what is holding you up?!

Bill walked up as I finished. Weak and shaky, I grabbed Bill's arm and he escorted me back to the pew. As relieved as I should have been after speaking, I merely felt numb. My mind remained layers away from the actual events, the full load of my grief not yet breaking through. The blankness of my thoughts, instead of scaring me, softened the blow of my new reality. Months would pass before I consistently left behind my Lee-in-the-present-tense, finally recognizing that Lee was . . . did . . . lived . . . only in the past tense.

Pastor Jim continued his retelling of the events of that harrowing night, and I tried to focus on his words.

> After dinner, Lee put the dishes in the dishwasher, and cleaned the table, and set up the programmable drip coffeemaker for early Friday morning. He did this regularly for Tina since she is the early riser in the

> home. She usually gets up early, reads her Bible and prays before the rest of the house rises. He would set up the programmable coffeemaker so that she could have coffee waiting for her when she got up.

The coffeepot story rewound me again to the morning after Lee died. Pastor Jim and his wife Sue sat with me in the eerie quiet after I got off the phone with the organ donor staff. In the midst of that emptiness, the coffee pot suddenly came to life. Jim and Sue were startled by the noise; then—as I explained Lee's coffee pot routine—they were touched by the story of my husband's act of service. I suppressed my sadness at the thought that Lee would never again be there to make coffee for me.

Trying to focus on the present, I tuned back in to Pastor Jim.

> The path from my house to the Carson's house is well known. My teenage daughter was in Tina's high school, weekly girls' discipleship group. I had dropped her off and picked her up several times at Tina's house. I was always happy—and I told my wife—that Tina was her mentor and discipler for the times that she had her. I thought how good it was that my daughter had a model example, as Lee would take care of the kids while Tina had her girls' discipleship group.

My eyes held fast to the pastor as he spoke, but my mind sidetracked to happier times of Lee watching the kids as I spent time with "my" dear teenagers. These teenage girls had wonderful families of their own, but spending time with them in Bible study was precious to me. When I turned my attention back to Pastor Jim, he was in the ER with me.

When we arrived at the hospital, Tina went right up to the receptionist in the emergency room and identified herself. There was no one else in emergency, so you know Lee got total attention immediately. She identified herself and asked to see Lee, but instead we were ushered into a waiting room. They were still working on Lee. And we continued to pray the whole time we were in there.

Sometime later, and I'm not exactly sure how long, a doctor and nurse came in and told Tina that Lee could not be resuscitated. And that the doctor had tried everything. Since Tina is familiar with the medical terminology, they talked back and forth. Just at that moment, Tina was in her "nurse mode," where she wanted to know what had been done and what had been tried. They had technical language: medications and stuff that I didn't know anything about, but she did. And then Tina asked to see Lee right away.

When she entered the room, she was no longer the nurse, but Lee's wife. She began to cry deeply, and hold his head, and kiss him and say that she loved him and wanted him back. In between, she prayed for God to help her and give her strength. When she lifted up her head, she told me, "Lee is not here. The real Lee is gone."

I gave her some time to be alone with Lee. I went outside the door and closed it. I heard her through the door go all-over crying, and that kind of heaving crying that's so deep, telling Lee how much she loved him. When she came out, I told her that the last thing Lee experienced on earth was her helping him. And the last image that he had, was her face.

[11]

Lee's Memorial Service, Continued

AS THE EULOGY CONTINUED, I became aware of Claire and Bennett, who were in constant motion during the service, bobbing up and down throughout the first two rows of relatives and friends. My children were happy to be surrounded by everyone who loved them. For the first time in my life and theirs, I was almost oblivious to where my children were or what they were doing.

Whereas I had difficulty comprehending the event even as I sat still, my kids soaked up the words in the same sponge-like way that they absorbed the adults' attention all across the pews. Later, after the service, Bennett asked me, "Why didn't he talk about playing Lincoln Logs?" Although Pastor Jim had reiterated the events of Lee's death, he had left out my six-year-old's highlight of the night.

Lee's family chose to write down their thoughts, memories, and feelings for the service. Pastor Jim read these written eulogies, beginning with the memorial written by Lee's mother Lois.

> As I recall, Lee was a bundle of energy from day one, and as a toddler he was into everything. The report from nursery school said, "Little, but mighty." Lee's years in high school and elementary were also action packed. He loved backpacking in the Sierras with the Boy Scouts and his Dad. He enjoyed swim meets in high school and went out for various teams.
>
> When Lee went to the Air Force Academy, he enjoyed so much what was going on there; and I enjoyed from a distance participating in that, and admiring how diligently Lee worked. The highlights were his graduation there; and at pilot training, the events that went on, that we will never forget.
>
> My tenderest memories are from his wedding with Tina, and the births of Claire and Bennett. Lee was a good father and a good husband. He showed his love of the Lord through many thoughtful deeds to many friends and his family.
>
> I will miss his smile which was like liquid sunshine, and that twinkle in his eyes. But I take comfort in Romans 8:38 which says, "For I am convinced that neither death nor life, neither angels nor demons, neither the present nor the future nor any powers, neither height nor depth, nor anything else in all creation will be able to separate us from the love of God that is in Christ Jesus our Lord."

The Bible verse that Lois chose was a favorite of her mother—and Lee's grandmother—Irene's. Previously a precious hope to hang onto during her mother's funeral,

Romans 8:38–39 became a comfort to Lois in the sudden loss of her son.

Lee's father Bob wrote of precious memories, frustrating escapades, and father-son bonding.

> Lee, my son, gone now, but never to be forgotten. How do I put into words the love and respect for a man who was my best friend and collaborator on projects large and small over the years?!
>
> My fond memories include his great desire to explore: at age three, climbing out of his bedroom window at two in the morning to look around the neighborhood. By digging on the side of the house and finding buried treasure. By hiking and climbing in the mountains where I could share some of his experiences. Skiing in Colorado and California, which I tried, but never succeeded. Flying through the sky as both a military and commercial airline pilot.
>
> Lee did everything all out, swimming hundreds of laps year round at 5:30 a.m., race swimming, marathons on the flat and up Pike's Peak, triathlon races, and scuba diving in the Pacific Ocean. Lee also liked motorcycling. Lee's passion for flying began early, and he worked very hard for an appointment to the Air Force Academy, the first from his high school. He made it through first-year training and later Air Force Survival School, parachute jumping, and modified SEAL [Sea, Air, and Land Forces] training with the Navy. The academy awarded Lee a BS degree in 1981, and he took an MS degree while serving in Ohio where he met and married Tina, an Air Force nurse. Later they both served at Nellis Air Force Base in Nevada, where Lee trained pilots to fly the Stealth F-117.

> We always wondered why he was never home! Lee served eight years in the Air Force after four years at the academy, then went on to fly for American Airlines based in Chicago and San Jose, as a flight engineer and first officer, for a total of fifteen years.
>
> I miss Lee. I'm proud to be his father. I miss Lee more than I can say. He helped me be a good father. He loved his mother and his sister. He tried my patience at times. I miss Lee. Lee is flying for the Forever Airline now. No flight delays, fair weather always, and landing at that big airport in the sky. Fly high, my son. I love you. One day, I'll be a passenger on your plane.

Lee's younger sister Chris, whose optimism and obedience often contrasted Lee's childhood choices, wrote a precious tribute.

> It has always been a pleasure to be Lee's sister. He was my first friend and playmate. Lee grew up into a man I deeply admired and respected, especially as a husband, father, military officer, and quiet servant of God.
>
> My fondest memories of Lee have a common theme of movement, speed, and daring. These themes were reflected in his preferred mode of transportation at different ages. His red two-wheeler became a ten-speed bike, then a motorized skateboard, then a motorcycle, a faster motorcycle, a customized VW bug, a jet, and finally an airliner. I remember some thrilling motorcycle rides, and even being a passenger in a small Cessna where he piloted.
>
> I took comfort in the predictability of Lee's character. He was analytical and methodical, yet peppered

> with kindness. He made me feel safe. I miss Lee terribly, especially not growing old with him. It was a blessing to have had him grace my life for these few years. I look forward to seeing him in heaven. Naturally, he got there first. When airlines pass overhead, I think of Lee and know he is with God and is at peace.

Lee's brother-in-law Loo, Chris's husband, also contributed to the written eulogies.

> I first met Lee in Fullerton [California] back in 1987. After our first conversation, I realized Lee and I share many similar hopes, beliefs, and interests; and I looked forward to learning more about him. He later became my brother-in-law, and over the past seventeen years, I grew to respect, admire—and most of all—to love Lee like a brother.
>
> He has helped me greatly over the years with his many insights and life experiences. And Lee was always ready to lend a hand with any problem or project. He was truly a servant of God. While our lives have recently been busy with work, young children, and the general cares of this world, I had hoped to spend more time with Lee as our children grew up—a time when he and I would have more time and energy on our hands. I looked forward to our growing old together. I looked forward to developing a long and rich history of shared experiences, from our children's first pimples, dates, and weddings, to our own graying and thinning of hair.
>
> As I reflect on my vision for our future, I am indescribably saddened by his early departure from our lives. But now Lee is in a far better place, and I take comfort in knowing that Lee and I will meet again someday. And in that far better place, we'll catch up on old times. I will

> deeply miss my brother-in-law. I will deeply miss my dear friend.

The family tributes were tender and so true. While I smiled at memories and relished the sentimental thoughts, I was too numb to cry. I tried to savor the tributes, knowing that this was all in honor of Lee. The number of written messages surprised me; I did not realize that so many people had written about Lee for the memorial service. Even my former neighbor Rick, Lee's friend and fighter-pilot colleague, sent a tribute.

> When I first met Lee, it was in Tucson in 1983 during A-7 training. He was a runner, an ultra-athlete. He asked me to go for a run with him, a run up Telegraph Pass Trail, which was a mountain. Seeing how it was 100 degrees, but it was a dry heat, I said, "Okay." So we ran and ran and ran uphill. At the top of the trail, we were out of water.
>
> "No problem," Lee said. "We'll just fill our bottles with water from this creek."
>
> "Oh yeah? No problem?!" I said, really thinking, *What kind of a fanatic is this guy?!*
>
> Lee and I ran together numerous times after that, too many to count. I remember running with him in Panama, northern Canada, and all over the US. He was my roommate at our first Maple Flag, which was a baptism of fire in the world of flying fighters. We competed and commiserated over upgrades in our status as A-7 pilots. We spent lots of hours discussing the state of the world, the Air Force, women, and the state of our small little slice in all of the above.

I introduced Lee and Tina to each other. The memories of the details of that time are fading with time, but I specifically recall how well they hit it off. I remember how annoyed they both were at me that I had the audacity to bring a lieutenant nurse and a lieutenant fighter pilot together at an Air Force bar. Such a concept. I was at their wedding. It was an honor. I remember going to the basement of the Officers' Club and hanging out with them after the wedding.

Lee will always be intricately tied to the very best memories of my youth. We came of age together. Even though we hadn't spoken in a long time, I always assumed that he'd be there when the time came for us to speak again. He was that kind of friend, the kind you know is always there. But he's not there anymore, at least in this life, but I know he'll be there in the next life, waiting for me to go on some insane run with him when I get there. That's a comforting thought. It's always good to know someone is blazing the trail for you. Thanks Lee.

After reading the tributes, Pastor Jim read a brief history of Horatio Spafford, who wrote the hymn "It Is Well with My Soul" in 1873. My numbness held on as we sang the hymn as a congregation, and I did not choke or tear up as I usually do.

Kelly, my favorite male soloist at our church, sang the next song, "Untitled Hymn (Come to Jesus)." Again, numbness prevailed and I listened without tears. I may have had the only dry eyes in the sanctuary as Kelly's rich tenor voice sailed on through the last verse. I could not fathom what it meant for Lee to leave the world and meet Jesus.

Next to speak was Pastor Doug, the youth pastor from our previous church, North Valley Christian Fellowship.

My name is Doug Buron, and Lee and Tina served as youth workers; we call them youth shepherds. They were marvelous. . . . They were marvelous. I met them first at a potluck that we had for new people visiting our church. Lee told me about being an Air Force pilot and flying for American Airlines. I saw them a couple weeks later and, exercising my perfect recall, I asked him, "So tell me, what was it like being in a submarine?" True story.

Um . . . Lee and Tina both. Tina had a way of being able to connect with people with a gentleness and tenderness and a being-there. I was asked this week, "How could Lee be a youth worker with a pilot's schedule?" And for those of you who know them well, it's like, you get whatever you can get. And it's worth it.

I talked to a young man today that is in the army training at Fort Hood whose life Lee is still affecting—from way back then. He makes a difference in people's lives, and you've seen it.

When we were getting ready to move to Oklahoma, he came over and helped us install a lawn in our backyard. He had the time. He wanted to come and help.

I thought I was going to come up here and mention some things that a lot of you didn't know, but from hearing these stories, a lot of you did. The memory I want to share with you today is one that stands out most in my mind. We went on a thing called a Summit Adventure, which is a wilderness trip. And we took twelve kids out into the wilderness on a hike. I trained for two months because, though I am a perfect parabola, I do have a hard time going uphill.

> So I trained [sarcastically shaking his head]. . . . It was frustrating; it was hilarious. Like you were saying, Tina, he would just run circles around you. Like going on a hike with a mountain goat.

Doug's comment about Lee on the trail sent me off into a reverie of my dear Lee and all those miles we had spent backpacking. I saw Lee on the trail in front of me—his muscular legs marching ahead, his backpack firmly supported by broad swimmer's shoulders, his tanned arms swinging rhythmically—as he hiked at a never-wavering, constant pace. In his classic youth-pastor style, Doug's next sarcastic comment yanked me back to the sermon.

> *Uh, Lee, how you doing?!* His energy, his enthusiasm—I hadn't seen that part of him before. He was like Tigger. You know, ready to go—he is in his element. I guess it had something to do with his training, being out in the wilderness.
>
> I talked to him a little bit about his survival training. I didn't get a whole lot back, but for those of you who don't know it, it operates something like this. They drop you off in the wilderness, about two hundred miles from the nearest road, and they give you two toothpicks, a leisure suit, the Casper, Wyoming phonebook, three feet of fishing line and a slinky, and then they say, "If you can make it to Las Vegas, you passed." That's kind of what he was able to do. He had that sort of training, and being up there in the mountains was absolutely incredible.
>
> It was a challenge for a lot of these kids. But seeing him relating with them and teaching them, and instructing them, helping them . . . there was one girl that was so excited; she wanted to keep up with Lee. The second half

> of the trip we carried her on her pack. True story. Lee arranged it—told us how to do it. Even then, he was bearing the burdens of other people, encouraging everybody all the way along.
>
> With a man like Lee, you take whatever you can get. I believe Lee came to Christ because he knew it was dangerous. He knew it was dangerous.
>
> In the book of John, chapter 10 verse 10, it says, "The thief comes to steal, kill, and destroy but I come that you might have life, and that you might have it to the full," or "you might have it more abundantly" [KJV]. There is a battle mentioned in that one single verse, "The enemy comes to steal, kill, and destroy." All you have to do is pick up a newspaper to know that that's true. Lee and Tina have spent their lifetimes engaged in that battle, stepping in the gap for other people.

Listening to Doug's sermon, being challenged to live for Christ, laughing at his jokes; it all seemed so familiar. I almost felt as if it were my usual night at youth group—until the differences registered in my consciousness. *Why is he talking about us? Why is he mentioning our names so much? Why is Doug wearing a suit?!* Slowly my mind registered the event. *No, this is not youth group. Doug is in a suit. Lee is so very far away.* Before I could pursue that line of thought, the fog settled in again between me and my reality, and I listened as Doug continued.

> There are three things that you can learn from stories like this. A book written by John Eldredge [2003] talks a little bit about this. This is from him: three eternal truths that we can learn, because the

work that Lee and Tina have done is an eternal one. It's not just making things better or making things safer, but it's an eternal work that goes beyond.

Things are not always what they seem [Eldredge, 2003]. We need to take a new look at the world around us. I always told young people, in twenty-nine years of youth ministry, that we are one missed heartbeat away from eternity. How on earth could it be Lee's?! We don't know, but we do know that things aren't always what they seem. Look with the eyes of faith.

We are at war [Eldredge, 2003]. There is somebody who is trying to steal our soul, to steal our life, to steal our joy; and we are at war. Lee and Tina have been engaged in that battle. Becoming a Christian is dangerous. There is an old story from C.S. Lewis [1950], *The Lion, the Witch and the Wardrobe.* And in this story—it is a fantasy—one of the kids is introduced to the Christ figure in the story: it's a huge lion named Aslan. And as the one child introduces the other to Aslan, the child who hasn't met Aslan before is scared to death and says, "Is he safe?" And the other child said, "No, but he is good." And God is certainly that.

We all have a vital role to play [Eldredge, 2003]. That is where God is calling each one of us, to pick up our opportunity and to make a difference. We all have a vital role to play, because Christ came that we might have life and have it more abundantly. 2 Timothy 4:7 says this, "I have fought the good fight. I have finished the race." (It's amazing that he could finish a race.) "I have kept the faith. Now there is a crown in store for me." And Lee has been crowned. We miss him, but he has left a legacy. He has made a difference in the lives of people who carry that with them their entire lives. He made an eternal difference. [Doug then turned toward me.] And you continue to.

I looked at Doug in surprise, and again my thoughts were disconnected from the reality of the event. *Why is he in a suit and talking to me in the middle of his sermon? Why did he say Lee's and my names when he was preaching? That's embarrassing.* Although I listened intently, the words and impact of the service were difficult for me to comprehend. I was in shock.

On the Saturday before the funeral, Lee had originally scheduled time with our neighbor friend Abbott to get advice on a computer system that would scan and preserve family photos. Ironically, instead of computer shopping with Lee, Abbott spent that Saturday scanning Lee's photos and preparing the slide presentation for the memorial service. Per my request, the accompanying music included choruses that Lee and I sang to our children at bedtime every night. As he introduced the pictorial celebration of Lee's life, Pastor Jim relayed my comment that I would miss Lee's perfect pitch and incredible singing voice. Seeing our photos on the big screen pierced through my mental fog, and I tearfully watched our lives pass by in past tense.

Afterwards, Pastor Jim asked if anyone would like to take a turn at the microphone to say anything more. An open mike was offered to the first person who stood up, in the back of the church. His name was Stephen; he was in the youth group when Lee and I were youth shepherds at North Valley Christian Fellowship.

> There's quite a few people here I know, but I know Tina because she took care of my Mom when she was sick. There was a time in my life where my wife and I were separated. I was on an airplane coming from someplace I probably shouldn't have been, and the ride was really, really bad. I had never experienced

> anything like this in my life. And I didn't know what was going on, but I was—I was really scared. But when the plane finally landed, I was excited, as anybody would be. But—the part that really made it for me was that—when I started walking up to the front of the plane, I looked up ahead of me when I was walking outside the door, and Lee was standing there. It was at that point that I knew that God had his hand on my life and I was just secure in knowing that Lee was flying the plane. I've never shared that before, but . . . and I've never been able to share with Tina, but I just knew that there was a reason why I was able to make it here tonight. So, thank you, Tina.

I turned my head to hear Stephen speak, fighting through the fog to make sense of memories and reality, none of which was clear to me. Then I heard the familiar voice of the next speaker, Dennis, Lee's fighter-pilot colleague. Dennis, his wife Sally, Lee, and I stayed in touch after all four of us had left the active duty Air Force. I could not look at Dennis for fear of breaking down into tears. Dennis commanded the floor in his confident voice from the center aisle of the church.

> Well, my comments aren't entirely brief, actually. I've known Lee for about twenty years, since we met in the National Guard. I've been talking to a lot of folks in the last few days about Lee and, if Tina will allow me, I'd like to share those.
>
> Lee and I first met in 1984 when I made it to the unit. I was the third of three Project Season guys, who were active duty pilots, to go out to Springfield and fly with the Guard and train, because the active duty didn't have enough cockpits. I had to meet with Mike, a huge, brawling Irishman. He was the John Wayne figure of the Guard

unit—bigger than life. Then came Lee—lean and tan and athletic, a very easygoing Californian kind of guy. And then I showed up, and the Guard unit had quite a bit of expectations, I guess, on the Project Season guys. I'm afraid I couldn't match those guys in brawn or brains or wit, but they were stuck with me. So for the next three years, the three of us—those guys having a big leap on me—shared rites of passage and the coming of age there flying A-7s.

We lost Mike to an accident on a bombing range. When we did, we took him back out to Oregon and laid him to rest there. A unit in Klamath Falls [Oregon] flew F-106s and did a four-ship fly-by formation with overcast skies. They flew over the funeral. At the appropriate time, number three pulled up in the missing man formation. There's a thing of beauty that number three pulled up into the clouds. Lee and I were together to talk to his [Mike's] brothers: two massive, brawling Irishmen like their brother. We talked to them about the tragedy that had befallen our unit and how the men flying together, came together to handle that tragedy—how it brings people closer together.

At the memorial service that we had there in Dayton [Ohio], our commander John Smith read out loud a poem that I'd like to read now. This poem was written by a young fighter pilot during World War II, John Gillespie Magee, Jr. He was an American citizen who was born to missionary parents in Shanghai and educated in Britain's Rugby School. He went to the United States in '39. At the age of eighteen, he went to Yale. Like other Americans of the time who wished to aid in the cause of freedom, he decided to enlist in the services of a nation actively engaged in war. Magee enlisted in the Royal Canadian Air Force in September

1940. He served overseas with a Royal Canadian Air Force Spitfire squadron until his death on active service in December 1941. His poem, "High Flight," composed in September of 1941, was scribbled on the back of a letter, which he mailed to his mother in Washington. Pilot Magee was killed a few months later when his Spitfire plane collided with a bomber-pilot trainer on the approach to the airport over Lincolnshire, England. He was nineteen years old. [Clearing his throat, Dennis then read Magee's poem.]

"Oh, I have slipped the surly bonds of earth,
And danced the skies on laughter-silvered wings;
Sunwards I've climbed and joined the tumbling mirth
Of sun-split clouds—and done a thousand things
You have not dreamed of—wheeled and soared and
swung
High in the sunlit silence. Hovering there,
I've chased the shouting wind along and flung
My eager craft through footless halls of air,
Up, up the long delirious burning blue
I've topped the wind-swept heights with easy grace,
Where never lark, or even eagle, flew;
And, while with silent, lifting mind I've trod
The high untrespassed sanctity of space,
Put out my hand, and touched the face of God."

We will miss you, Lee.

The next to speak, Judy, had previously lived next door to Lee and his family in Fullerton. Lee's first and only babysitting job was for Judy's two children. Later while at the Academy, Lee spent time with Judy and her husband Harlan when they lived in Boulder, Colorado.

> I was a neighbor out in California. The first image I had of Lee was of somebody whizzing by my window. And I think the biggest honor—I think he was on some sort of scooter!—I think the great honor to Lee today that I have heard from his community here is the same theme that goes over and over. It's about how he's always willing to help out with projects, and about his energy, and how he always leads and helps others. It's beautiful.

An American Airlines captain had a great tribute:

> I just want to ask everyone—My name is John and I had the opportunity to fly with Lee on many occasions—did anyone notice any of those pictures where Lee did not have a smile? I'll take that smile with me today.

A female colleague from the San Francisco crew base stood to speak.

> Just from American Airlines, we're really a close-knit group out here in San Jose. We're small, and Lee was always a joy to fly with. We always flew with him on turnarounds. I'm one of the turnaround queens, along with Connie. Every pilot in here loved flying with him. We went through great times together. He was a wonderful man. He'll be missed.

Finally, after all who desired to speak had done so, Pastor Jim closed the open-mike session and resumed his message.

> Well, I've got to say to all the kids here, you've been very good. This has been a long time for you to sit—especially Claire and Bennett. We are all gathered, united in our desire to pay respects, and united in our

need to do so. United in expressing thankfulness to God for the gift of life. Feeling cheated that Lee Carson is no longer here, but grateful that he came into our lives at all.

Thank God for the gift of life. We give thanks for the life of Lee Carson, who gave himself to his family. His memory will never be erased from our minds and hearts. Let us pray.

Lord, we thank you for Lee Carson whose life touched us all. For all the qualities and strengths he had. For all the memories we treasure. For his love, laughter, and loyalty in the relationships that mattered most. Lord of love, hear our prayer as we pray for those most closely affected by his death: for his wife Tina, his children Claire and Bennett, his parents Robert and Lois, and his sister Chris, who mourn the passing of husband, father, son, and brother. Lee leaves a legacy in his relationships as son, husband, father, brother, and friend. Thank God for even small mercies. Thank God for the life of a man whose memory will never be erased from our minds and hearts.

Heavenly Father, we thank you for the precious gift of family life and all human relationships and for the strength they draw from one another. Have compassion on those for whom this parting brings particular pain and the deepest sense of loss. May they know the gentleness of your presence and the consolation of your love as they cast their cares upon you.

Therefore, confident in God's love and grace to all who place their trust in the resurrection of Jesus Christ, we commend our brother Lee Carson to the mercy of God, our Maker and Redeemer. To the refuge of the earth, we entrust our friend's body. To the protection of our God in heaven, we entrust his soul. To ourselves, we entrust his

> spirit, his faith, which form the core of his being, the principles he lived by, and the relationships he cherished.
>
> We're going to miss you, Lee. And now please stand for the benediction.
>
> And now may the Lord bless you and keep you. May the Lord make His face to shine upon you and be gracious unto you. May the Lord lift up His countenance upon you and give you peace. Amen.

As the service ended with the Aaronic blessing, the benediction taken from Numbers 6:24–26, my shoulders relaxed and I soaked in God's continuity. These were the same words I had heard weekly growing up in the Lutheran church: God's words of grace, peace, and comfort that I could hang onto as I left the sanctuary to face my new life.

[12]

Initial Survival

THE MEMORIAL SERVICE was surreal, especially since I had slept only about eleven hours in the previous five days. I was blurred to the reality of the occasion by a mind that could not yet process the pain. The significance of the event broached my consciousness, but the finality of Lee's death was still to be worked through. The comprehension of that finality would take months, even years, to process. At this point, I was surviving just one minute at a time.

Whereas I could not retain much of the service, my children had paid attention. Bennett surprised me by reiterating part of my tribute, "Mommy, I remember your challenge: what is holding you up?" My children had been "lap-hopping" during the service; I could not believe that they heard or comprehended anything. I wondered how any of us could really grasp what was happening.

Thankfully, others were ushered out after the service while our family remained in the front two pews. From where I sat, I could see "my" teenage girls from my previous year's Bible study discipleship group. Seeing the confusion on their faces as they stood together, I went over to encourage them not to give up on God. We stood huddled together in a group, our arms wrapped around each other as they listened to my words with rapt attention.

Soon I felt Jamie, the friend who had helped me overcome my bathroom fear, tapping me on the shoulder to take me to the reception in the church's fellowship hall. Realizing that I would not make it through the crowd of people without being stopped, Jamie helped me duck my head down, leading me by the hand through the maze of people. My sister followed closely behind, ushering me through the crowd and waving people off as they tried to speak with me. An odd thought crossed my mind. *I feel like a rock star herded past throngs of waiting fans.* Thankfully, my numbness allowed me to joke about the situation, a coping strategy I very much needed, instead of falling apart at the reality of what was happening.

The sense of people clamoring for my attention was disconcerting. *Why do they want to reach out to me?!* My mind questioned this even as it attempted to shield me from the underlying horror that occasioned the event. The choice between accepting the outpouring of love and attention, and thus acknowledging the death and pain, versus wallowing in the numb protection of stunned shock was not yet a conscious decision for me.

The entourage moved out of the sanctuary and through the lobby. I knew that Lee's pictures and memorabilia lined the front entrance, but I avoided glancing at them, realizing that if I looked, I would fall apart. So I ducked my head as I was ushered through the space, across the patio, into the fellowship hall, past the buffet tables, and off to a side table where my escorts sat me down.

Maryanne—my former Bible study leader, couples group co-leader at our old church, mothering mentor, and dear friend—had coordinated an incredible reception. Christ Community Church had a tradition of hosting a full dinner after a funeral. Someone told me that Lee's service was the largest funeral they had ever hosted. Maryanne ensured that over three hundred people were welcomed and comforted by a dinner of turkey, ham, and all the trimmings. In her skilled manner, she coordinated the short-notice feast as a potluck, involving friends from our old church, the new church, and our children's public elementary school.

As people moved through the buffet line, a receiving line formed off to the corner of the hall where I was sitting. There had been no wake, reviewal, or receiving line, so this was the first chance most people would have had to talk with me. The line lasted for hours as people came to talk and reminisce with me. Those hours were a blur of love, comfort, and concern as I acknowledged the sea of faces from the twenty-one years of Lee's and my life together.

"How can she do this?"

"She hasn't eaten."

"She hasn't slept since it happened."

"Look, she's shaking. Can't they let her rest?!"

Friends and family continuously fussed over me. By that time, I was shaking with the sensory overload and shock. Jamie brought me a plate of food, but I never got a chance to eat more than a few bites. It would be weeks before I could really eat and digest food.

Even as I overheard the comments of those concerned about me, I felt God's supernatural strength buoying me up. As described in 1 Corinthians 1:4, the comfort I myself had received from God was what I was able to comfort others with. I knew that this receiving line was how I needed to respect the hundreds of people who came to honor Lee. Only God could sustain me through such an emotional maelstrom. Obviously, none of the events of that day were accomplished with strength or reserves originating in me. My source of conviction and energy was none other than my eternal God, who miraculously saw me through the crushing reality of my new life.

During the reception, Claire and Bennett played outside with the other kids. With all of their favorite people gathered in one place, my children enjoyed themselves. In that precious protective mechanism that kids have, my children were able to disconnect from their grief and enjoy the festivities as if nothing had happened. For the first time in their lives, I was able to disconnect from the responsibility of taking care of them. In uncharacteristic manner, I never checked on them or asked what they were doing. That evening marked the last event during which my focus was on just Lee and me.

One of the American Airlines captains who last flew with Lee approached me as I walked past the food line. In concern, he asked, "Did Lee get new tires for your Mitsubishi? Did he fix the antenna?" I did not know the captain by name or face, but Lee's concerns and plans for my old car had definitely been communicated to this coworker. What a blessing to know that Lee must have discussed his recent car repairs with the captain at work.

One gentleman who came to pay his respects was Craig, the father of one of Claire's classmates. Craig and Lee were two of the most involved fathers in Claire's third-grade class. Craig relayed how Lee and he had become acquainted as they accompanied the class field trip to the Almaden Quicksilver Mining Museum. I then remembered Lee talking about making this new friend. Having found someone else who lived out his priority of kids and family, Craig told me how distraught he was at losing someone he admired. I encouraged Craig to look at Lee's strength as something that came from Jesus. With both of us tearful at the loss of Lee, Craig dropped down to his knees. As Craig sensed God's touch on his heart, I tearfully told him that Lee would want Craig to recognize God's love and to consider Christ's impact on his life.

Comments by others touched me that day in ways that I never would have expected. At one point, my friend Pam commented "It's so strange how those pastors looked like Lee!" I shook my head in disbelief. In looks, temperament, style, and voice, Doug and Jim are not at all similar. They differ in almost every way—except that they both love the Lord and Lee. I finally realized that she was seeing Jesus in all three men. All I could do was pray that God would draw her to His heart also.

So many hours were spent with loved ones in that receiving line, but so little time was available to reminisce, commiserate, comfort, and catch up individually. My mind shielded me yet again from the full impact. The Lee-and-Tina partnership was officially broken. The reunion honoring Lee was over. I would never again speak as part of the duo we had been for over twenty years. For many people, that would be the last time I would see them; my connection to them because of Lee had been severed.

After the hours-long receiving line finally finished, I had the chance to breathe and eat. A few friends and family sat with me, encouraging me to eat, and discussing my tribute to Lee. In my sleep-deprived and emotionally spent state, I was acutely aware of God's energy mobilizing me.

Only God could take the wreckage of my widowed devastation, set me in front of 300 people, and let me speak with His poise and power. That was exactly what my friend Jamie recognized when she exclaimed, "Who *was* that woman?!" Jamie was teasing me, while fully acknowledging that God's strength upheld me through the service.

"I don't know, but you'll never see her again," I answered in exhaustion, still surprised at myself that I had survived the events of that momentous day.

Another interesting review after the service came from Pastor Doug's wife Debbie, who remarked, "The memorial service showed how to live a full Christian life."

In the weeks that followed, I received many cards and letters from people whose lives were touched by Lee's memorial. As would happen many times from then on, I was surprised at how God could use the worst event of my life to pour His love and intervention into so many precious hearts. I felt such a burden to contact people and find out how they were doing, but I was reassured by the realization that the Holy Spirit was responsible for the follow up.

God used Lee's memorial service to reunite people. Surprised to find each other again, one woman from my Bible study reconnected with her old friend, a former nursing colleague of mine. Another woman from my Bible study ran into Bennett's kindergarten teacher; former walking partners, they had lost contact. After the funeral, the two friends resumed walking together. Shortly afterwards, the teacher accepted Christ as her Savior, and the pair later attended our women's Bible study together.

Another of the blessings from the memorial service was how people honored Lee in their charitable giving. In lieu of money for our family, we asked that people who wanted to donate would send money directly to Lee's favorite charities, Compassion International and Children's Relief International. Just weeks before Lee died, over 200,000 people in eleven countries died in the Asian Tsunami of December 26, 2004. Families from our kids' public school, San Jose's Noble Elementary School, donated generously to the Compassion International Tsunami Relief Fund in memory of Lee.

Lee and I had long supported Children's Relief International, the parent organization for The City of Hope orphanage in Bucharest, Romania, ever since my 1996 participation as a mission trip chaperone with Pastor Doug's youth group. Family and friends sent thousands of dollars to contribute to the Bucharest orphanage and street-children ministry in Lee's memory.

While ministry continued in Lee's memory after the funeral, I was spent and exhausted. The five days after Lee's death had been a sleepless whirlwind of pain and confusion. My sister Rebecca, concerned for my well-being, made an appointment for me to see an internal medicine physician the morning after the memorial.

On the drive to the doctor's office, my whole body shook and I felt overwhelmed. Casting Crowns' "Voice of Truth" (Chapman & Hall 2004) song played on the radio. Noticing the calming effect the song had on me, my sister turned up the volume. In between sobs and sniffles, I tried to sing along and reflect on the lyrics. *Yes, Lord, I want deep faith—but can I survive the seemingly insurmountable pain required to develop such faith?!*

The doctor weighed me as I stood weaving and weak, almost falling off the scale. I then crumpled onto a chair, and sat folded in half with my hands covering my face. The doctor crouched down to my level, and she listened empathetically to the jumble of words and emotions that poured out. Rebecca filled her in with the facts of how little I had slept and eaten as I sobbed through my story. Dr. C gently discussed why she recommended sleeping pills and antidepressant prescriptions. I knew that I could not continue to live in the manic, adrenaline-fueled state that I had experienced for the last five days. I just wanted to sleep, but my body was functioning in survival mode. Despite physical and emotional exhaustion, I was hyper-alert with frequent tremors as my fight-or-flight response persisted. Even though I did not like the idea of medication, I knew I needed help to rest.

I remember the first real meal my extended family sat down to eat, lovingly brought over by a member of our church couples group several days after Lee died. The dinner was an incredible feast of ribs, potatoes, vegetables, and even extra, kid-friendly side dishes. Although I appreciated the effort, I could not bring myself to eat much. I felt no need to eat, although my family raved about how delicious the meal was. My sense of smell was dulled, along with my appetite, digestion, and hunger.

The emotional pain dulled my awareness of my own activities of daily living, let alone my children's needs. My sister made comfort foods that hearkened back to our childhood—bites of bananas on buttered toast with hot chocolate. She handed me small plates of nutritious foods every few hours. I never threw up, but I was never conscious of hunger or the need to eat.

I spent the days sobbing and crying almost continuously. I was still distracted from my own bodily needs, so much so that Rebecca continued to remind me when to go to the bathroom. I was concerned that I was urinating only once or twice a day, but I did not feel the urge to go. I finally realized that, as before, I was losing so much fluid through tears that not much was left to filter through my kidneys.

Sometimes I felt numb to scents and noise; at other times I was hypersensitive to every stimulus. Beautiful flower bouquets filled the living room, but the greenhouse scent that wafted up the stairs only signified death and funerals to me. Often when I walked onto the upstairs landing that looked out over the living room, the smell of flowers and sounds of people overwhelmed me, and I turned right around and returned to my cloistered bedroom.

During the sleepless nights, I often wandered through the house or listened to music in my bedroom. Sometimes I was caught up in the music and pulled into a place where earthly concerns and responsibilities did not matter. I was able to sing and worship the Lord, even as I grieved my loss. God is still who He is, and worthy of praising, even when I question what He allowed to happen. At times the music could take me beyond the grief to moments of healing and comfort.

One CD that I listened to over and over was *Three to One* (2004), a self-titled CD by a trio from our church. Two members of the group, Todd and Kelly, sang at the memorial service. The third, Dave, was the husband of my friend JoAnne. He had sung several German choruses on the CD, which tapped into one of the few areas of my brain that was not associated with Lee, and therefore not grieving. The German took me back to my childhood in Germany when I had learned the language in German school and spoke it with friends and neighbors, as well as with my mother's side of the family. I could sing those songs in German and momentarily become separated from my grief.

One song that echoed through my wounded soul on that CD (*Three to One,* 2004) was Kelly's version of Avalon's "You Were There" (*Avalon,* 2004). Kelly's pure, smooth voice presented the lyrics that challenged my sense of loss and abandonment. Because Kelly had also sung at the memorial service, listening to the song had a surreal quality, as if Lee's memorial was still ongoing. Ben Glover's lyrics to the song are directed at God and speak of His omnipresence. I replayed that song for hours on end, knowing that God was there in the midst of my tragedy but questioning whether I had the faith to truly believe those words.

In the early days after Lee died, I spent most of my time crying, often screaming and sobbing loudly. I did not care if my kids saw me merely crying, but I knew that my despondent, out-of-control bawling disturbed them. If I broke down in front of them beyond the usual sobbing, with the gut-wrenching wailing that comes from deep within, a friend or family member would escort me away from the kids, take me up to my room, and pray with me or just hold me.

I often sat cocooned on the floor of my bedroom's walk-in closet, talking with God. I wanted to be with God and I wanted out of this pain.

"I love you Lee!" I yelled in one of many screaming fits. So much of me agonized over whether Lee knew that I loved him. *He left so quickly; did he know that I really did love him?!*

"I love you Lee!" I screamed it out, as if he could hear me from the heavens.

Then I felt God asking, *Whom do you love more, Me or Lee?*

Oh that hurt! The great *I AM* tore away the best gift He ever gave me: my love, my precious Lee.

You, Lord, I conceded. I submitted. The agony and sorrow was beyond what I had ever felt before.

God, I surrender. Obedience costs. Sometimes it hurts so much.

But God, I release my beautiful, loving Lee to You. I say yes to You Lord. No holds barred.

God, You have my broken heart. I give You what is left of me, although I feel crushed and dead within. Thank You, Lord for paying the ultimate price for me. Remind me that it cost You so much more than I will ever know.

That closet gave me such a feeling of safety and security in those early days of grieving. It was also the perfect place for me to make private phone calls. God gave me loved ones to call who would lift me up when I was at my lowest. In the early morning hours, I would often phone my friend JoAnne in Germany, my Aunt Renate on the west coast, or my Aunt Carolyn in Minnesota. The time difference, plus the fact that my aunts are early risers, meant that I could count on companionship at any hour.

In the first few days after Lee died, JoAnne and her family had not yet returned to California on furlough from their German mission assignment. JoAnne was great to call in the middle of the night, because Germany was half of a day ahead of us. With her kids off to German school, JoAnne had time to talk while she packed. She read the Bible to me and prayed with me as the rest of my household slept.

My mother's sister, Aunt Renate, gave me practical advice and filled me in on details of how our family had coped after my father died. Her loving support, and reminders of God's help through my dad's death, calmed my worries. Whereas both of us marveled at the fortitude and dedication to God that my mother had displayed as she coped with widowhood, Aunt Renate soothed my insecurities about not being as strong as my mom. When I cried that I could not do this like my mom, she reassured me that I would get through this in my own way with God's help. She prayed with me and read me Bible verses. The empathetic sisterhood she had offered to my widowed mother thirty-two years ago became a deep reservoir of mature, Christ-like comfort that she poured into me.

Aunt Carolyn, my father's sister, filled me in on how her mother, my Grandma Biltz, was doing. On January 6, 2005, the same night Lee died, Grandma broke her hip and then had a heart attack. She was admitted to the hospital and scheduled for stress tests the next morning before having a hip replacement. Somewhere between the night of January sixth and the morning of the seventh before the stress tests, Grandma had chest pains.

"I'm too young to die!" ninety-four-year-old Grandma pronounced in defiance of the many medical issues that threatened her life during that hospitalization. On January seventh, doctors presented Grandma with the choice of transferring to the university hospital for angioplasty or undergoing a hip pinning. Grandma chose the hip pinning. Although less extensive than a total joint replacement, the hip pinning at the local hospital required a long recovery. Afterwards, she transferred to a nursing home for several weeks of rehabilitation, but Grandma never returned to her two-story duplex home.

Although Grandma adored Lee—and perhaps because of that—my aunt and mother chose not to tell her about his death until after her surgery. My mom and I used to joke that if Grandma would stop witnessing to people, her job on earth would be done, and God would take her home. In fact, I journaled one of Grandma's telephone comments to me: "The best thing about my life is that I'm a Christian. I'm so glad! I witness everywhere I go."

During an earlier hospitalization at the University of Minnesota, Grandma had befriended one of the assistants in the hospital. She talked with the woman, and later wrote to her. Grandma discussed much with the nursing assistant, telling her about the Lord and what He meant in her life, and then encouraged the woman to return to Michigan and reconcile with her husband.

In January of 2005, my aunt was coordinating a move for her brother, my Uncle Paul, who had also broken his hip in a fall and would need to move to a one-level apartment. She was in the midst of two moves, two hospital stays, and multiple arrangements, yet Aunt Carolyn found time to listen to me and comfort me. She understood my irreverent, and at times morbid, sense of humor as we laughed, cried, and commiserated about family issues together. God had again blessed me with friendship and support through my family.

Though the support never faltered, I still struggled, even as I tried to understand. "For my thoughts are not your thoughts, neither are your ways my ways, declares the Lord. As the heavens are higher than the earth, so are my ways higher than your ways and my thought than your thoughts." Isaiah 55:8–9 is a favorite verse, but I still do not get it. The irony of God's plan is incomprehensible to me. A forty-five-year-old endurance athlete, father of two young children, in apparent perfect health with no cardiac risk factors versus a ninety-four-year-old widowed grandmother with a twenty-five year history of cardiovascular disease, multiple cardiac catheterization procedures, and the inability to undergo bypass surgery because of her high surgical risk. Which person would you expect to have a fatal heart attack? More than once I argued with God. *So, did you take the wrong heart?!*

One day, sitting in my bedroom during a grief meltdown, I wanted to die. I told God that I was done and could not go on. I was at the end of my rope in despair. Although afraid that I would try something desperate, I also recognized that I had no energy to harm myself. I was angry that God would not just take me, since I was giving up. As I lay on my floor curled up and hoping to die, God prompted me to call someone for help.

There was only one no-nonsense person I thought of to call, Pastor Doug. In retrospect, I recognize that Doug was an antidote to my self-pity, but at the time I just wanted to complain about God to someone who could handle my honesty. I knew Doug would listen and give bold advice.

"Doug, I can't do this!" I wailed petulantly over the phone.

"Yes, you can," Doug countered in his deep, firm voice.

"No, I really can't. I'm giving up. I'm done." My whining continued, but Doug, a pastor and father of three daughters, was not deterred.

"No, you're not." Never one to sugarcoat the truth or sidestep a confrontation, Doug matched my insistence with truthful resolve. "You were a highly trained officer in the Air Force. You are not disabled; you are temporarily stunned."

"This isn't temporary. Yes, I *am* done. I want God to take me. I can't survive without Lee." My complaining escalated to defiance.

"Yes, you can. God has not left you. You have a future to look forward to. You're young. You'll get married again."

"Doug, if you were here in person, I would punch you for saying that! That is horrible to say." Doug is the irritating older brother I never had. And yes, I really would have punched him had the comment been made in person. Appalled that he would suggest what I considered a betrayal of Lee, I nevertheless listened as Doug went on.

"Godly people will give you lots of advice—"

"That's for sure. So many people tell me what to do now," I acknowledged as I interrupted.

"You are a woman of faith, and you need to trust your instincts. Don't listen to all the advice-givers, but go to God. Do what God says to do."

"But this is so hard. I don't want to do this."

"Neither did my mom," Doug went on. "She was widowed with fourteen- and seventeen-year-old sons. She tells about the time she went to her bedroom and faced her two choices: lie down and die or get up, go on, and face life. She chose to face life and went back to work as a nurse."

"But I have nothing left. I am done with this life," I groused.

"You have to get back in the game," the former football player urged. Doug did not stop encouraging me, even to the point of goading me on in his brotherly manner. Then his wife Debbie joined him on the phone, and they both prayed for me. Sweet fellowship with trusted friends.

After hanging up the phone, my despair lessened. I got up off the floor and went downstairs. Bennett was sitting at the piano and asked me to help him. I sat down next to him and played the accompaniment as he practiced his piano piece. We had such sweet fun together, and Jamie grabbed a camera to capture the moment. The incident made me realize that if I pushed myself just a bit farther—past the point of my desperation—to get back in the game, God would take me the rest of the way.

I hated football analogies, but I thought about it anyway. Life could still have small fragments of fun when I was willing to leave the locker room (the safety of my grief-cocooned bedroom) and rejoin the game (parenting and spending time with my kids.) Yes, it was halftime. I was losing and griping to the coach. I told God that there was no way I could go on after being so shattered. And God, the Ultimate Coach, told me to get back in the game. At age forty-three, I had half the game—half of my life—to finish yet.

I decided to go out for the second half.

[13]

The Team

GRIEF IS NO RESPECTER of chronology. Time is distorted when the mind processes the irretrievable past, tries to understand the present loss, and fears the unknown future. Dealing with the present encompasses the irony of recognizing the loss while still trying to ignore the truth of what has happened. Denial protects from the excruciating reality and gradually recedes as one recognizes and deals with the truth. The struggle between accepting—yet fighting—the reality takes large amounts of emotional energy. The reality of the loss has to permeate every layer of life. That onion takes a long time to peel.

For the next five weeks, I was essentially in shock. My system was in fight-or-flight response, with a stimulated sympathetic nervous system that slowed my digestion, sped up my heart rate, and sharpened my senses. My nonessential functions slowed while the adrenalin from the shock sped up everything needed for survival. While my insides churned at high rates in this new survival mode, my exterior did not move much. My brain was trying to protect my conscious self from the shock of what I knew in my heart to be true.

"Catatonia is a safe place," I wrote in my journal as my new motto. I may not have been as rigid as a catatonic, but I moved very little as I sat crying in a daze, passing the hours in mental solitude. One morning, my mother put on my socks and combed my hair because I was unable to do that for myself. I had my usual place on the couch, where I curled up with a blanket. I alternately wept, talked, or sat in stunned silence.

The scheduled support that would sustain me in the upcoming months began even before my family members left town. In the memorial service, Pastor Jim mentioned that people could contact my friend Jamie to offer help. Jamie, my kindergarten mom friend, led the charge with three others: Maryanne, my mothering mentor; JoAnne, the missionary who by that time had returned from Germany; and Rebecca, my sister and childhood grief partner. Together this foursome linked, phoned, delegated, planned, and coordinated to set a machine of logistics in motion. "The team," as we called these helping friends, started regular meetings to coordinate care for my children and me.

The team was divided into three sections: kids, meals, and me. A phone call to my number gave the following message: "If you are calling for meals, call Maryanne at —. If you are calling about the kids' schedule, call Jamie at —. If you are calling about Tina, call JoAnne at —." Maryanne arranged for meals three to four times a week, prepared by friends from the kids' school as well as our previous church and CCCM. Jamie coordinated rides to school, activities (both extracurricular and playdates), and homework help for both children. JoAnne planned the schedule for twenty-four-hour care for the three of us, household help, and appointments with doctors and counselors. Early on, the team even scheduled caregivers for me while the kids were in school. After my sister flew home, the three friends continued to provide practical support and comforting love within a protected enclave.

My home became a refuge from the sensory overload of real life. Guests were filtered and allowed in only according to my energy level. "My people" answered the phone; all calls were dutifully recorded on the ever-growing notepad. Even dear friends were sometimes turned away from the door as my team encouraged me to rest. The team formed an impregnable fortress to shield me as I lived in my shell-shocked state. I was allowed to grieve any way that I needed to: wander aimlessly, sob, sit in an unresponsive state, cry on someone's shoulder, or whatever else I needed to do.

Nighttime, mealtime, daytime with the kids at school—for me, it was *all* difficult. In the morning I would awaken and, for a split second, I would not remember that Lee had died. Then, suddenly conscious of life in my new nightmare, my tears would begin again. The future was not something I could plan for; each day was survived moment by moment. Sometimes this meant that I could get through a few hours staring out the window; at other times, I just held my breath and got through one minute at a time. The time warp was disconcerting, but I was too numb to notice the specific days or events that passed by in those early weeks of grieving.

January of 2005 was cold and rainy in San Jose. I was always freezing, so I wandered around the house with a blanket over my shoulders. When my jumbled thoughts consistently interfered with my speech, I developed a stutter. I had significant tremors; my hands—even my whole body—shook uncontrollably. I sobbed so hard that I could not keep up with the mucus running down my face, let alone the tears. Those unrelenting tears eventually caused eczema patches on my cheeks.

My internist Dr. C diagnosed my symptoms as a sympathetic storm. I begged her to tell me how long it could last. She had seen this type of adrenalin surge last as long as six months in a hospitalized patient. She stressed that these symptoms were all related to grief, and that what I was going through was physiological, not pathological. She explained to me how my adrenal glands continued to release epinephrine, the fight-or-flight hormone. Always the nurse, I asked where my dopamine and serotonin were; those were the neurotransmitters that would have calmed my system down. Beta blockers had been prescribed to slow down my sympathetic nervous system and lower my heart rate. Even at unusually high doses of the medication, my heart beat more than 110 beats per minute. Some nights my heart rate was 128, even after I took a sleeping pill and beta blockers. Whereas my blood pressure had always been low, it became significantly elevated.

Although I dealt with a high heart rate and catecholamine surges, thankfully I never had the chest pain that characterizes takotsubo cardiomyopathy, or what is more commonly called broken heart syndrome. Scientific literature describes takotsubo cardiomyopathy, or stress cardiomyopathy, as acute chest pain and breathlessness in response to a stressful episode, such as the death of a spouse (Sharkey, Lesser, & Maron, 2011).

My tremors, stuttering, high heart rate, and elevated blood pressure lasted for five weeks, during which I was not safe to drive. My team of friends scheduled carpooling to and from our appointments. They ensured that my children did not miss school or extracurricular activities.

Given my high heart rate and lack of appetite, I kept losing weight. The team knew my weight and how elevated my blood pressure was, but would not tell me. Whoever accompanied me to the clinic, usually my sister or JoAnne, turned me around so that I could not read the scale at the doctor's office. I was afraid of how much weight I was losing so I wore my heaviest clothing to the appointments. It made me nervous that my friends worried about my weight. They were on me about my weight, in my business, and about God's business. Very humbling.

I felt like a sheep being led around by my handlers. Concern and information about me was passed among caregivers. My friends talked over and around me, but I was too devastated and numb to participate. I knew I was weak and unaware of much that was going on around me, but all I could do was acquiesce to what they asked me to do and try to breathe through the emotional pain. I was an exhausted, ravaged, walking corpse. I sat there knowing what I should do, for example, pour glasses of milk for my kids, but I could not muster the energy to accomplish even the simplest activities of daily life.

A big shock came for me when I pulled a pair of jeans out of my drawer and tried to put them on, only to have them slide off my hips. I recoiled in horror at the thought that this agony had wasted me away physically as quickly as it had done mentally. Then I started to laugh as I realized that they were Lee's jeans, which, of course, were too big for me. With friends and family doing all of our laundry for us, it became humorous to see where our clothes ended up. I got Lee's jeans and Claire's underwear. My socks ended up in Bennett's dresser, along with Claire's shirt. Our funny game of "Whose clothes ended up where?" was a nice diversion. It also helped me let go of my perfectionism and independence, replaced instead by gratitude for the help.

Not only the laundry, but all other household chores were done for me, first by my family, and after they went home, by my friends. The help was phenomenal. I thanked God that he sent me loved ones who valued keeping the kitchen clean. The "old me" tried to keep my kitchen clean, and when my friends worked so hard to do the same, despite all that was going on, I was grateful.

Along with the blessing of laundry and cleaning, meals were sent three times a week in disposable containers and left outside in a cardboard box on the front porch. When meals were delivered, we did not have to answer the doorbell to see anyone or return any pans or dishes. Jamie wrote a note to post on the porch: "Your willingness is so appreciated! Thank you for the meal. Please just place items in the box and they will be collected soon (no need to knock or ring the doorbell). Thank you so much! The Carson Family."

Like the Israelites who asked, "What is it?" when God blessed them with food in the desert (Exodus 16:15–16, 31–32,) we called our food "manna." Delicious, wholesome, warm meals were sent with much love and prayer. Some families sent loving notes or gifts for the kids. On Valentine's Day, someone sent a pink, glittery, heart-shaped candle with dinner. I set it on a pretty dish in the middle of the dining room table, and it symbolized to me that life could be pretty and feminine again, even after such devastation. That day I also received a chocolate rose from someone who just left it at the front door. Like so many other loving acts we received, I did not know who sent it, so I could only ask God to bless the giver in return. I cried at the thought that my true valentine was gone, but I also thanked God for how He sent dear people to love and care for us.

"I didn't know so many people loved us!" Bennett exclaimed delightedly after a delicious dinner and gifts arrived from our vacation Bible school leaders. The kids were surprised at the support we received. The support and lessons on gratitude that my children gained from the meals and the household help blessed and comforted me deeply.

The garage was a place that I avoided because so many memories were tied up with the sports equipment, bikes, and cars. While Lee was alive, the garage was his territory, his "man cave." One day I carried the trash out and stopped—dead in my tracks in the dead man's cave.

"God, I can't do this! I can't go on!" I screamed at the God of the universe as I looked around the garage at everything that reminded me of Lee and what he had enjoyed. I wailed in total meltdown. "How can he be gone?!"

JoAnne rushed out to the garage. Realizing that she could not get me to move, JoAnne held me as I sobbed. Tears and mucus streamed down my face and onto my chest as I wailed and moaned. I wanted to die. I had no energy or desire to go on with my life. Nothing in my life—not even my children—seemed worth living for. I wanted only to be with Lee. I screamed these thoughts out to God, as JoAnne held me and cried with me. After I stopped, JoAnne started praying for me. No magic words or sudden solution, but in her friendship she stood by me through the agonizing loss and allowed me to grieve and vent.

JoAnne was my meltdown manager. She explained it to the kids using potty talk, which they loved.

"Do you want to be in the bathroom with Mommy when she poops?" JoAnne asked the kids. (Thankfully this conversation did not occur at the dinner table.)

"Eeeeew! Yuck!" Claire and Bennett chorused.

"In the same way, Mommy needs some time to get her yucky stuff out by herself. Just like Mommy washes her hands and comes out to be with you after going to the bathroom, she will stop crying after she gets her yucky feelings out. Then she will come back to be with you as usual." JoAnne later told me that the kids understood the analogy. I was sure they savored the potty talk part of it.

When I went downstairs to dinner, I compared my meltdown to their tantrums. "You know how Mommy helps you get to time-out or to your room when you lose self-control? That's what Mrs. M [JoAnne] was doing, helping Mommy to her room when she lost self-control because she was sad and mad about Daddy dying." That was my "Eeeeew–yuck" moment: I hated being my kids' role model for loss of self-control.

Cathartic, soul-wrenching sobs of grief disturb even the most stoic of souls, and I wanted to keep to myself when I broke down like that. In the beginning my caregivers escorted me out of my children's range when I lost it, but later I was able to excuse myself for weeping episodes. I used the shower as a private place to wail, until my skin got so dry that I had to shorten my showers.

After bawling in the shower, I would drop into bed by 10:00 p.m., emotionally exhausted. Delusional in my hope of sleep without medication, I would try to fall asleep on my own, giving myself a midnight deadline to take a sleeping pill. I usually spent those hours sobbing, agonizing over painful memories, fearing that people would stop praying for me, hoping to die, and yet fearing that I would live. On the other hand, I feared not making it, thinking I would become the one who died within a year of my spouse because of a broken heart. So many lies of Satan's accosted me in my bed at night. I was fragile and heartbroken. After hours of this, I would give up and take the sleeping pill, crying myself to sleep. For months, I cried myself to sleep every night, convinced that I would never fall asleep without tears again.

A sleeping pill usually bought me a few hours of slumber, but I never slept the full night. Many times I woke from a sound sleep, sobbing as grief pervaded both conscious and subconscious realms. Or I woke up in the middle of the night and wandered shell-shocked through the house. In those first few weeks when friends and family stayed with us, my caregiver would wake up and come out of the guest room to sit, pray, or talk with me. My friends graciously gave me the space I needed, yet they gave me the rock-solid assurance that I was never alone in my pain.

Jamie often "worked" the night shift with her six-month-old daughter Kylee. One night, after the kids went to bed, Jamie and I had a slumber party on the floor of my room. In our pajamas eating grapes (Jamie ate only healthy food), we enjoyed heavy theological discussion interspersed with silly girl talk.

Jamie spoke from the perspective of the stay-at-home moms, "You know, I thought we lost you last fall."

"I really was going to go back to work, especially since Bennett had started first grade and was in school all day." The reasons I gave seemed like a far-distant normal, a vantage point that would never be the same again.

"You were looking for a job, weren't you?" she pried gently.

"Yeah, I know, Jamie. You were right. I am so glad that I didn't go back to work. Can you imagine what I would be doing now?!"

"You came so close," Jamie stated in hushed tones, the significant consequences of that decision remaining unexplored by either of us.

"Okay, Jamie, you can say it: 'I told you so.'"

"No, no," Jamie demurred, her gentle nature finding those words hurtful.

"No, come on, Jamie, just say it to me. 'I told you so.'"

"Tina, I can't," she replied with a grin.

"Yes, you can. I deserve it." My begrudging admission was delivered teasingly. "You were so right. Come on Jamie, say 'I. Told. You. So.'"

My attempts to goad her into giving me a hard time were unsuccessful, as I knew they would be. Her smile changing to a chuckle, Jamie tried to choke out the words as we both dissolved into laughter.

She and I then went on to reminisce about how we had met our husbands. It was so much fun just to talk. Our normal lives were so filled with children: her Kenny and my Claire who had started kindergarten together and were still good friends in third grade, my Bennett two years younger than our oldest kids, Katelyn one year younger than Bennett, and her baby Kylee. We rarely had time to complete a conversation, let alone talk about topics other than the kids.

Jamie and Kylee slept together on the guest room futon. I think I spent more time awake at night than Kylee, but Jamie never complained. Kylee was so precious to me. I could hold her and enjoy her deep brown eyes and sweet smiles, as I tried to connect vicariously to her innocent wonder at the world. At six months, Kylee met her milestone of sitting up on my dining room floor, and we took pictures in celebration. Kylee, my forever happy friend, forced us to realize that the future holds the promise of joy, despite our current pain. She was the only one in my world who was not grieving.

[14]

Kids in Pain

THE CLASSIC ANALOGY for helping children grieve is the use of oxygen masks on a jet. In the event of rapid decompression, oxygen masks will pop out of the overhead console. As a parent, you are instructed to grab your own mask first, put it on, and only then help your children get their oxygen masks on. The rationale is that you will not be able to accomplish this task once you are hypoxic; too little oxygen renders you incapable of even basic tasks.

In Air Force nursing flight school, part of our training involved time in the decompression chamber. We were given a ridiculously simple, almost insultingly easy worksheet on a clipboard; then we were sent into the chamber. Wearing oxygen masks, we were asked to pull them off once we reached altitude and then complete the worksheet. The goal was to focus on what our symptoms of hypoxia, or too little oxygen, were. One of the first symptoms of hypoxia for many of us was the loss of color vision. The world became black and white. Despite intense attempts to focus on simplistic questions, such as simple addition of one digit numbers, we were confused and had difficulty concentrating. The physiological manifestations of oxygen deficiency were fast in onset and insidious in nature. There was a warped recognition of the need to put the oxygen mask back on, after which the task was haltingly accomplished in slow motion.

In times of rapid decompression, as well as in seasons of grieving, you must help yourself first before you have the strength and presence of mind to guide your children. This is contrary to the basic parenting instinct of taking care of your child before yourself. For example, a mother will starve herself if it means her child will get food. Basic survival instincts in the wild, as well as in the modern world, direct resources to the survival of the children even at the parents' peril. Only by going against your basic instinct, in grieving and hypoxia, can you be well enough to take care of your children.

"My name is Tina Carson and I am mentally incapacitated," I joked with my team. I wrapped my arms around myself and flapped my hands on my back as if I were in a restraint jacket. My joking hid the terror beneath that statement; I knew that I was unable to care for my children, and I feared being taken away from them.

Claire and Bennett were out of school for a total of three days after Daddy died. The day after the memorial, my children went back to school. I remembered Evelyn Husband's descriptions of family life after her husband died in the shuttle crash. Evelyn sent her kids back to school soon after their father died, and she emphasized the importance of establishing normal routines (Husband, 2003, pp. 200–2).

Despite the comfort I felt in following my role model, I still agonized as I saw my kids walking out the door. I wondered how they could return to their usual routine after such a life-changing loss. Poor Bennett looked so neglected going back to school that first day: a hole in the knee of his pants (he refused to change once dressed), overdue for a haircut, long fingernails that he had insisted (but then gave up on) clipping himself, and dull, tired eyes. Claire's long hair was unkempt and uncombed, her tomboy outfit a mismatch of blue camouflage pants and a horse T-shirt.

My heart ached for what my children had lost, and for what I could never have protected them from. While school had not changed for all the other children, it would never be the same for Claire and Bennett. That first day back, both uncles were outside with the kids, waiting for their ride to Noble Elementary School. I cried and watched from the window, as if I were hidden away in a cage of mourning. Mr. J, the father of one of Bennett's classmates, had offered to drive my kids to and from school. In a moment of zaniness that got even me laughing, Uncle Fred (my brother) and Uncle Chris (my sister Rebecca's husband) lifted the kids onto their shoulders and started chicken fights. Seeing my kids laughing and playing was the most soothing balm I could imagine.

Before he died, Lee and I had decided to apply his grandmother's inheritance money toward the purchase of a piano. Lee's grandmother played the organ at the church where her husband pastored, so a piano seemed like an appropriate tribute to her legacy. I followed through with that plan and arranged for Bennett to start piano lessons. Claire had been playing piano for years, but she practiced on a keyboard I had purchased at a garage sale. The night before the piano delivery, Bennett helped me move the couch in preparation.

As I read Bennett his bedtime story, he repeatedly leapt off the bed in excitement over the piano's arrival. When I tucked him in, Bennett softly said, "I want Daddy to be here."

I cried with him and concluded, "Life is not fair . . ."

"But God is good," Bennett finished the second half of the motto I had repeated to the kids many times. I usually meant it in response to childhood whining about who got the bigger brownie or why her crayon was broken and his was not. How ironic that the phrase I used so regularly became a painful reminder of how we were to live.

The piano, a used Yamaha upright in a shiny ebony finish, arrived while the kids were at school. JoAnne and I greeted the delivery with much fanfare.

"We're grieving," JoAnne announced, as she ran out to the truck with the camera, "and we have a first-grader who needs to see this."

The two delivery men moved the piano from the truck to the lift, lowered the lift, and rolled the dolly into the house as JoAnne took pictures of every step. I was too weak to go outside, so I sat in a chair to watch. The delivery men must have thought we were nuts as we cried and blubbered.

"Do you play piano?" the older gentleman asked kindly.

"Just a little," I responded tearfully.

"They all say that."

No, really little, I thought to myself.

"Could I play you a song?" the other man asked.

"I'd be honored," I said from my chair as I held my head in my hands.

A few notes—and I knew: Ludwig van Beethoven's "Fűr Elise." Solemn and amazing. A unique rhythmic lilt in this player's version. Beethoven might not approve of such liberties in the rhythm, but I was touched. More tears. Finished, he walked over and gave me a hug.

"You have no idea how much this means to us. Thank you," I said through tears.

Bennett came home from school and squealed in delight when he saw the new piano. He sat down excitedly, and we snapped more pictures. Claire also squealed, but as someone who regularly protested piano practice, she announced that she would play only one note. When we started taking pictures, she became angry at the camera. Finally, when we left her alone, she began playing with enthusiasm, her little-girl frame sitting erect and centered on the piano bench. In contrast to Lee's concern that the piano would merely be a piece of unused furniture, it was regularly used for practice, by our kids as well as Jamie's. Four kids taking turns on the instrument brought joy and music to our grieving house.

At dinner that night, Claire, in her usual no-nonsense manner, commented, "Lose a dad. Get a piano." As I teared up, she added, "I'd rather have a dad."

"Me too," I sobbed.

Claire and Bennett had lots of tantrums. They lost control of their emotions easily, just as I did. After a team member had been in Claire's room and moved her toys, Claire went off on an angry tirade and threw stuffed toys at her bedroom window. Given the dozens of stuffed animals on her bed, I knew the tantrum could go on for a long time. I watched the objects of her wrath hit the window, fearing that Claire would break the glass, but thankfully she threw only soft, plush toys.

Then suddenly, I remembered Lee and his Dad replacing the windows in our house several years prior. Overcome by the memory, I dissolved into tears and retreated back to my room, only to hear Claire scream. She ran into the bathroom, looking for something else to throw, and yanked the towel bar out of the wall. Then another memory came back to haunt me: the last time the towel bar came down, Lee had said he would not be able to fix it next time. How painfully true that was now. More tears.

Claire's raging continued, so I called Emily, my neighbor friend and the church librarian. I used our code phrase, "I need an extra pair of hands." Of course, the shrieking in the background was a clue that things were out of control at our house. Emily found me slumped on the hallway floor sobbing as Claire was throwing toys. Emily read to Bennett and then helped him get ready for bed. Claire maintained her screaming fit for over an hour. I alternately subjected myself to the room of rage and flying objects, or sat exhausted and crying in the hallway. Later I overheard Claire say to Bennett, "When Mommy's sad, anything goes."

Nighttime rages were not uncommon, nor was the exhaustion I felt in dealing with grieving children, as we ended yet another day without Daddy. My daily prayer with the kids was, "Dear God, remind us that Daddy loves us, but that you love us more." That was a difficult concept to swallow, that God's love could eclipse Daddy's. How could I possibly get my children to believe that truth when I was struggling to comprehend it myself?!

One morning Bennett and I stood in the backyard, I in my robe and he in his little boy pajamas, watching a flock of geese fly high in the distant sky. I achingly remembered watching Lee fly his A-7 in formation at the Dayton Air Show and wondered how many formations he had flown in. *Oh God, I miss him.* As we watched, the geese smoothly moved from the classic V formation into an arrangement that looked like the letter T.

"Look Mommy—they made a T! T for Tina!" Bennett exclaimed, pointing to the sky with his tiny index finger.

Breaking into goose bumps at the significance of the flock's maneuver, I asked incredulously, "Bennett, do you know what that is?" I had heard of but never before experienced a sign from a dead loved one. "That is a sign."

"From Daddy?"

"I don't know if it was sent by Daddy himself or if God did it because Daddy asked him to. I don't really understand how it works, but that is definitely a sign from God that Daddy still loves us. Do you remember our prayer? God please remind us that Daddy loves us, but—"

"You love us more," Bennett chimed in with the last half of our family prayer.

One morning I went downstairs and all the lights were on. An intricately crafted valentine for Claire lay drying on the table. My little nightwalker had been at work on his arts and crafts. How did I miss that? An antihistamine had helped me sleep the first three hours of the night. Then, after returning my crying six-year-old to his bed, I had taken half of a sleeping pill, which bought me two hours of sleep. Groggily looking around for my nighttime crafter, I started to wonder if I was capable of caring for my children. *Am I safe with those sleeping pills?* I did not hear Bennett get up and go downstairs. *Are the kids safe? Will I ever sleep a full night again?*

Bennett presented Claire with his sleep-sacrificed treasure: a ribbon-trimmed, construction-paper valentine. When Claire saw two of her special stickers on the front of the card, she exploded.

"Why did you use my special stickers from the Jungle? You didn't even ask! They cost me fifteen points each!" She screeched her explanation of the stickers she had "purchased" at the children's arcade within The Jungle, an adventure playland she had visited on a recent outing.

Crushed in agony that his gift had actually hurt her, Bennett cried out in fear and pain. Both children ran to their rooms and dove onto their beds, sobbing. I followed, leaned up against the hallway wall, and slid down as I too sobbed in anguish. As I would come to recognize, a seemingly normal sibling rivalry episode could incapacitate all three of us. The ominous iceberg of grief undergirded every interaction and threatened to sink us with the sting of our loss in the everyday ups and downs of life.

All three of us ended up sobbing over the valentine episode, just ten minutes before the carpool arrived. We managed to sort it out somewhat, with Bennett realizing that he had made a good choice of stickers, because those were Claire's favorites. Claire realized that, because she never put them away for safekeeping, the stickers ended up in the kids' craft drawer for use by anyone. Bennett had not violated her space after all.

Claire later appreciated Bennett's efforts and refused his offer to cut out the stickers. "I like it just the way it is," she sincerely expressed. Like eggshells to a hard countertop, our wounded, hypersensitive hearts shattered quickly in response to everyday matters.

Issues that had never existed suddenly became important, like when Bennett became stressed about his cluttered room. A messy room had never bothered him before, but now, as he tried to process his trauma, the toys and books strewn across his room irritated him. As a recovering neat freak myself, I understood. Oma (my mother) and I worked on his room, trying to clean up without invading his space. We straightened up several things, and then Oma gave him a couple of jobs to do when he came home from school. She asked him to vacuum, and then he had to put all of his cards in a bag and label them. Accomplishing those tasks and seeing his room cleaned up seemed to calm him.

Even as we worked through some situations, meals remained the most painful time of the day. Lee's empty chair was a prominent and raw reality when we sat at the table every night. I was angry that Lee and I had worked so hard to make mealtime special as a family, only to have the loss magnified with him gone. *If we had not worked so hard to be together as a family, it would not hurt so much,* I thought dejectedly. Sometimes I sat with tears streaming down my face throughout the entire mealtime.

On JoAnne's prompting, I changed where I sat at the dinner table, moving from my usual seat to Lee's seat. I made it a deliberate gesture, to visually and symbolically establish that I was the authority and the new head of the family. "I'm going to sit in Daddy's chair now," I announced weakly.

"This must be the guest chair then!" JoAnne announced, enthusiastically jumping into my old chair. As excruciating as it was for me to take Lee's place in his chair, it was an important shift for us in our family structure. The process of becoming $n = 3$ instead of $n = 4 - 1$ would require many slow, deliberate, and painful steps in the upcoming months and years.

The "best-worst" game was a nightly routine that the four of us had shared as a family. Playing the game without Daddy was agonizing, but like so many of the things we did together before Daddy died, I knew that continuing the routine was essential for my children.

Dinner was always our time of conversation. One night within weeks after Lee's death, Claire, in her assertive voice, announced, "Mommy, I have two questions."

"What, Claire?" I responded, gearing myself up for one of her usual challenges, as evidenced by the tone of her voice.

"Where is the body?" Claire had obviously been processing the "what" and "where" of Daddy's death. Her question sparked a discussion of Daddy's cremation and what we would do with his ashes.

Emotionally exhausted after addressing Claire's first question, I braced myself for another doozy and asked her, "So what is your second question?"

"Can I have some more pasta?"

"Sure!" I laughed as I dished up more penne, or "tubes" as my children called them. How classic for a grieving child!

One minute she processed a painful concept and the next minute she popped out of her grief to attend to matters of everyday life. Her seeming ease of transition made me wistful. *If only I could switch gears like that.*

"Mommy, was Daddy dying your worst?" Claire asked every night. She seemed to need daily validation that this was still my worst event.

"Claire, yes. Daddy dying is the worst of my life," I reassured her yet again. Like a toddler proving object permanence, Claire asked the same question over and over to ensure that my answer was still the same. For weeks, I mentioned Daddy dying as the worst of my day, not only because that truth consumed my everyday thoughts, but also to reassure my children that we had survived the worst of life. Sharing the best of our days became an exercise in gratitude for the many things that people had done to help us.

One night Claire had an additional question. "Mommy, when you get to heaven, who will you be happier to see, Daddy or your dad?"

"Claire, I would run to your daddy, because I love him so much. Besides, I had only eleven years with my Dad, and I had almost twenty-one years with your Daddy."

Claire transferred much of her emotional pain into physical symptoms, somaticizing her grief. She did not verbally express her feelings about losing Daddy, but she frequently complained of physical ailments. Once it was a pulled calf muscle—lots of pain, whining, and attention-seeking behavior. I learned to recognize the physical symptoms as minor and to realize that her comments actually described her emotional pain.

Claire's dramatic outbursts always related to the iceberg of grief beneath her physical malady. "God, why does it have to be me? This hurts so bad! I hate this!" Claire cried out these questions in relation to her current symptoms, a cough and congestion, but I recognized them for objectified expressions of grieving. These were somaticized manifestations of her grief, but in a protective, self-defense mechanism, she attributed all pain to her physical ailment. One night I sat with her for over four hours as she cried out these grieving wails, ostensibly about her ear congestion, but obviously about the trauma of losing her father. All that I could do was hold Claire and pray for her. I prayed for her aloud, but my silent recurring prayer felt desperate. *God mend her, because I can't.*

Shortly after that tough night, Claire accused me, "Mommy, you are so lazy because you won't drive for my field trip!"

"Sweetie, I would love to, but I am too sad about Daddy right now. I still can't drive." She had no concept of my debilitated physical condition.

"All you do is sit around, talk to your friends, and hold Kylee!" To Claire's mind, I paid more attention to Jamie's daughter than to my own children. My heart ached for the shock she was going through. I felt so inadequate as a parent.

Even everyday events elicited my feelings of parental helplessness. Bennett's first grade student-of-the-week poster, a pictorial and verbal presentation of our family, was due in February. I did not know how to deal with this, but Bennett did. The family picture he chose was a picture of

Daddy feeding him in the high chair. The family picture he drew showed the three of us with sad faces. All I could think of was, *Lord, please heal his broken heart.*

Even in those difficult days, not all was bleak. My friend and former neighbor Terry drove more than three hours with her daughter Amy, Claire's best friend, to stay with us for a long weekend. Claire and Amy used their artistic skills as they processed their grief together, cutting out snowflakes and posting them in the upstairs hallway. They taped a banner with huge letters across the wall: Lee and Tina. Their generous hearts poured comfort and encouragement into me, even as they supported each other.

One night Terry gave Bennett a huge brownie for dessert. As always, Terry loved to spoil Bennett and get him to eat things that I would not normally let him have. Eyes wide with excitement, Bennett exclaimed, "That's twice as much as Mommy gives me!" We all cracked up.

"I'm claiming grandma privileges," Terry laughed.

"Terry, you aren't even a grandma! Nice try," I chided.

"It's okay," Terry countered.

"I know I have to give up control, but I don't have to watch!" I exclaimed as I left the room. Little brownie boy was so happy.

Sometimes a special treat would soothe, but other grief moments required more. "Mommy, on January 7, 2006, can we have a minute of silence for Daddy?" Bennett had a longer-term outlook than the rest of us. A moment of silence had been held at his school in commemoration of the 9/11 victims, and Bennett thoughtfully applied that to his own loss. His little mathematical mind was working ahead to ensure that Daddy would not be forgotten.

I responded halfheartedly, wondering how I could possibly live through this for one full year. "Bennett, that's a great idea. Let's do that!" I achingly wondered if there would be many minutes in the upcoming year during which I would *not* think about Lee.

At times, the kids comforted me. On the way to church, Claire offered, "Mommy, I have a Bible verse for you."

"What's that?" I asked.

"I will have faith in the Lord who strengthens me." Claire announced. Wow. She was applying God's Word to my life. I was proud and humbled at the same time.

At bedtime one night Bennett read me Psalm 63:8: "'My soul clings to you; your right hand upholds me.' Mommy, it was on the wall [on a plaque] so I found it in my Bible." Treasures from my kids' wounded hearts to mine.

One day, Bennett surprised me with a question. "Are you going to change that?" Bennett pointed out the computer's log-off message: "Log off Lee Carson."

Yeah, that one stabs the heart. I struggled with my thoughts. *Lee is eternally logged off of this world.*

"What should we change it to?" I questioned, trying to keep my voice from revealing the pain I felt.

"How about your name?" Bennett asked.

A simple change in terms of keystrokes, yet a monumental shift in family life.

[15]

More Team Support

IN MY JOURNAL, I recorded all the help I received on Friday, February 11, 2005. In a stunning display of God's outreach through many backgrounds and faiths, friends from seven churches and one Sikh temple helped me out on that day alone.

> *Journal entry, February 11, 2005.*
>
> *This would be a dream come true, if it weren't my biggest nightmare—i.e. childcare, housecleaning, cooked meals, personal secretaries, chauffeurs, financiers, even a humorist—and plenty of time to spend with you, Lord. Lots of Christian music—tapes, CDs, even personally created ones. Journaling with a hand that still works. I am thankful, God, but this is still so hard. Help me to stop striving and just Psalm 46:10—be still before you, Lord.*

Friends from my church and women's Bible study helped me out with household tasks. Sandy brought me soup, helped me with benefits paperwork, took me to a counseling appointment, and walked around the park with me. Joyce brought me bath oil and soup, and changed the bed linens for us. This involved rearranging over one hundred stuffed animals on Claire's bed, but with two daughters and four grandkids herself, she was experienced. Linda loaned me Christian music CDs to listen to. Kelly, my friend who came the night Lee died, visited Costco to get groceries. She also bought "camis and jammies" (camisole tops and pajamas) to fit my new skeleton-like frame and keep me warm. Dori gave Claire a lift to horseback riding lessons.

Darren, Bennett's former vacation Bible school teacher, took him out for a haircut. With no air bags in the teenager's older car, it was Bennett's first time sitting up in the front seat and he was thrilled. Plus, Darren bought Bennett a large-size smoothie, a double-sized treat that made my little guy feel very special.

Many people helped with daily activities. Jamie's husband Kien carpooled the kids to school; Mr. J, the father of Bennett's classmate, carpooled them home. Bennett's kindergarten teacher donated theater tickets to a *Little Mermaid* musical in Sunnyvale, and Jamie drove the kids to the performance. Our neighbors, who were not even on the meal schedule, brought me a delicious meal of curry; the garam masala chicken was great comfort food to me. My next door neighbors, Donna and Rod, called me with the information I needed on automatic garage door installation. Andrea from my church brought us dinner, a kid-friendly pasta dish.

As always, there was the ongoing planning. Jamie arranged the kids' schedules and set up weekend playdates.

Teri, a friend from church, and Lourdes, a friend from the kids' school, coordinated the meals that people planned to deliver. JoAnne worked on my schedule, and my sister helped with financial details.

After recording all the help we received in one day in my journal, I wrote the following prayer:

> *Journal entry, February 11, 2005.*
>
> *God, you own the cattle on a thousand hills and the hearts of so many from different churches. Thank you for pulling your team together! Forgive my arrogance at the thought that I could put these people together. Whenever I give myself credit, you softly chasten me, "You are so lucky to be seeing so much of my tapestry."*
>
> *God, I stand humbled. You are my provider and my redeemer.*

On that same day, I received a card from my friend and former InterVarsity Christian Fellowship staffer Jane. She wrote, "May grace roll over you again and again like the waves of the ocean. Grace and grief, grief and grace with some waves crashing with much more force than others. Jesus' shelter to you in the midst of your own tsunami." The analogy was so applicable. The world was grieving the Asian tsunami; I was carried away in the flood of my own grief. I felt as if a tsunami of sorrow had engulfed my heart and threatened to sweep it out to the depths of an unreachable ocean.

One of the CDs I listened to repeatedly was Michael W. Smith's (2004) *Healing Rain.* So many of the songs on that CD spoke to my wounded heart. I would run up to my room to escape the phone/mail/people, play the CD, and repeat it endlessly as I sang and sobbed to those songs.

Not having to spend evenings cooking in the kitchen allowed me to appreciate features of life I had not noticed before, like sunsets. I would pull up a chair by the bedroom window, and either play a worship CD or observe in awed silence, as God painted yet another fleeting masterpiece on the patch of sky past the rooftops of my neighborhood. I savored the cloud formations. The distant jets and contrails, visible from my bedroom window, stabbed me with the recognition that Lee was so far away, much farther than if he had merely been flying a jet on the horizon. So distant from Lee, yet I felt so close to God.

Back in 1997, my friend Daphne and I shared our struggles when she quit her counseling internship to have a baby, and I gave up my nursing career to be a stay-at-home mom. We spent time encouraging each other in faith as our lives paralleled with the pregnancies and deliveries of our boys. Daphne gladly joined the team as my counselor. In one of our many conversations, I agonized over all that I had never mended in my relationship with Lee.

"I love him so, but I am sorry for not being a better wife," I sobbed.

"When the voices of condemnation come, ask Jesus to show you where He was," Daphne advised in her calm, reassuring tone.

"What do you mean?"

"Do you remember the story you told me about the time when you were on Maui?"

"I remember telling you about when I cried on the beach." In mid-October of 2000, Lee and I flew to Hawaii to vacation on Wailea Beach, Maui. The afternoon we arrived, I went for a walk on the beach alone and ended up sitting on a rock, crying. Here we were at a resort rated in the top ten worldwide, on our favorite Hawaiian island with every promise of an incredible trip, yet our marriage was having problems. Our communication issues, challenging children, and cares of life in general were overwhelming us. We were so irritated with each other that we did not even want to spend time together once we arrived. I wondered if Lee and I would even be able to endure each other for the duration of the trip.

As I sat crying on the rock and calling out to God for help, a couple walked right up to me. Recognizing God's intervention, I did not even wait to be spoken to. Instead I blurted out, "Will you pray for me?"

They asked me what they could pray for. "My marriage," I replied, and then I felt stupid. Lee and I had so much to be grateful for: health, children, home, finances, family, and church—but we were still having marital problems. There was no adultery, alcoholism, gambling, or other serious issue destroying our partnership. I felt as if I had no excuse for having marriage frustrations, when others coped with so much more. I asked if these strangers would pray for Lee's and my communication and parenting. The woman held my hand and the man placed his hand on my shoulder. These total strangers prayed, and I sobbed as I felt God's touch on my marriage. Without even offering my name, I thanked them afterwards and walked back up to the room. Not that our marriage healed instantly, but God was changing our attitudes and habits so that our close relationship could be restored. We ended up working on our problems and having a great vacation.

"Where was Jesus in that?" Daphne reminded me of the story I had told her.

"Daphne, I know. God sent that Christian couple to me at just the right time. His provision and His timing. I got it then. I don't get it now."

"Just ask Jesus to show you where He is when you hear those voices of condemnation."

Like the title of the Casting Crowns song (Chapman & Hall, 2004) I listened to so often, I needed to listen to God's voice of truth.

At one point, an acquaintance called to ask me to have lunch with her. I knew she meant it kindly, thinking it would be good for me to get out, but she had no idea of how I was really doing. I politely said no, but then went to my journal to rant.

Journal entry, February 13, 2005

Dear Friend, you call and ask me to meet you for lunch. No, Child of God, I am not quite there yet. You don't know, do you, that I spent most of January basically on bedrest?! From the bed to the couch and to the bathroom—when I remembered. The fight-or-flight response seared through me, setting every nerve on rawest edge. Narrowly focused on the unknown danger, I snapped, cringed, and feared the crunch of my bones when loved ones hugged my scrawny frame. My heart raced at over 120 beats per minute, barely calming to the heart-slowing medications I swallowed so desperately. Fine tremors wracked me.

Let's lunch in a year when perhaps my mind will clear. Right now, my friends have to do yucky errands with me. You offer to help, but do you really mean it? Are you strong enough to pick up a death certificate from the mortuary and walk into Bible study as if nothing had happened? Or hang onto the paperwork that I need when we go into the Social Security office, gently keeping it, because for me to see my sweetheart's name on our marriage license would set off another wave of grief? Or manage my anxiety attack in line at the Social Security office when I hear only foreign languages and panic at the thought that the clerks do not speak English? (Thank you Emily, my team member who does yucky errands, for that kind of friendship and help.)

One Thursday in February, I was on the phone with my mother-in-law, and she asked if I was alone. I realized that even though I was home alone, my team of friends from women's Bible study was hard at work. Teri dropped a roll of film off to be developed at Costco. Neighbor Emily dropped a CD off at my therapist's office. Emily's daughter Annie and her dog took Claire out for a walk. Jamie drove Bennett to gymnastics class with her kids. Kelly, my helper on the worst night of my life, called to change my doctor's appointment. Someone was cooking dinner for us, and of course, many were praying for us. God had truly mobilized an army to help us. So, yes, I was alone in the house, but God made sure that I was not without help from His precious ones.

While being alone at home was rare for me, sometimes God's help crowded the house. Pastor Kim, our youth ministry leader, once brought twenty-five teenagers to clean up my yard. They filed into the house with smiles, carrying guitars and songbooks. We worshipped our amazing God together, filling the house with music and a joy that had been sorrowfully lacking.

"This is what our house is meant for," I said to Kim, fighting yet another flood of tears, as I remembered how Lee and I had enjoyed hosting youth events in our home.

After worship, I left to spend time at Kelly's house. "Otherwise, if you don't leave, knowing you, you'll be out there leading a Bible study," Kim had cautioned me earlier.

I drove over to Kelly's, and the teenage army went to work. They did crafts with my kids, vacuumed inside the house, and overhauled the yard. They pulled out a tree-sized bush, banished my "snail hotel" plants, cleaned the patio, yanked out dead tomato plants, deadheaded flowers, and trimmed everything, as well as the much-needed chores of lawn mowing, edging, and raking. They added new tan bark and spruced up everything in record time.

I was overwhelmed by the outpouring of love and support. I am a giver not a taker, and accepting help graciously was a tough lesson to learn. Over at Kelly's house, we prayed that God would help me to be a gracious receiver. We also prayed for God's blessing on these teenagers and their leaders. I was in the midst of a sob-fest when they called me back to the house early.

What I loved about those teenagers was that no matter how emotionally unstable and weepy I was, they welcomed me in. And so it was when I returned to the house. So many had done so much for me; I was overwhelmed. Claire handed out cards we had made up earlier for each teenager. We just wrote "Proverbs 11:25" on plain index cards so they could look up the verse themselves: "A generous man will prosper; he who refreshes others will himself be refreshed."

On another day, my sister took me to the laboratory to have blood drawn. Braced for a long wait, I carried my journal with me. As usual, the waiting room was crowded, except for the chairs underneath the television, where we took a seat. After about twenty minutes, our number was called up to the sign-in desk.

"I'm sorry, but your health care benefits are terminated," the receptionist said softly.

"What?!" I blurted out loudly as I began to escalate.

"Our computer shows that you are not eligible for insurance coverage."

"He just died on the sixth! It hasn't even been thirty days!" I increased the volume as my meltdown progressed. "He just died! They can't cancel my insurance!"

"We'll just pay for it then," my sister calmly offered. "Her doctor needs these labs to be drawn." Meanwhile I was sobbing at the counter and, as all eyes followed me, I left my sister to work out the details. I stomped back to my seat under the TV, where I became the prime viewing spectacle for the crowd. The man sitting next to me vacated his seat as I returned. I sat crying with my head in my hands, feeling as if this was one more thing that proved my life was over.

My hyper-acute senses picked up on everything. "See, I'm not the only crazy one," I whispered to my sister after she returned. I nodded toward a father with his agitated son. As father and son waited close to an hour to be called back for the blood draw, the developmentally disabled son shuffled side to side with a repetitive, circular nodding motion of his head.

Although distressed myself, I still assessed my surroundings and felt empathy. An elderly gentleman sat in a wheelchair across the room from us. His caretaker kept fussing over him, moving his arms and legs opposite from how the patient had placed them. I wanted to scream at her, "Leave him alone! Let him stay where he feels most comfortable!"

As our number came up again, Rebecca and I walked back into the laboratory, where the shuffling son became distraught and started screaming. The father and the lab technician discussed the situation and decided to forgo the blood draw, even after the long wait. I wanted to go over and comfort the boy, who I saw as a toddler trapped in a large teenager's body. "Can't you see how to handle him?" I wanted to scream. "Just acknowledge his fears and give him some control over the situation." Instead, I moved to the side as the agitated boy loped out, followed by the dejected father whose waiting for over an hour had been for naught. The old me knew how to handle the situation; the new me stepped aside with an aloof awareness that the frightened boy was not my responsibility. My self-absorbed thoughts seemed as heartless as a chilled vial of blood. I did not like the cold, callous new me.

The laboratory technician from the registration desk, at whom I had previously screamed, was gloving up and desperately looking to take any patient but me. Unable to skirt into another booth, she tentatively came toward the counter in front of me.

"I'm sorry for being rude . . ." I began.

"That's okay." She said quietly, trying hard to be absorbed in her setup and avoid further conversation.

"No really, I'm sorry," I continued. "I may be crazy, but I am not afraid of blood draws." We went on to talk and she visibly relaxed when she realized that I was not going to freak out at the needle.

On the way out, I kept my head down, but I still noticed a mother who shielded her toddler's eyes and pulled him toward her as I walked by. I rushed out the door, embarrassed by my outburst.

Crazy and cruel—is that the new me?

[16]

Paperwork to Die For

BASED UPON THE AUTOPSY, the coroner's report stated that Lee died within minutes of acute coronary artery occlusion. The report estimated that his atherosclerotic cardiovascular disease had taken years to form. After hearing that I was a nurse, the coroner spent time discussing the autopsy results in detail over the phone.

"He had atherosclerosis?!" I asked doubtfully, amazed that Lee could have fatty plaque deposits on the inner walls of his arteries without any symptoms.

"It was extensive. All the way up his carotids and in the Circle of Willis." Dr. V, a Santa Clara County coroner, described locations in the brain where Lee had plaque.

"How could that be? Did he really have it all over?"

"Yes, down the aorta and in both femoral arteries." Dr. V described all the anatomical areas of blockage he had found during Lee's autopsy.

"So where was the clot again?" I needed to have the details repeated to break through my disbelief.

"It was a large clot in the left anterior descending coronary artery." Dr. V patiently repeated his diagnosis.

"Your basic, average heart attack." I conceded softly, still stunned that this was my husband we were discussing. "We always called those 'widowmakers.'" The coronary artery we were discussing feeds the muscular front wall of the left, or pumping, side of the heart. A clot high up in that artery is sometimes the first and fatal symptom of heart disease, hence the colloquial term "widowmaker."

"My daughter had the same type of heart attack." Dr. V shared the story of his daughter, a young mother of small children, who was on limited activity after surviving a similar heart attack. My heart went out to the family, and I prayed silently for Dr. V's daughter, even as I recognized my twinges of jealousy for wishing that my husband had survived.

In the wake of Lee's death, one early paperwork priority was signing up for Social Security benefits. My family made an appointment for a telephone interview to avoid a trip down to the office. I was still barely coherent, so my mother and stepfather gathered documents and set up the table so that everything was at my fingertips. They dialed for me and sat expectantly, wondering if I would be able to recite the facts without breaking down.

"I just need to verify details over the telephone and we can get you set up to receive benefits," Keith from the Social Security office in San Jose said confidently. He went on to ask details—numbers, dates, and facts. I blankly recited the information and read the facts from the many documents my parents shuffled in front of me. Suddenly I heard weird noises from the other end of the line.

"Excuse me—we have something happening at the counter that I have to deal with . . ." Keith's voice trailed off to the sound of yelling and strange noises. In the ensuing audio chaos, I had no idea what to do.

"What happened?" Mom questioned, realizing that something was not right.

"Some guy is going nuts at the counter. Keith had to go check it out. They're yelling and . . . should I hang up?" I sat there numbly, considering whether or not I should remain on the line.

Keith returned a few minutes later. "Sorry about that. I had to take care of a little incident." My mind, still obsessed with images of my own trauma, creatively summoned an image of a crazed patron assaulting a Social Security representative and being tackled by security guards. Horrified at my imagined scenario, I vowed never to go to the office in person.

"Let me try again here to pull up Lee's work history." Keith asked me to repeat Lee's Social Security number. "Okay, now I have it. Let's see. Very consistent. Steady growth in income. Nothing out of order."

"Just like his character," I responded, the tears once again pouring out of my eyes. This was so hard, but it was just the beginning of the paperwork.

Another task I needed to do early on was to transfer money into the checking account from savings. As a military couple, Lee and I had several accounts at banks all over the country. I knew of the accounts and banks, but I used one account primarily. Lee was the one who had managed the paperwork, kept track of all the logistics during moves, and maintained our financial overview. Our primary bank did not yet offer online banking, so Lee had done transactions by phone. I was panicked the first time I had to track everything down and initiate the transfers myself. I carefully pulled out his detailed lists of accounts and decided where I needed to transfer money. My hands shook as I tried to focus on the transaction. Not yet voice activated, the system required me to punch in long strings of numbers.

My mind flashed back to a conversation Lee and I had shared several months earlier.

"Lee, I really think you should change your access code," I had urged.

"Why? I've had this one for twenty years," was Lee's reply. Like his hairstyle, he was resistant to change anything that worked for him.

"That is the point," I urged. "Identity thieves count on that. If someone got into the accounts, they could access everything because you use the same number. Experts say you should change your access codes regularly."

"This works for me. If you want to change your code, you can, but I am leaving my number on the main accounts." As usual, Lee had held his ground.

That conversation came back to haunt me as I attempted the first money transfer after Lee died. My hands shook as I tried to remember the access code that I had changed in connection with my membership number. When my mind blanked on my newer access code, I reverted to using Lee's bank membership number and his standard access code.

"Oh, God, forgive me! Lee, I am so sorry!" I moaned in sorrow, recognizing my lack of appreciation for the gift of

Lee's reliability. I was thankful for his consistency because—despite my grief and confusion—I still remembered the numbers that we had used for decades. I felt so guilty for being irritated with him months earlier. I tried to think of what he would say to me now, as I was struggling with this financial transaction.

"Come on. You can do this. It's easy; it's not brain surgery!" was the encouraging response I imagined from Lee as my trembling hands fumbled at the number sequences. So many things he had always done for me seemed frightening, but my imagined conversation was right, they did not require highly advanced skills, and I would be able to do them. Thinking of Lee and what he would say, or how he would respond, infused me with the much-needed confidence that I would survive.

On another day, when my children were farmed out on playdates, I called my bank to start on the pension paperwork transfers. Bleary eyed and mentally foggy, I was overwhelmed by the packet: 401(K), IRA rollover, wire transfers, successor trustee, and routing numbers. In my previous life, these would merely be facts to analyze. At this point, they represented a new reality that stabbed me in the heart: twice the retirement funds for half the people. I felt like only a half person who, without my one-and-only, could no longer look forward to retirement.

My thoughts convulsed with fear at my solitary future. *Who is going to ski with me? Run with me? Empty the coffee pot with me? Swim with me? Backpack with me? Sing next to me in church? Sweetheart, I miss you in a million ways!*

My paperwork responsibilities were endless. I met with my lawyer John to review what I needed to do to finalize the trust. John tried to recall, even looking it up in his records, how Lee had found him, but neither of us remembered. My only memory of setting up the trust was the day we went to sign the paperwork. I was one week overdue in my pregnancy with Bennett. Rain was pouring down as we drove over the mountains to John's office.

"Do we have to do this now?" I complained petulantly. "We are going to die on these wet mountain roads! Why couldn't you pick a lawyer on our side of the Bay? Can't this wait until after the baby is born? Is it worth dying on this slippery, winding road for a stupid trust?!" I went on and on. As usual, I could not antagonize Lee enough to fight back with me. In his typical manner, he was able to ignore my emotionalism and stay out of the argument. Instead of changing his mind, Lee met me with his quiet resolve to get the job done.

We signed the paperwork that day, thus memorializing the date of that argument in the title of our trust. Now that date stands in memory of one of our disagreements, and I am reminded that my shortsightedness was thankfully overcome by a loving husband who always provided for his family.

Although I had met the lawyer only once, I recognized John at my appointment after Lee's death. As we talked about death and dying, he shared the story of his daughter's death. He began to tear up, so I grabbed the tissues from my purse and offered him the pack.

"That is usually my role," John said, "to give out tissues to my clients."

"It's okay," I reassured him. "I'm a widow. We always carry tissues."

John and I reviewed all the paperwork necessary to complete the trust. I was so thankful for God's choice of this kind professional to walk me through the maze of paperwork yet to be filed. In closing, John asked if he could pray for me. I agreed, expecting a long, formal prayer worthy of a huge courtroom audience. Instead, I was impressed by John's brief, heartfelt words to a Savior he obviously treasured.

First time I ever had to pay for a prayer, I thought wryly as I left the office.

In addition to the packet of paperwork I needed to send to my lawyer, I had a packet to send to Lee's company. The main holdup was the lack of a finalized death certificate.

Empathetic American Airlines employee Nikki was the office manager for the San Francisco Chief Pilot. She repeatedly called me and asked for the official copy of Lee's death certificate. "Pensions [Department] is breathing down my neck." She explained why the company could not accept a pending death certificate for payout of benefits and pension funds.

I assured Nikki that I was not withholding the death certificate from the company, and I explained why the finalized death certificate was so delayed. Because Lee's death had been treated as a murder scene, the death certificate could not be finalized until all laboratory tests were completed. The lethality of my broccoli casserole and the antacids taken from Lee's bedside were still to be analyzed. All of the samples, specifically the toxicology blood tests, were sent to a California state agency and processed as court evidence. The death certificate needed to have every toxicology screen completed, every antacid tested, my broccoli casserole exonerated, and Lee's clean blood confirmed. Whereas the autopsy report was mailed out within weeks, the death certificate took over three months to finalize, and then I spent another year sending out death certificates to straighten out accounts and settle paperwork issues.

Given my ongoing paperwork pressures, the mail was a strange combination of potential enemy and comforting friend. The cards and letters kept pouring in with prayers, words of love, and precious comfort. On the other hand, I was terrified of the many paperwork hassles that came in the mail. One letter from the Social Security Administration threatened to discontinue benefits the following week because my visit to show documentation was overdue. During one three-day time span, my medical, dental, and COBRA insurance plans were all erroneously canceled. Albeit the usual bureaucratic verbiage, I panicked at the thought of having my benefits cut off. Even if I had been functioning normally, the paperwork would have been overwhelming. To my grief-stricken psyche, administrative snafus loomed as if they were threats of starvation and homelessness.

My biggest fear in life had always been to be widowed and dependent on Social Security. That threat had become reality, but I had to change my perspective on what that meant for my children and me. I read and reread God's promises of provision in the Bible. Even if all else fell through, I knew that my heavenly Father owned the cattle on a thousand hills

(Psalm 50:10) and promised to provide for widows and the fatherless (Psalm 146:9).

One standard I developed to maintain my financial privacy was to hire people who were "twice removed": nobody in my immediate circle of friends or family, nor anybody they knew. I did not want any social connection with the financial professionals I hired. I did not want to run into them at the grocery store, a church function, or dinner party. My lawyer was in place, but I needed to select a financial advisor and an accountant. After reviewing qualifications and interviewing several candidates, I hired Mr. A, a certified financial planner (CFP).

Mr. A's unique qualification, in addition to the CFP certification, was a master of divinity degree. Decades ago when his father died, Mr. A helped his mother with the paperwork and coordinated details with her CFP. The CFP was so impressed with Mr. A that he encouraged him to pursue financial counseling as a career. Mr. A completed his seminary degree, later turning down a pastorate in order to pursue financial training. Instead of shepherding a church, he chose to work as a financial pastor in his career as CFP.

In my first session with Mr. A, he wrote two columns on the white board, "With Lee" and "After Lee." Simplistically, it looked like two columns on a page. In actuality, there was a vast divide, a life-and-death difference. Mr. A listed the financial amounts Lee and I had worked with in the left-hand column; this represented a lifetime partnership of earnings, with retirement and education savings. In contrast, the other side depicted a gaping void of finite resources to be dealt with all alone. On that right-hand side, Mr. A presented the plan for future finances, given my expenses and income after Lee's death. Through tear-filled eyes, I told him that I was having a hard time getting across the big white space between the columns. I was so impressed that Mr. A would take the time to understand our financial picture as a couple before Lee died. The respect and understanding that he demonstrated for Lee's financial management confirmed God's choice of Mr. A as my CFP.

June sixth marked my receipt of Lee's final paycheck, dating as far back as December. American Airlines refused to direct deposit the check into our joint checking account. Same bank, same checking account, same wife, same paycheck routine for fifteen years. But no, they had to send a check in the mail. The amount they sent was a surprise, because it included pay for the last two weeks of December, for Lee's first trip of January, and for reimbursement that Lee was due for vacation pay and monthly carryover time. Grateful for the money, I still marveled that the company had made me wait six months for Lee's final paycheck.

In addition to the paycheck, the month of June brought many paperwork responsibilities. By then, my raw emotions had soothed significantly, and I no longer needed daily support to take care of my children. Although not apparent to me at the time, I was gaining emotional strength and independence as I managed the stacks of documents to fulfill the trust requirements. Once again, I had to copy every bank statement, every account receipt, every stock holding, and every financial document for the five months since Lee had died. I had to provide detailed lists (credit card statements and checkbook registers) of all that I had purchased in that five months. I was overwhelmed trying to track down paperwork I had not filed, envelopes I had not opened, and records I needed to find and photocopy. Copies of all this made up yet another packet of over fifty pages, which I sent to the lawyer. It was basically a repeat of what I had done in January. What seemed to be simple paperwork exercises had tax implications, legal ramifications, and audit potential. As always, the paperwork seemed endless.

[17]

Fancy Therapists

CAROL WAS MY FIRST grief counselor. Originally from Minnesota, she was widowed when her forty-seven-year-old husband died of a heart attack in 1982. She raised four boys on her own, and changed careers from a teacher and principal to grief counselor and hospice bereavement director. Someone had given me Carol's phone number, and within weeks of Lee's death, I was counseling with her on a weekly basis.

Emily, my tall, elegant friend who helped with "yucky errands," drove me to many of my counseling appointments. She was my neighbor, church librarian, and wife to Abbott, who had developed the computer slide show for Lee's memorial. Their two daughters frequently babysat for us. For years after Lee's death, their family loved and supported us in uncountable ways. No matter what came up, I knew that I could call them for advice, support, and logistical help.

About two weeks after Lee died, Emily chauffeured me to my first grief therapy appointment with Carol. We got lost trying to find the San Jose offices for Hospice of the Valley. As we drove into the parking lot after finally finding the office, we saw a license plate that read "1GR8GOD," a great reminder of a great God who had all of this in His plan.

My first session with Carol involved telling her my story. Still in shock, I told the whole story more as a spectator than a participant. I described the mental videotape that continually replayed the events of the resuscitation and asked when this would stop tormenting me. For the first of many times, Carol did not give me the timetable I so urgently requested.

As she greeted me for one of my weekly sessions, I realized that I was not coping well. You know it is a bad day when your therapist proclaims, "Oooooh," with ever-so-long Minnesota vowels. "You look different from last week."

No kidding, I thought. *I'm trashed. I can't do this.*

For the first three months after Lee died, my mourning routine was no jewelry, no makeup, and dark clothes. It was not so much that I wanted to look as bad on the outside as I felt on the inside, but that any effort was too much. I barely found the strength to comb my hair once a day, let alone style it. I wore the same gray and black clothes, automatically grabbing the darkest and dingiest clothing I found in my closet. I looked as dead as I felt, and I did not care what anyone thought.

My take-home message from one of Carol's sessions: it was okay to still feel so connected to Lee.

"You don't think I'm in denial?" I asked tearfully.

"Why do you say that?" Carol asked in her calm, encouraging voice.

"Because I am just doing all the things we decided together to do."

"Like what?"

"Well, over Christmas, we sat down and planned everything out." I went on to explain that I was implementing decisions that Lee and I had made together as if I were on autopilot with my life. As I talked with Carol, I realized that I was forced to do these things on my own now, instead of together as Lee and I had planned. "Bennett was going to start piano lessons and Claire was going to start horseback riding lessons. They have now started those after-school activities. Lee and I decided to get a piano, a dog, and a new car. Isn't that denial if I just keep doing the stuff Lee and I were going to do?" By this time my tears were sobs.

"Following through on your plans is not denial."

"But isn't it denial that I still feel like I'm married?"

"I felt married to my husband for two years after he died," Carol admitted. "That is normal. You will still feel connected to Lee."

"But when will the pain ease?" I choked through sobs.

Carol replied in her soft, gentle way. "The pain will ease, even though sometimes the suffering seems to go on forever."

I could not understand how the incredible hurt could ever diminish, but Carol's perspective made me hopeful. In her validation of my connection to Lee, Carol eased the pressure that I felt from others—pressure to move on. But then there was a question on my mind. I was too new at grieving to ask it, and too panicked to consider the answer, but it entered my thoughts nonetheless. *What do I do when I go beyond the point that Lee and I had planned? How do I go on without him?* That question was not something I was ready to address yet.

Instead I told Carol about the piano, and about the joy and music it brought back into our house. She reminded me of how children are able to move in and out of grief.

Then Carol told me that she was going on a one-week vacation.

"I guess that is God's lesson to me that I am not in control," I said, choking back the sobs and panic of not being able to see her soon. After Carol's even-keel explanation of who to call in the event of an emergency while she was gone, I continued with caustic undertones, "Okay. Thank you for being part of God's healing plan for me, even if I can't see you as much as I need to." My thoughts swirled. *How can she go on vacation and leave me at a time like this?!* As usual, Carol did not respond to my sarcastic humor; she knew better than to feed my cynicism.

I walked out of the room after my counseling session and promptly got lost. I had walked those office halls before, but I could not remember how to get past the seeming maze of conference rooms. My physical sense of feeling lost in the building mirrored my emotional sense of abandonment. In futility, I surrendered to the pain and gave up. I shuffled into one of the many dark conference rooms, sank with my back against the wall, and slid to the floor sobbing. Someone soon came in, lifted me onto my feet, and escorted me out to the waiting room where Emily stood by to give me a ride home.

My need for grief therapy was obvious; but I knew, as did my team, that my children also needed grief therapy. Although recently retired, Judy had returned as the interim school psychologist for Berryessa Union School District shortly before Lee died. God had placed the right person in that job, just in time for my kids. Despite her busy schedule as the only psychologist for the three middle schools and eight elementary schools in the district, Judy saw my kids weekly after Lee died. She told me her own story; twenty-two years earlier, her thirty-nine-year-old husband had died of a heart attack. The couple and their three children had skied at Lake Tahoe all day and were eating in a restaurant when he collapsed. Judy and her children watched as an Air Force doctor and an Air Force nurse tried unsuccessfully to resuscitate her husband.

Judy was an incredible resource to me on everything from kid tantrums to grief. She met with my kids and regularly updated me on their coping skills. She developed an action plan for both kids, which dealt with their anger and sibling rivalry. What a gift from God to have someone in place who understood what we had been through and could advocate for us within the school system.

The San Jose Hospice of the Valley grief support groups were divided into age groups: six- to eight-year-olds, nine- to twelve-year-olds, and teenagers. My children could join their grief sessions immediately but, although the parents' grief group met concurrently, I was not eligible to join until I was three months out from my spouse's death. Initially, Emily drove us down to the office, and I would sit in the lobby while the kids went to their groups. I tried to complete my Bible study lesson as I waited, but often I just sat crying. Somehow I sensed that it was a safe place to fall apart, so I usually did.

When Claire and Bennett started their grief groups, twenty-five children participated in the kids' groups. One family of children had lost a brother, but the rest of the children had each lost a parent. Both of my children had tantrums about going to their groups, but once they arrived at the office, they calmed down. One week Bennett watched a Care Bears video, which made Claire jealous. He made a Care Bear for the craft that week, but did not want to keep it. I saw the number forty-five on the back of the bear.

"What's the number for?" I asked, recognizing the number as Daddy's age.

"It's for how old Daddy is," Bennett volunteered, his blue eyes and round face peering at me intently. "My Daddy is the oldest." With that comment, he was done discussing the grief group.

Sitting in the lobby, I overheard laughter from Claire's group. At one point I even distinguished Claire's excited chatter coming from the noisy room. When Claire came out, she did not want to mention anything. She remained sullen and even started a tantrum once she got home. Later she told me that her group leader had experienced the loss of father, sister, brother, and child. With that one comment, I knew that Claire was connecting with the group. Not that she wanted to discuss anything, but I was comforted by the fact that others understood her grief. So much pain for so many families.

Three months after my husband died, I joined Hospice of the Valley's spousal-loss group, which became a vital support for me. It was a relief to finally meet with other parents while our kids met in their groups. Carol, the bereavement director and my personal counselor, was our group's facilitator. Carol's gentle, experienced leadership ministered effectively to our wounded hearts. We became a tight-knit group of five widows with kids between the ages of two and fourteen. All but the twin two-year-olds were in grief groups together. The circumstances of our husbands' deaths varied widely—sudden, prolonged illness, cancer, heart attack—but we traveled the difficult journey of young widowhood together. Much of what we discussed related to parenting challenges. As Carol informed me later in my one-on-one sessions, having children delays and complicates grief. Our group of five widows explored our losses, validated new insights, reviewed decisions, and shared our lives as we spent almost a year together in grief sessions. The amazing women I met in that group remain friends and role models to this day. We met each other at rock bottom and have been privileged to watch each other's unique transformations to living again.

Kim, Betsy, and I—all widows with children in the same grief groups—sent our children to Camp Hope in Livermore, California, for the same weekend. The widow who started Camp Hope, California had come through the same hospice office several years before we did; she also counseled with Carol and attended the same support groups with her children. Camp Hope, California continues to be a phenomenal weekend camp for grieving children, staffed by professional counselors and therapists who volunteer their time.

Claire's camp counselor was a psychologist with a doctorate degree who specialized in counseling teenage girls. Claire connected with her counselor and opened up in ways she had not previously allowed herself to do. Of course, this breakthrough was relayed to me by the counselor, not Claire. Unfortunately, the counselor was from San Diego, too far for Claire to follow up with regular sessions.

From what we three widows observed as parents, the weekend was a remarkable blend of grieving and healing, of sadness and play. When I picked the kids up after their camp weekend, I was met with the usual responses. Bennett talked at length about how much he enjoyed the weekend, and Claire did not want to talk about it.

Therapy continued to be important for all of us, and my private sessions with Carol were something to look forward to. I knew we would explore difficult issues, but I also knew that she would lend clarity and focus to the incredible hurt I felt. Carol validated the deep pain of my suffering from her perspective of personal and professional experience. I could trust her, even when I felt there was no hope for my future.

Carol and I spent many sessions discussing my previous losses. As a "second generation widow," I had the "luxury" of being able to review how my mom had handled widowhood and how I had grieved the loss of my father. With Carol's wise guidance, I reviewed my past and decided what to incorporate or change in my own widowhood grief journey.

"This pain of your suffering will gradually be replaced by the sad reality." Carol spoke with an understanding tone. Her heartfelt wisdom resonated within me, even though I was often too fresh and numb to comprehend her words.

"I can't imagine this pain ever ending," I sobbed.

"It becomes different. It hurts so badly now, but it will change."

"I just can't do this," I tearfully protested. What followed was Carol's assessment of my suicide risk. She asked me relevant questions to determine whether I was a threat to myself physically or merely despondent in my grief.

"Depression is a normal part of grieving. You can't always tell them apart, but grieving is limited."

"Not with me. This feels as if it will hurt forever." I once again dissolved into sobs. As always, Carol validated my grief. Then I relayed to her the incident that had prompted my internist's recommendation to start on antidepressants.

One of my lowest nights was spent curled up on my bedroom floor. Alternately crying and lying despondently still on the floor, I watched the time go by on the alarm clock.

5:00 p.m. *I should think of something for dinner.* (This was after the three months of manna.)

6:00 p.m. *This is when I should get up to feed my kids.*

7:00 p.m. *Now I really should get up.*

8:00 p.m. *I have to feed them, but I just cannot get up. I cannot care for my own children.*

After hearing about my struggle to get up off the floor to care for my children, Carol recommended medication for me. "I usually don't advise that a client start on antidepressant medications for grief," Carol explained her philosophy, "but I think it is indicated for you."

"So I'm a total basket case, worse than your average widow?!" My attempt at humor fell short with Carol, as it often did.

"My concern is that you be managed for antidepressants by more than a family physician. In my experience, a psychiatrist should manage antidepressants."

"But I am seeing an internist, not a family physician. And you still want me to see a psychiatrist?"

"Yes, I think that would be best before you start on medications."

"I'm so messed up that I need a shrink besides you and my regular doctor?!" It was easier for me to joke about being mentally incapacitated than it was for me admit my need for more help.

"Yes, if you go on medication, I think you should be managed by a psychiatrist." Carol once again bypassed my efforts at dark humor.

"Okay. I'll see a psychiatrist." *Add that to the list of all my appointments.*

I did see a psychiatrist, who increased my antidepressants. To my estimation, I was on enough Paxil to kill a horse. He gave me the research to back up the indications, efficacy, and safety of the high dosages. Apparently his staff was not in the loop with the research results. When I called for a prescription refill, the pharmacy technician said he could not fill that high a dose. The nurse then called me back to inform me she could not authorize that dosage either. Finally the psychiatrist called in the prescription, and I received my meds. Down to around one hundred ten pounds on my five-foot-seven inch frame, I was not some behemoth needing large doses. My goal on antidepressants was to be able to get up off the floor and care for my children. In that sense, the meds were effective.

During a family therapy session with Carol at the hospice center, my children were assigned to draw pictures. Instead, they got distracted by a big marble-track setup. They rolled marbles along the track while Carol and I talked.

"I have never seen anyone with as much support as you have," Carol said in amazement. That was quite a statement coming from the hospice bereavement director with twenty-two years of experience in grief counseling.

"You mean, you haven't seen anyone as messed up as me?!" I joked feebly.

"No, I mean the support you have. Your team is incredible." Carol was characteristically no-nonsense in response to my attempts at humor, which were minimal at best early on.

"Well, that is to God's glory," I acknowledged.

"That is how the church is supposed to operate," Carol observed.

"I feel guilty that I am still so trashed even with all of this support."

"But you need it and God knows that." Always the encourager, Carol never agreed with me when I was hard on myself.

"But you know what?" I hated the lesson that I was being forced to learn. "God is teaching me that even if I was in Banda Aceh [one of the sites devastated during the Indian Ocean earthquake and tsunami on December 26, 2004] with no house, no family, no church, and no fancy therapist, Jesus would still be worth clinging to."

"Fancy therapist?!" Carol questioned.

"Yeah, didn't I tell you? My mom calls you my 'fancy therapist.'"

"Why?" Carol questioned with a puzzled look that replaced her usual empathetic expression.

"When I tell my mom about all the support I have with counselors and grief groups, she tells me, 'We never had any fancy therapists when I was a young widow!' So, Carol, that makes you my fancy therapist!" I pronounced triumphantly as I laughed. Carol always had a subdued and moderate response to my usual weeping, scarcely consolable state, so I was not surprised that her response to my laughter was subtle as well.

Along with Carol's help, one of the therapies that really helped me was meeting with members of my church prayer team for sessions of Theophostic prayer. The concept of Theophostic Prayer Ministry (E. Smith, 2008) comes from the Greek roots for *theos* (God) and *phostic* (light). Basically, this was time spent in Christ-centered prayer, relying on God to shed His insight into my emotional wounds. My prayer team encouraged me to continue and deepen my personal relationship with Jesus Christ in the midst of my emotional turmoil. The two intercessors helped me face my pain in prayer; they prayed for God to reveal the truth to my heart and mind. We prayerfully reviewed the wounds of my childhood, delving into the traumatic memories surrounding my father's death. God blessed me with Bible verses and new perspective as He comforted me in the loss of both my father and my husband.

Another grief group I joined was GriefShare, a grief recovery support group that incorporates videos and a workbook. Facilitated by volunteers, the series is presented nationwide. Although GriefShare is faith-based, atheist and Buddhist members of my group enjoyed the program as well.

Some of the wisest practical advice I ever received about grieving came from the GriefShare videos.

During this time, I continued to see Carol on a weekly basis. "Now is not forever," Carol read one of the hospice center's therapy mottos to me as I stared at the quote on the bulletin board.

"It *feels* as if this will last forever," I moped.

"You will have a future."

"I don't see it. I can't even imagine having joy again."

After my young widowed parents' group completed a year of sessions at the hospice center, we went on to a monthly group called Step by Step. Vicki, another hospice therapist, facilitated this group, which combined the widowed parents with other widowed people. Vicki pushed us beyond our comfort zones to get us to face life again. Rather than discuss our children's grief, which we widowed mothers usually reverted to, Vicki forced us to focus on ourselves.

One of Vicki's assignments was to brainstorm the activities we wanted to accomplish and write them on individual sticky notes. Then we were supposed to display the notes in a prominent place and begin working on them. My brainstorming notes eventually moved across the country with me and hung inside my bathroom cabinet as reminders of what I could do. For example, I took a community education cooking class and reconnected with my former roommate Barb.

I called Vicki the "kick-me-in-the-butt" therapist, and I started seeing her for one-on-one sessions. She helped me to recognize who I was before Lee died and to correlate that with who I still am. She helped me explore moving options, discuss dating episodes, and venture out into new activities.

Her assignments were tough, but reflected an awareness of what I was capable of doing.

One of my assignments was to host a dinner party for twenty people. That was no big deal when Lee was alive, but I did not believe that I could do it without him. To my surprise, I accomplished the task and enjoyed it. I hosted a potluck for the widows and children from our hospice groups—halfway through a floor remodel and with a non-functioning toilet on the main floor. In our focus on eating together, we were slow to notice that our dog Cooper jumped up to the counter. Cooper ate half of the chocolate silk pie before we stopped him, a feat we laughed over repeatedly. The kids made it to the upstairs bathroom in time, our hospice group members had fun together, and I recognized the old me starting to emerge.

[18]

Fence Butt, Butt Slides, and French Kisses

TERI, MY BIBLE STUDY FRIEND from church, chauffeured for my therapy appointment one afternoon, and we shared precious time together without children. Teri, Joanne (before her family became missionaries in Germany), and I had participated in a cooperative preschool together with our youngest children. As moms, we had grown close to each other and to all of our children, but, other than the preschool, our time together had been limited to short greetings at church. Not until Lee's death did our friendships grow beyond our love of children, becoming deeply personal.

As she drove, Teri and I commiserated about being in the sisterhood of the fatherless. Teri's father had died when she was an infant; all that she knew was life with her widowed mother. As her words sunk in, I realized that I straddled both worlds: the widow club with Teri's mother Madeline and the sisterhood of the fatherless with Teri. Madeline was a role model to me, a prayer warrior from my former church whom I had met in Bible study. I always looked up to her, but never thought I would someday walk in her shoes. The dreaded "W Club"—nothing I ever aspired to or wanted to join.

Clouds churned in the sky above us as Teri drove home through varied patches of rainy and sunny weather.

"Do you tell your kids to look for rainbows in weather like this?" I asked.

"No," Teri said. "I don't tell them to, but we do."

Just then we noticed a huge, low, fat rainbow stretching east to west over San Jose. Looking toward the eastern hills, I asked, "Where do you think it ends?"

Teri smiled serenely without answering.

"Well," I asserted smugly, "it's either over your house or mine or church, and I choose to believe it's over all three."

When we reached my driveway, Jamie greeted us with Kylee in her arms. "Do you have a key?" she asked worriedly. "We're locked out."

I never thought to take a key! In this strange new life of mine, people were always coming and going through my crowded household. I smiled inwardly as I retreated to memories of other times our family had been locked out of the house.

One of my favorite locked-out incidents occurred while I was in labor with Bennett. The hospital obstetrics ward was full, so the staff asked me to wait for a bed. I was trying to keep the contractions going, so I went out to the stairwell to pace up and down. Lee had to speed his pace to follow me as I marched up the stairs with the vehemence only a two-week-overdue pregnant woman could muster.

A nurse tracked me down and asked, "Do you by any chance have a mother and a toddler who are locked out of the house?" Lee grimaced at the realization that, in his haste to flee the house, he had locked all the doors, leaving toddler Claire and my mother in the backyard. Totally absorbed in my memory, I smiled as I remembered Lee's stunned face.

Abandoning my precious recollection to return to the present, I answered, "It's okay. There's a spare key hidden on the other side of the fence."

This would involve some effort, as the key was hidden behind the locked seven-foot-high fence door. Jamie stood there holding six-month-old Kylee in her arms. I demurred, feeling like a princess who could not be asked to do anything. After all, I had just worked on my new motto of "It's not my responsibility" during my therapy session.

"I'll do it," Teri said eagerly. So she stood on the gas meter and then jumped up to meet the fence at waist height, as if mounting a balance beam. Only that is where any similarity to a graceful gymnast ceased. Teri got stuck halfway over the fence as she stretched down to open the gate's locked bolt. She teetered precariously with her stomach wedged against the top of the fence.

Jamie and I looked at each other helplessly. Jamie held the baby in her arms. In my weakened state, I knew I could, at most, be a bag of bones to cushion Teri's fall. Looking up, we both stared open-mouthed at Teri's small posterior in that slow-motion moment before she fell.

Jamie suddenly let out a "FENCE BUTT!" warning cry. We both cracked up, stepped back, and (selfishly!) kept laughing as Teri fell straight down onto her backside.

"Are you okay?" Jamie and I called out simultaneously, even as we continued to laugh.

"I'm okay," Teri assured us.

"You better be," I joked, "because I don't have worker's comp for my team!"

When we finally got inside the fence, the house key was difficult to remove from the underside of the downspout where Lee had hidden it. That was so typical of my Lee, duct taping the key so tightly that we almost did not get it off. I was the one who finally yanked the key and tape off the gutter. I thought wistfully about how his hands had last touched that duct tape; not much more in my life would have last been touched by him.

The next Wednesday morning at Bible study, Teri was reading announcements from the podium when Jamie leaned over from the row behind me and whispered in my ear, "Those are her fence-butt pants!" It was all I could do to stifle a burst of laughter at the memory of a small, teetering fence butt high above me.

My Bible study friends shared humorous moments with me in the midst of challenging times, but God also brought laughter from unexpected sources.

One night Lee's high school classmate and swim team buddy John called me up. I could tell that he was missing Lee, because he talked about their usual topics of interest: the progression of interest rates since the 1980s, Alan Greenspan's tenure and its effect on US and foreign economies, and the Asian economic crises of 1997–98. Try as I might to keep up with his brilliant train of thought, I was maxed out by the time John mentioned M1 and M2.

"John, I don't even know what that is! I've never had an economics class."

At that point John realized that he had lost me. He was hoping I could discuss the issues like my MBA man, but that was not my arena. It was an interesting window for me into what the guys must have discussed at our dinners. Whereas I had rarely spoken with John before Lee died, his wife Laura and I had shared interesting, long discussions on topics like children, thyroid glands, cancer, and remodeling projects.

John finally gave up on the economics review and asked whether I had found help with financial matters. Prompted by concern for our family, he relayed a few widow horror stories about financial mismanagement to me. I told him about my practice of hiring people who were twice removed from my social contacts to manage my finances. I described some of my decisions, and he supported my choices.

Then John switched gears to talk about Lee. "Lee could be so mature and yet so immature."

"What do you mean?"

"Well, he had his whole life planned out, and he knew what he wanted to do after high school. But then he could be so immature, too. Did you hear about the swim team in the locker room?" John laughed.

"Lee told me that you guys used to do butt slides in the showers."

"Yeah, but Lee came up with a unique twist on it," John laughed louder now.

"What do you mean?" I wondered how much technique there could possibly have been in executing butt slides in the gym showers.

"He didn't tell you?"

"Not really. He just said it was really funny. What did Lee do?"

"Well, if *he* didn't tell you, then *I'm* not going to tell you!" John laughed again, maintaining his loyalty and keeping Lee's butt slide technique secret. Then he added, "Do you have *any* idea what a lady killer Lee was?!"

"Well, I always thought he was gorgeous," I gushed.

"He was such a lady killer in high school. Believe it or not, people got us mixed up back then," John said with disbelief.

California blondes with swimmer's shoulders and incredible tans—I am sure those boys got lots of attention, as Lee did for decades, staying youthful and fit into his mid-forties.

"Girls used to come up to me and ask if I was Lee," John continued, "and I would answer, 'I'll be Lee if you want me to!'"

Just one day after I heard about my "lady killer" husband, our carpool guy Mr. J called to tell me that my seven-year-old son had tried to French kiss a girl after school. Appalled, I assured Mr. J that I did not condone such behavior, nor did I know where Bennett had gotten this idea.

Once off the phone, I got angry at Lee for the first time. "Okay, *Mr. Lady Killer!*" I shouted to the heavens, "This is supposed to be *your* job!"

Of course, when I nonchalantly asked Bennett where he heard about French kissing, he innocently replied, "From Claire."

Claire had heard the french kissing definition from her Minnesota friend. The reactions of my two children vividly illustrate the difference between boys and girls. Given what she had heard about French kissing, Claire asked me relevant questions, either to clarify or to find out about how it applied to Daddy and me.

Bennett, on the other hand, heard the information and in a testosterone squirt (as I call it), had to check it out. So he chased after a girl at school with his tongue hanging out and yelled, "Let's French kiss!"

I was appalled that nobody had told me. At that point I was participating in the carpool and showing up at school several days a week. I wondered why they did not tell me. Because I was the poor widow who did not need more bad news about her kids? So her kids could continue to misbehave?! I asked Mr. J to please tell me when things like that happened, because I needed to correct my children. Bennett and I talked about his inappropriate behavior after school, and then he called to apologize to the girl he had chased.

Alone in my room afterwards, I yelled at the wall again, "Lee . . . *Mr. Lady Killer!* You leave me to handle the kids by *myself?!* I told Bennett he can't French kiss until he's in love with someone in college. *Ha!*"

[19]

Grief Hurdles

LOOKING BACK to the first week after Lee died, I remember my continuous mental review of that horrendous scene in my mind. My brain replayed the events over and over, like a living-dying horror movie that would not release me: Lee's vomiting, diarrhea, loss of consciousness . . . CPR, calling 911, waving down the ambulance . . . his body lying there, patches hooked up to the monitor, paramedics all over my bathroom, a crowd around my husband, the gurney in my hallway . . . walking into the ER, the ER waiting room, hearing the news of his death, spending time with his body in the cast room. My thoughts recited the details repeatedly, adding torturous questions. *What happened? What did I do? What could I have done? Could they have saved him? Did this really happen?!*

The trauma had not yet fully penetrated my conscious mind. Numbness and shock would be my protective friends for weeks, even months, as the harsh reality had to work its way slowly through my mind. Only months later, once the adrenalin storm had worn off and my conscious thought had begun to process the reality of my loss, did I start to notice Post-traumatic Stress Disorder (PTSD) responses. "Triggers" are what I called the events that elicited in me the fight-or-flight response. Initially, the triggers did not necessarily penetrate my conscious thoughts; I just responded physically with PTSD symptoms. I would suddenly break out in a sweat, feel my heart racing, and become anxious. These episodes pounced on me without warning. Much of this I explored with my therapist Carol.

After a while, I learned to recognize my triggers; this was my first step to overcoming the PTSD. These triggers were not necessarily conscious memories. For example, the sole of a firefighter's boot could set me off. Early on, I did not specifically remember a firefighter's boot from the night Lee died, but that memory later came back violently with PTSD symptoms.

One night my kids and their babysitter jumped and played in their shoes and coats in my bathroom, leaving footprints in the tub. Later, my kids long asleep, I came home and noticed black footprints in my bathroom; once again, the searing pain of Lee's death washed over me. A mere footprint, but it brought back all the trauma. Crying in fear and panic, I slumped onto the floor as I relived the CPR scene.

Another time, we were at our church's family camp when the worship team's bass player Jeff had a stroke. The paramedics were attending to him in his tent. As I walked over toward his wife Mary, I saw the paramedic's boot sole at the door of the tent. I felt the by-now-familiar panic rising up in me, complete with fast, thumping heartbeat and sweat running down my neck. Taking deep breaths, I kept walking toward Mary. Pushing past the panic, I was intent on getting to Mary. I cried out to God nonverbally, and He miraculously gave me the strength to ignore my memories, join the assembled group, and start the prayer for Mary's husband. God answered our prayers with Jeff's miraculous recovery; within weeks, Jeff returned to play bass for the Sunday morning services.

With every PTSD event, I tried to identify the trigger and then breathe and pray through my symptoms. One night as I was driving our babysitter home, I saw a fire truck in the middle of the road with lights flashing. I recognized it as a trigger; the fire truck memories from my traumatic night were ready to erupt. After becoming aware of the trigger, I breathed deeply and told myself the truth. *That is not my fire truck. They are helping someone else. Not my husband. Not his ambulance.* Somehow, it helped ease my symptoms, my heart rate calmed, and I drove the babysitter home as usual.

In terms of PTSD and triggers, I braced myself for the class to renew my advanced cardiac life support (ACLS) certification. I knew no one in the class, and I gave myself permission to run out of the class if need be. Sure enough, a trigger presented itself on the test. One of the first questions read, "You come across a forty-five-year-old man who became unconscious after a heart attack." I felt the panic rising up in me as I thought through my personal answer to the question. *You do CPR and ACLS but nothing helps and your life will never be the same again.* Then I breathed deeply and told myself that this was not Lee; it was just a question on a test. I forced myself to answer the question factually and move on to the next question. Problem solved, until I came to the CPR recertification station. Doing CPR on the mannequin did not bother me; after so many years of nursing, this was routine. However, as I was doing the sequence of compressions and breaths, I looked at the mannequin. These dummies did not have the usual flesh tones; newer models, they were gray in color. Suddenly the gray hue reminded me of Lee's color as I performed CPR on him. It was the color that triggered my speeding heartbeat, sweating, and lightheadedness. The tears rolled down my cheeks, but I kept my head down and continued as the instructor evaluated the group's performance. Once again, I recognized the trigger, felt the symptoms, and breathed through it.

The PTSD triggers were usually recognizable to me, and the symptoms became familiar. Occasionally, something new set me off, but I became less debilitated each time. Years after Lee's death, while backing out of my driveway one dark early morning, I saw my neighbor on a gurney being loaded into an ambulance. The lights flashed in the dark, and memories of that night returned to me. I knew this trigger and started talking to myself. *It is not your ambulance, not your husband, not that night. Look at him, he is breathing and talking to the paramedics. He is okay. It is not Lee.* With deep breaths, I shook off the panic and drove away.

Activities that forced me to face my grief, but did not elicit symptoms of PTSD, were what I called "grief hurdles." Often, these seemingly ordinary events loomed large in the shadow of death and loss. Something as everyday as walking into the master bathroom could render me incapacitated, because it was the site of Lee's heart attack. Jamie stood by me as I faced that early grief hurdle of using my bathroom again, just hours after administering CPR to Lee in the same place. After facing that, my bathroom did not bother me.

I like the term "grief hurdles" because it reminds me of my high school track days and my unsuccessful attempts to run hurdles. I would face the hurdle, think through the strategy, plan out my steps, lope out at a predictable pace, reach the necessary height, but still hit the wood with my trailing leg. No matter how hard I worked, what strategy I tried, or how helpful my coaches were, clearing the hurdle was tough. I usually ended up with a bruised knee, if I was left standing at all. In the same way, grief hurdles were things I knew I had to get past if I wanted to live a life that was not debilitated by grief. I could choose to face grief hurdles . . . or not. It required courage to deal with the challenge head on, and—just as you cannot change course above a wooden hurdle—so it is with a grief hurdle. Once committed, you have to complete the task, even if you wipe out or smash a knee. And you need to do it yourself.

Even now, I face my grief hurdles alone, irrespective of what goes on in others' journeys. Just as in hurdling, looking over at the next lane while grieving is irrelevant to the measured steps I must take. Hurdles are spaced at equal intervals, but since the runners have staggered starts in the longer races, the hurdles are set at different points around the track, depending on the individual lane. In the lane of my life, I may face a hurdle at a certain point, while my neighbor's lanes are free and clear of obstacles. Succumbing to the temptation to change lanes and avoid my hurdle would disqualify me. Similarly, I cannot jump into someone else's life lane to circumvent my personal obstacles. My lane, just as my life, has hurdles designed and spaced for the race I am running. I cannot focus on someone else's lane; I must face and run my own course.

One early grief hurdle was making coffee again. A coffeepot is just a small kitchen appliance—until your world is turned upside down. In that hypersensitive dimension of grief and loss, I recognized the symbolism of our coffeepot. Lee and I both loved coffee, and sharing a pot was a morning ritual we savored. We would joke about racing to the pot to fight over the last cup. On Lee's days off, he did not want to get up early with me, but he usually set the automatic timer to make a pot of coffee for my early morning Bible time. Oh yes, the appliance had been used after Lee died. Relatives had used it and washed it. But not me. Just looking at that coffeepot unhinged my tear ducts, as I recognized that my dear Lee's act of coffee service to me would never happen again.

Kim, a dear friend and our church's youth pastor, stopped by on a Wednesday afternoon to visit. Since Kim would be teaching the junior high youth and would need energy that night, I offered her a cup of coffee. As a hostess, I mustered my strength to face the pain of my coffeepot.

"Do you want me to make it?" Kim offered willingly.

"No, I have to make it."

"I can make it if it's too painful."

"No, it's something I have to do, or I will never make coffee again."

"Okay. Whatever you need me to do."

"If you could just stand by while I face this . . ." I described the significance of drinking coffee with Lee as I pulled out the container of coffee. The coffee was a special home-roasted blend my Sunday school co-teacher had given me for Christmas. The joke was that we needed more than caffeine to keep up with the wild second grade boys' Sunday school class we taught. That everyday, normal life of a Sunday school teacher seemed so far away; simply making a pot of coffee seemed impossible now.

"I don't even know how to make half a pot," I sobbed as I poured the water into the coffeepot for the first time since Lee had died.

"That's okay," Kim encouraged as she gently hugged me. Her calm presence gave me the assurance that I could get through it, and her shared tears over a simple cup of coffee helped me clear a huge hurdle of grief pain.

"Do you know that God says you are twice held?" Kim asked.

Shaking my head no, I listened intently as Kim explained her statement. "Yes, you are twice held. Let me read this to you from John 10:27–30, 'My sheep listen to my voice; I know them, and they follow me. I give them eternal life, and they shall never perish; no one can snatch them out of my hand. My Father, who has given them to me, is greater than all; no one can snatch them out of my Father's hand. I and the Father are one.' Do you hear how it is two hands that you are held in?"

Although a familiar Bible passage to me, I had not previously understood the symbolism. Kim presented the metaphor of being twice held: once in Jesus' hand and then again in the Father's hand. That reassurance of not being let go, by either my heavenly Father or by His Son Jesus Christ, was the safety net I needed to hold me up. Kim let me cry on her shoulder as she reassured me with God's Word.

One grief hurdle that I did not want to face was running again. Lee and I ran for our first date and many other times throughout the next two decades. I thought that the memories and loneliness would be too great for me to be able to run again. One day I grabbed my running shoes and attempted to put them on the closet shelf, thinking I would leave them there forever.

"Do you want to clean the dog poop off first?" my friend Linda, another of my co-op preschool mom friends, asked in her warm, gentle way. An occupational therapist by trade, Linda was a member of my team who walked with me and encouraged me to get outside often.

"Okay," I growled as I noticed that the shoes were dirty. I disdainfully picked the shoes up, stepped out to the backyard, and tried to wipe them off in the grass. The excrement was dried on and, as much as I stabbed at it with a stick and sprayed water on it from the hose, the shoes would not clean up. The effort and the grief exhausted me, and I slumped onto the concrete patio in a puddle of tears.

Then I realized, as any runner knows, that the best way to get dog poop off your shoes is to run it off—so I marched into the house. "Linda, let's go for that walk," I managed through gritted teeth and tears.

Another grief hurdle overcome. I knew that the next time, those shoes would not be so difficult to face. And someday, I would be strong enough to run again.

One February day, Daphne and her six-year-old son Zechariah—the son she was pregnant with when I was pregnant with Bennett—came over to walk with us. Both of my children wanted to go to Penitencia Creek in nearby Berryessa Park where they had last been with Daddy. Not so long before, we had enjoyed our usual family outing at the park, with the kids on bikes, Lee on scooter, and me running. He would take the kids down to the creek and let me run laps around the park as a workout. That would never have sufficed as a workout for him, so he usually ran later after we got home from the park. I still remember Lee smiling at me as I returned from my laps to see him and the kids playing. Idyllic. Now a far-gone memory.

Ouch. Facing those memories was another grief hurdle. But facing it with Daphne and Zechariah helped. My kids commented on what they had done and where, in the park with Daddy. They lived in the moment: running, laughing, and playing in their favorite park with their friend. Theirs was not the grieving, memory-retrieving outing that pierced my heart as we walked.

Back at the house, other experiences elicited memories to grieve through. Inconceivable, that a pantry could be a source of pain, but when I was grieving, everything hurt. One night, after Maryanne, my mentor mom and meal co-ordinator, completed the kids' bedtime help, I was ready to face another grief hurdle.

"Maryanne, thanks for putting the kids to bed. Could you help me in the kitchen?" I asked, grabbing a grocery bag.

"Sure. What do you need?" asked my logical and efficient friend Maryanne, who was just the team member for this kind of help.

"Can you take some of these groceries home?"

"Don't you want to keep the food?"

"No, I just want to get rid of odds and ends I know I won't use." More specifically, I needed to get rid of Lee's food items.

"Are you sure you don't need that?" asked Maryanne, as I started filling the grocery bag.

"This is Lee's 'spicy' as the kids call his Tabasco sauce. I don't need it now. . ." I trailed off in a stream of tears at the realization that Lee and his Tabasco sauce were gone. The salsa, Tabasco, beer, jalapenos, and tortilla chips—all of Lee's favorites were pulled off the shelf, out of the fridge, and out of my life. So much to relinquish. Agonizing memories. Overflowing tears. Another grief hurdle cleared.

[20]

Toothbrushes and Transitions

JANUARY 22, 2005

Lord, today I threw out his toothbrush.
My husband of almost nineteen years,
Taken away from this earth in a mere three hours.
God, you may be sovereign, but I still don't get it.
I miss that toothbrush parked next to mine.
How many times did we stand side by side
accomplishing such a mundane chore?
An everyday little chore that we thought nothing of.
As usual our idiosyncrasies revealed our differences.
Solid, unwavering Lee brushing consistently
according to his routine.
He stood firm, unwavering in front of the mirror.
Then there was me.
I squeezed the toothpaste from the middle—
splotch!

Lee was irritated and could not understand why I
couldn't just roll it up meticulously.
"See, like this," he said, using the handle of the toothbrush to flatten the toothpaste tube repeatedly.
"Big deal," I thought, holding firm to my squeeze in
the middle.
Then there was my technique:
Brush vigorously, but don't stand in one place.
Oh no! I was on the move—on the go.
Pacing, multitasking as I brushed my teeth.
Lee could not relate to that technique.
Sweetheart, today I moved my toothbrush to your
spot.
Silly to make a shrine of where your toothbrush
parked.
Yet, so much of me wants to save everything I have
from you.
I love and miss you so much, Lee!
But thanks for giving my toothbrush the closest
parking spot.

Writing helped me cope with my difficulty in throwing out Lee's toothbrush, as well as with other frustrations. In Job 16:2, Job rebuked his friends for being "miserable comforters." When well-meaning friends similarly made clueless comments, I documented them in my journal. I tried to record my interpretation of the origin of these comments, with the recognition that what seemed like heartless jabs were actually misguided words prompted by concern. Thus I wrote, thinking that if I could write my reaction down, the nasty responses would never come out of my mouth. People were not being cruel on purpose; they just did not think before they spoke.

These are some unintentionally hurtful comments offered by friends, family, and acquaintances.

"Oh, you look so bad! I saw your face, and you look like you are ninety years old." This was actually shock and concern, not criticism, from a dear friend.

"You look good."

Now really, are you lying or saying that to compliment me?! Why does it matter how I look? Sometimes it took only a little makeup and people felt better about looking at me.

"This shock could put you into menopause!"

And who would care at this point?!

"What should I do with this? Where do you want me to put it?" she asked insistently, interrupting my phone conversation as she waved the funeral dress in front of me.

Now there is a dress I do not want to see again.

"You should be PTA [Parent Teacher Association] president next year. You'll really get the vote now."

How nice that my friend and fellow PTA member did not have her life turned upside down. Although I sat on the PTA board as secretary, my new parenting responsibilities eclipsed my school priorities.

"Oh, I got this sexy red nightgown for my birthday. My husband loved it."

How nice. I may never have a husband or sex again. Do you really have to rub it in?!

"How are you?"

I knew this question was motivated by concern for me. My responses were usually "Surviving" or "Today is okay" or

"It's tough." I could never fake feeling better. The kids hated hearing my "Surviving" answer, but I thought it was the most realistic way to answer the ubiquitous question.

"I wonder what her faith will be now." A friend of mine overheard this comment at my children's school.

Faith is the only thing that I hang onto now.

Then there were painful written words that stabbed my hypersensitive wounded heart. A mailed ad for a credit card, with rewards that came addressed to Lee, proclaimed, "Your everyday life just got more rewarding."

Yeah, every day in heaven must be a lot more rewarding than anything Lee ever experienced on this earth. His life, but not ours.

Slogan on Lee's favorite breakfast cereal: "May help reduce the risk of heart disease." I had to remove that box from the cupboard quickly, because it smacked me in the face with the reminder of Lee's heart-healthy diet.

This slogan was printed right next to his name on a subscription offer: "We miss you and want you back."

I agree.

"We invite you to return to our upcoming Family Life Marriage Conference in San Jose—" I rudely interrupted the phone caller to mumble that I was a widow and please take my name off the list. Then I hung up and dissolved into tears.

One painful item was our dual-alarm clock, which dated back to 1986. Merely an inanimate object, the clock radio represented years of awakening together. The dual-alarm feature symbolized our marriage: although set for two different schedules, it functioned as one unit. Lee was my partner, the other alarm on my clock. We were set to the same station, yet not always in synchronization. A bit of a relic electronically, the appliance nevertheless still worked well. Because it was a reminder of waking up with Lee, I knew I had to change it. So I bought a single-alarm clock radio/CD player. The kids and I sat on my bed as I took the alarm clock out of the package and tried to figure out how it worked. Bennett, taking on Daddy's role of Mr. Electronics Expert, crawled under the bed and figured out how to get the cord threaded through the headboard.

Along with the alarm clock, I made another change in the master bedroom. The quilt my mother had sewn us for our tenth wedding anniversary was washed and stored away for our children. In its place on my bed, I used a thrift-shop special. Such a deal for a summery, pale floral, queen-size quilt, but after I treated the stains and washed it, many small rips appeared.

The classic, cream-colored, quilt background matched Lee's dress shirt exactly. That was *the* dress shirt, not that he did not have more, but this shirt was worn only to weddings, reunions, and other occasions that necessitated a sports coat—and that was usually under duress. He was most comfortable in running shorts and a singlet, not ties and sports coats. I cut up the shirt, along with some fabric scraps from projects I had made for Claire's bedroom, and I patched the quilt. This "new" quilt lay on my bed, awkwardly patched and pieced by hand, not unlike the pieced patchwork of my awkward new life. But what a precious investment of my time and treasured memories it represented.

Many of Lee's items were boxed and saved for our children. Ratty old T-shirts, which Lee had refused to part with, were now relegated to heirloom status. He was likely in heaven laughing at my sudden preservation of what I had previously begged him to throw out. Items not saved were given to friends and family or donated to thrift shops.

The distribution of Lee's items pervaded my thoughts and dreams. One of my vivid dreams had my parents, Lee, and me sitting together when Lee asked where his inversion boots were. Every time we had moved, Lee set up a pull-up bar in the garage, where he did sit-ups and pull-ups in his inversion boots. In my dream, I was horrified by the realization that I had given away items that Lee needed. I agonizingly tried to remember the thrift shop where I had donated Lee's boots, and I panicked at the fear of not finding them.

Whether donating Lee's possessions or making a purchase, I often faced strange and difficult challenges. One of the memorial keepsakes I purchased required some of the "cremains," the cremated ashes. I was scared to open the urn, so I called Emily, my friend who could handle anything and everything, to come over and stand by. I had been forewarned that the ashes can be more than just dust; they may contain larger bone fragments. I was hesitant as I opened the urn and pulled out the plastic bag. Removing the cable tie, I was surprised to see only the finest of sand. Not even a lump or coarse grain; it was only ash. Only the identifying marker from the funeral home was in the bag; otherwise it looked like mere tan dust. I carefully poured out the cup of cremains I needed into a plastic zipper bag, trying not to think of the significance of the dust settling onto my fingers.

It is not Lee, I told myself. He was in heaven, and this was just leftover nothingness. Ashes to ashes; dust to dust. I closed off the plastic bag and returned it to the urn.

"Thanks Emily. Sorry to call you over, but I thought I might melt down and need help to get through this. It wasn't as bad as I thought." Once again, what I thought for sure would cause a meltdown was not as difficult as anticipated. A widow never knows when the ambushes of grief will come.

Later I went to the post office with a package, mailing off the cremains to be preserved in a souvenir. With my energy returning, some days I felt ornery, and this was one of them. I wanted to bite someone's head off—preferably someone who was nicey-nice or nosey-nice. I wanted someone to ask me a question, just so that I could be nasty. I imagined such a conversation, although mailing my package was business as usual without any small talk.

"Oh, what are you mailing today—Christmas gifts already?" the nosey-nice counter clerk might ask.

No, just my husband's cremated remains, I wanted to snap back irritably. My fantasy whorl of self-pity seemed strangely soothing. At least it kept me occupied in the usual long lines at the Berryessa Post Office.

But no. The only questions I got were the usual ones. "Do you need insurance on that?" she asked sweetly.

"No," I answered calmly, stifling the urge to add a comment. *You couldn't reimburse me for what this is worth.*

"How fast do you want it to arrive?" the clerk continued.

From my grieving time warp, I wanted to scream. *Time, as well as nothing else, matters anymore!*

"Any flammables?" she asked.

"No," I said, biting my tongue on an additional retort. *It's already been flamed. Ashes to ashes; dust to dust.*

"Any valuables?"

"No," I lied. *It is priceless, but nothing really matters anymore.* How do you wrap your grief, or perhaps your last shred of coherent thought, around the fact that you packaged some of your husband's ashes and mailed them across the country?!

Even though I had only ashes left of Lee's physical body, I had his wedding band, and of course, my own rings. Another transition to consider was how long to wear my wedding rings, a very personal decision for widowed people. In Germany, a widow wears her ring as well as her husband's, moving them from the traditional married position on the right hand to the left hand. I remember my Oma, my German grandmother, wore her rings that way for the rest of her life. Other cultures have different traditions. I knew that I could not wear my rings forever, because I needed to save them for my children.

Ever since I said goodbye to Lee in the hospital, I wore his ring on my left hand. His ring was so huge that I had to wear it closest to my hand. The rings clanked against each other as his ring rolled around on my finger. Lee's ring hit my rings so often that it knocked a diamond out of my wedding band. When I decided to take my rings off at about ten months out, I chose to make a personal ceremony of the event. I went to the little chapel at CCCM, where I knelt before the rustic wooden cross, the diamond ring I had worn for over twenty years relinquished in half an hour.

October 4, 1985. Lee proposed to me as we sat on the couch in my townhouse living room. In the dim light, Lee pulled out the sparkly diamond ring that fit me perfectly, just like the man who came with the ring.

On our wedding day, March 22, 1986, Lee proudly put the second ring on my finger, a half gold, half diamond-studded band that interlocked and matched up with the engagement ring of the same pattern. The rings symbolized how our lives were intertwined as husband and wife.

November 29, 2005—the day my rings came off. My twin niece and nephew's third birthday. My cousin's twenty-eighth birthday. That day should also have been my Air Force nurse friend Chellé's forty-fifth birthday, but her life had also been cut short, robbed by a brain tumor that took her life in 2004 at age forty-four.

I set aside that particular day to commemorate an ongoing relationship that no longer existed. What I believed was destined for at least sixty years lasted less than nineteen. *Nothing I can do about it. The marriage is over.*

And so the wedding rings—mine worn for over twenty years, and his on my left ring finger since January 7, 2005 in the hospital—came off. The symbol of an ongoing, vital relationship would be replaced with living, loving, lasting memories. As I knelt before the cross, I cried and read chapter fifty-four of Isaiah aloud. God is my maker and now, my husband. Then I read 2 Samuel 24:24: "I will not sacrifice to the Lord my God burnt offerings that cost me nothing." So I removed our rings and placed them at the foot of the cross.

"My God, I surrender. I sacrifice it all to you." I offered it verbally and physically with my free will, although it had all been swept away from me without my choosing.

Closing my eyes, I recited my wedding vows aloud, flashing back to the first time I had done so. I ended with "until death do us part." I acknowledged verbally that my marriage to Lee was over. I prayed for the ones who would wear those rings next, that they would be blessed by God.

Tears and pain. Waves of grace and grief, grief and grace (as my friend Jane had so eloquently written) at the foot of the cross. The cross was the ultimate sacrifice, I realized. My Jesus sacrificed for me.

"Thank you, amazing God. Forgive me for daring to compare my sacrifice. It does not begin to compare." Then, emotionally spent and cried out, I waited for what God had to say.

The Aaronic benediction from Numbers 6:24–26, used to close Lee's memorial service, was my answer. I read it aloud to myself, needing to hear and absorb what I heard. "The Lord bless you and keep you; the Lord make his face shine upon you and be gracious to you. The Lord turn his face toward you and give you peace."

I knelt—blessed by God, crushed by pain, weakened by sacrifice, and in awe of the incredible gift of Christ's sacrifice on the cross.

[21]

Life Is Not Fair

"LIFE IS NOT FAIR, but God is good." I first came up with that pronouncement when my preschoolers wailed about perceived injustices: one of them got less ice cream in the dish or fewer turns on the swing than the other child. I would assure my precious offspring that the egregious offense was perhaps not equitable in outcome, but in the scheme of the big picture, God is still worth serving. Little did I realize that our family motto would challenge me for years to come.

"Mommy, why didn't a homeless man without a family die instead of Daddy?"

"Mommy, that man is fat and wears oxygen. Why doesn't he die of a heart attack instead of Daddy?" (Thankfully, this was out of earshot of the person toward whom she had expressed jealousy.)

"Mommy, if Daddy was so healthy, how could he die of a heart attack?" My eight-year-old presented never-ending questions that wounded me to the core. The fading freckles across the sweet porcelain of Claire's pale skin hinted at the inevitable, upcoming external changes that would occur whether Daddy was present or not. Claire's ever-precocious level of understanding, combined with this life trauma, gave her an "old soul" character that was unsettling. *How could I answer her questions, when I was asking God the same things?!*

"Life is not fair, but God is good," became my standard response. I tried to explain to my children that we do not know why God does what He does, but He is worth trusting anyway. Then I would run to my prayer closet and cry out to God with the same agonizing questions.

I stopped asking *why* questions early on, though. Given my strong will, I know that if God told me why, I would not like the answer. My thoughts were so self-centered. *Who cares if people come into relationship with Christ because my husband died? I want my husband back. So what about anybody else?!* That was the pit of my selfish core expressing itself. I knew it was wrong, but I could not stop the egocentric pain. I knew that it was not my job to ask why, much less to understand the master plan. My job was to be obedient in the face of much pain. So I started asking God to help me obey, even when I did not understand. That was a painful realization for me to process, and even more hurtful to communicate to my children.

Sometimes I just needed to be alone to think. My first walk alone to nearby Berryessa Park was a milestone. Nobody was available to walk with me that day, so I went on my own, trying to beat the distant storm clouds. So many recollections of walking to the park throughout the last nine years flooded over me. My tears rolled as distinct memories threatened to overwhelm me.

Stepping along the flood-plain berm, I looked up at the green hills and remembered the same walk with Lee when I was pregnant with Claire. April of 1996. I was days overdue, and we had tried to imagine what life would be like as parents.

Memories discharged in wounding assault: Baby-joggers—single, and then double. Bennett on his tricycle on the sidewalk. Toddler Claire throwing rocks into the stream with Daddy. Roller blades. Scooters. Bikes. Running with Lee when our kids were finally in school. Milestones. Transitions. Basic, everyday family life. I grieved the loss of all of them as the tears flowed freely. So many memories. So much of our future cut short. *I miss you, Lee.*

Six weeks after Lee died, I put the kids to bed by myself. My occupational therapist friend Linda hung out for standby help. I was proud to accomplish the bedtime routine without assistance, but also grateful that Linda was there for potential backup. Lots of tears and sadness, but I did it. Later I went to bed—more sobs, despondency, fatigue. The physical and emotional exhaustion threatened to consume me. My thoughts still reflected my pain.

> *Journal entry, February 17, 2005.*
>
> *I do not have the will to go on. I only have the Way, the Truth, and the Life. Lord, please take me to be with you. I can't do this, God. I don't have the will to live. Take me to be with you. Lord, both Lee and I had a hard time handling these kids together. How can I do this alone?! I can't, Lord. If somebody else could do the kids, so I could be with Lee.*

I spent a fitful night of interrupted sleep, even after prescription and over-the-counter sleeping aids. By morning, I just wanted to die.

At 7:00 a.m. that morning, the phone rang. It was John, a man from church I did not know, but I recognized the last name. He and his wife had been in our church newcomers class, and his daughter had worked with our kids in Sunday school. He spoke of Jeremiah 29:11, assuring me of God's future and hope for me. I was stunned at the incredible gift of encouragement that God sent me through this essential stranger. I told John that I had lost the will to live, but his words were helpful to me. I hung up the phone, shaking my head in stunned awareness of how God had brought His love and hope to me from such an unexpected source.

On my first day all alone without any help, I poured my heart out to God in my journal.

> *Journal entry, February 18, 2005.*
>
> *I just ache. Heavy, searing pain that shreds my life apart. Deep, agonizing sorrow that sweeps across every aspect of who I am. Piercing loneliness and overwhelming fear threaten to overtake me. Sweet Jesus, you paid my ransom. This alone is too much for me to handle. I cannot comprehend the cost of the cross. In love you paid that cost for us.*
>
> *I, in my anger, attempt to push through this, but I am stilled. "My grace is sufficient for you, for my power is made perfect in weakness." 2 Corinthians 12:9. Oh, but the rest of that verse is too hard for me: "Therefore I will boast all the more gladly about my weaknesses, so that Christ's power may rest on me." So hard to do!*

Verse ten is even more difficult: "That is why, for Christ's sake, I delight in weaknesses, in insults, in hardships, in persecutions, in difficulties. For when I am weak, then I am strong." The ironic nature of an Almighty God who dwells in puny, imperfect people.

Lord, sorry, but I'm not delighting in this. I am filled with excruciating pain at the loss of my Lee. God, please fill me with you.

Almost two months after Lee died, there were still people who did not know about the events in our lives. One day when Jamie and I walked to the park, we were stopped by a neighbor.

"Hi there!" she called out as she walked toward us with pruning shears in her hands.

"Hi, Ada!" I responded. To the kids, I referred to her as The Rose Lady, because of the incredible rose garden she grew along the sidewalk.

"Hi. How are you?" Her breezy reply indicated, as I feared, that she had not heard our news. I had not had to tell anyone about Lee since those first few days after he died, and I dreaded it.

"What's new?" The Rose Lady asked breezily.

"I don't know if you heard what happened to us, but . . ." I stalled initially and then blurted out, "Lee had a heart attack and died in January."

Her face distorted as she cried out vehemently, "Damn! He was like family to me!"

"Really?" I mumbled, recognizing that she knew Lee only through short talks as he ran by or walked to the park with the kids.

"And then there is my old man who has had lung cancer for six years, and he's still smoking and he keeps going." Her acerbic words cried out at the injustice of a young father's death. All I could do was clam up, fight the tears, and walk on, leaving yet another person to grapple with the *whys* of life and death.

One day I was chatting with our mail carrier as I picked up the mail while dressed in my running clothes.

"Hey, what ever happened to the guy who was always running around here?" she asked. "I haven't seen him in a while."

"Which guy was that?" I asked. The pit of my stomach churned in recognition of whom she was asking about.

"The one with the cute tush!" She answered enthusiastically.

"That was my husband Lee. He died two months ago of a heart attack." I choked out the words as her face twisted in horror. She protested that it could not be true, given how he was in such good shape. I concurred with her and gave her more of the details. The mail carrier went on to tell me about the brief, frequent conversations she had enjoyed with Lee. I smiled with the realization that my husband had touched many lives, even with short conversations on his way to the park for a run. As always, the *why* question was left hanging in the air, unanswered and indescribable.

March 3, 2005 was Lee's birthday, our first one without him. I let the kids decide what we were going to do. They decided to celebrate Daddy's birthday with a chocolate cake. After the hospice grief group meeting, the kids were excited to bake a chocolate cake together. All I could do was cry at the thought of all the cakes I had baked for him in the last twenty years. Ice cream cakes. Raspberry-filled layer cakes. Chocolate layer cakes. Airplane cakes with chocolate chips for bombs. Special cakes for my love. So many memories. So many tears. My shattered heart ached for a forty-sixth birthday that would never be.

The kids decorated Daddy's birthday cake with frosting and tubes of gel, alternately fighting and having fun globbing, squeezing, and smearing. I took a picture of their masterpiece. Stabbing knives twisted into my bled-out heart. *Where is our guest of honor?! How can he be gone?!*

Both kids insisted on singing "Happy Birthday." That really sliced me sideways, and I dissolved into tears by the end of the song. Bennett began to cry and came over to sit on my lap. Once consoled, he went back to dig into his piece of chocolate cake. Then Claire, whose face had been distorted in pain as she repressed any verbal acknowledgment of her grief, came to sit on my lap. She shed no tears (oh, my sweet Daddy's girl!), but at least she accepted comfort from me.

After several months of manna, our miraculous provisions came to an end. I slowly transitioned from relying on others—and becoming tearful at something as simple as a baked cake—to taking full responsibility for my children's nutrition. I resumed making dinner for the kids, but I took lots of shortcuts.

"You're a terrible mother!" Bennett said, shaking his head at the cold cereal on the table one evening. "Where's dinner?"

"This is it." I said firmly, adding, "Daddy always said he'd be fine with peanut butter and jelly sandwiches or cereal for dinner." I did not mention that I found Lee's comments abhorrent, because I worked hard to ensure that dinner was nutritious and, most often, homemade. Oh, how low the proud me had fallen.

As I reminded Bennett, "You had eggs, fruit, and toast for breakfast. Your lunch was hot lunch at school, and this dinner of cold cereal and melon is nutritious." I still felt guilty. *The old me would never have done that.*

Other reminders of my changed life came in the mail. Lee's biography from the memorial service was revised to fit the USAFA alumni magazine obituary requirements. In the past I had read those obituaries and felt sad for the amazing young lives cut short. Here I was, living a life of loss after my husband's life ended too soon.

I cried out to God in my pain. *Lord, it was not too soon for you, was it? You knew from the beginning of time that Lee would be here for just forty-five years. Oh, but Father, I loved Lee for a lifetime, not just for the twenty-one years I knew him. I said "in sickness and in health," but I did not expect death. Thank you, Lord, for a marriage without regrets. God, it was not perfect, but no marriage is. Lord, what a gift Lee was for my life!*

Even after expressing my beginning level of acceptance to God, I was still incensed that our marriage was not lifelong, as we had expected it to be.

After the kids went to bed, my nights loomed long and lonely. I often changed into pajamas early and lay on the bed reading. Instead of tackling household chores, I read in bleary-eyed exhaustion. I usually ignored duties like writing up PTA minutes in favor of "curling up with Jesus." That is what I called my time spent with Jesus when I came to Him in abject loneliness, despair, and exhaustion. I grabbed my

Bible, fought the tears, and prayed for Jesus to curl up with me and show me something in His Word.

One particular time God communicated with me, not from His Word, but with a question that dug into the depths of my heart. *Remember the pictures of Dad?*

I was reminded of a previous conversation with my sister Rebecca when she had asked, "You know how we each had pictures of us with Dad in our rooms?"

Sifting through my childhood memories, I recalled the pictures she spoke of. Petite, cute Rebecca sat on Daddy's lap on the bow of his coworker's boat. Daddy's loving arms stretched around Rebecca in an image frozen forever by the 8 × 10-inch print that hung in her room—a picture that bore witness to a father's love for his daughter.

Then there was the picture in my brother's room: Daddy, the toddler Fredric, and our Great Dane puppy in a candid action shot. A man, his boy, and a dog: family fun and contentment, captured and preserved for all time.

"No, I never had a picture of Daddy and me in my room," I answered my sister in quiet contemplation as I recognized the inequity for the first time. My sister remained quiet in surprise as she realized that truth.

I never pursued that thought again until God brought the question to my mind. *Why do you think that you did not have a picture of you and Daddy displayed in your room?* My sovereign God continued as He spoke to my heart.

"Because I was so ugly!" I retorted immediately. I remember a picture that always hung in our hallway of Daddy with his arms around both of us girls. All three of us were laughing. I had always hated how I looked in that picture.

Pre-braces, my crooked teeth stuck out all over the place. My overbite was so large that I could not close my lips around my teeth. "Bucky" was the nickname the school kids had used to torment me.

I realized that I had always assumed that I was too ugly for a picture of Daddy and me to be hung in my room. God gently touched me with the realization that this was an outright lie. (Plus, now as a widow, I understand how "widda brain" could have been the reason that I never ended up with a Daddy picture in my room. "Widda brain" is a term coined by my online widow support group to describe the absent-mindedness that results from the trauma of losing a spouse. After all, it took me three years to get pictures of Lee and our children hung up in their rooms.)

I began to sob, and I asked God the Father to replace the lies with the truth. I prayed that He would show me how I am a loved child of His.

I did not come up with any specific memories of my father loving me, but God did encourage me. After Bible study the next morning, I came home to an answering machine message from my Grandma Biltz. When I phoned her back, I was once again encouraged by her perennial optimism. She mentioned that she prayed for me regularly, which I assured her that I needed and appreciated.

"I wish I could do more for you," Grandma said wistfully.

"Well, Grandma, can you do me a favor? I need to hear that Dad loved me," I requested, choking back the tears.

"Oh, Tina," she said, the compassion and concern flowing out of her aged, gravelly voice. "Don't you know how much he loved you?!"

"Can you just tell me?" I asked, obviously crying.

Grandma went on to speak about the love, joy, and pride that her son—my father—had shown for the three of us children.

Another affirmation from God to me. Another father wound healed by the comforting touch of God.

Life is not fair, but God is so good.

[22]

Baby Steps

"BABY STEPS," my grief therapist Carol would often say when I told her what I was doing or complained about how slowly I was moving forward in my grief. As a runner, all I could think of was how my life was such a far cry from my former pace. I used to run—and run—through life. At this point I had to take baby steps. Just as short walks had become the extent of my exercise, normal activities of daily living were almost too much for me to deal with. For the first three months, I was lucky to accomplish combing my hair once a day. I remembered to shower only when I needed a place to wail uncensored, in peace and away from my kids. Everyday tasks seemed to require herculean efforts.

When the doctor allowed me to start driving again at about five weeks out, I was terrified. Daphne came along with me for the first drive, carefully monitoring my stress level and watching to see if I had any tremors. What a relief it was to be able to drive my car with my kids again. They were excited to have Mom back in the driver's seat, even if it meant I was the one forcing them to go to their despised counseling sessions.

Sometimes when I felt overwhelmed, I sat at the piano to plink out my favorite hymns, "I Need Thee Every Hour" and "Be Thou My Vision." One day as my fingers struggled through the notes of my favorite 1970s worship song, "For Those Tears I Died" (Stevens-Pino, 1971), Bennett came and joined me. I told my son that after my father had died, nobody in my family talked about him, except for Grandma Biltz. We did not have counselors or anything like that, so I just cried at night, grieving alone in the darkness of my room. While explaining this to Bennett, I suddenly realized that the song "For Those Tears I Died" had become my childhood anthem of God's presence throughout my grief.

Besides baby steps, another "Carolism" I learned to live by was, "Just put your toe in the water." Swimming into life again was overwhelming, and Carol helped me make necessary changes in small strokes. As my strength returned, so did my desire to deal with my household. I got to the point where I wanted to do things myself and not have so many people coming through the house.

My team was supportive as I eased back into life. I gradually let go of my daily team support and transitioned to full care of my children. At first, the team backed off from full-time help to provide only homework and bedtime help. After a couple of weeks, we transitioned to on-call help only. I called for help several times when I was overwhelmed with sibling rivalry and unable to cope with screaming kids. My children and I were so fragile that little frustrations quickly accelerated into emotional blowouts. When I resumed putting them to bed by myself, I felt that routine and family life, albeit not yet normal, were returning to our household. Carol, as always amazed by the assistance I received, guided my decisions about how much help I needed and how to ease back into my role as mother.

One night the kids were in my bedroom wrestling. It was like old times: they ran, somersaulted on the bed, jumped off the furniture, and tore around my room. In the midst of their carrying on as usual, I realized that nothing seemed the same as before. I missed Lee so much that I just lay on the floor and cried. Claire grabbed Daddy's picture and set it next to me.

I cried all the more, telling her, "It's okay to cry. And if you want to cry, I'll hug you and be here for you."

Claire shrugged me off with her usual retort, "I don't want to cry. I don't want to be sad."

The next day I went shoe shopping for the kids. I was overwhelmed and felt incapable of normal life responsibilities. But children's feet do not stop growing. Their lives continued, even as mine had stagnated. Their needs pushed me to accomplish activities of daily living, even when I preferred to curl up and die. Carpools to school, extracurricular activities, counseling appointments, homework help, laundry, groceries, bill paying, and yard work—I gradually resumed my responsibilities, even though much of it was accomplished with numbness and low energy.

Whenever I felt as if I were getting back to some semblance of normal, a grief hurdle would set me back. On March 22, 2005, what would have been our nineteenth wedding anniversary, I took the urn of Lee's cremated ashes into the empty chapel at my church. Heavier than it looked, the urn was my last connection to Lee's body.

As I held onto the urn of my husband's remains and approached the altar in the chapel, I considered my women's Bible study from that spring. Our women's group had delved into Beth Moore's (1995) study on the Old Testament tabernacle, and I was absorbed in the study of the sanctuary, sacrifices, and burnt offerings. At that moment, I could not stop making the comparisons between the Bible study and my own life. A firstborn male without defect—a pure, unblemished ram. My beautiful, unblemished husband. No, Lee was not perfect, but he was the best of what I had to give. Lee was God's best gift to me and the charred remains of his earthly body were the sacrifice I offered. This gift was a sign of my devotion to a God I did not fully understand, but whom I completely trusted.

I spent twenty minutes kneeling before the table under the chapel's rugged wooden cross. Initially, I clutched the urn to my heart, but then I placed it upon the table, releasing my vestige of control over a gift that ultimately, and for eternity, belonged to my Savior.

I sobbed as I read Genesis 22, the biblical account of Abraham taking Isaac up the mountain for the sacrifice. Bible readings present such an apparent compression of time. As Abraham journeyed with Isaac and the servants, they were on the road for three days. Then Abraham and Isaac continued up the mountain without the servants.

Trudge, trudge, trudge up the hill. What conversations took place? How heavy was Abraham's heart? Was Isaac a clueless teenager?!

That January and February of 2005, I felt as if I understood a bit of the ache and pain of the seemingly interminable trudge up the mountain. Yet here I was, offering my prized treasure to my Creator. I cried and prayed through the three pictures of Christ hanging on the chapel wall: at His baptism with the dove, at the well with the Samaritan woman, and washing a disciple's feet.

Then I read Psalm 71:20–21: "Though you have made me see troubles, many and bitter, you will restore my life again; from the depths of the earth you will again bring me up. You will increase my honor and comfort me once again."

Happy anniversary, Sweetheart.

After processing my jumbled thoughts with God's Word, I picked the urn up off the table and brought it back home. *Closure with the urn. For now.*

That night our church held a Seder, the Jewish celebration of the Passover meal. A French gentleman from Chosen People Ministries led the service. Dressed completely in black, I cried intermittently. I vacillated between aching for Jews to come to *Yeshua HaMashiach* and for the loss of what March twenty-second meant to me. The service was respectful, yet so painful. The salty tears and bitter herbs of the meal felt like my current lot in life. I mentally rewound to past anniversaries spent with Lee. I projected what we would have been doing together and felt the stabbing loss of future anniversaries. This anniversary was a date never to be celebrated again, a relationship never again to be savored. So much of me was gone forever.

Easter Sunday had been my goal as the time to come out of my mourning period. At least that is what I planned when

Easter had seemed far off. Christ's resurrection, new birth, new life, God's promises kept. I decided to put some effort into how I looked, which was easier said than done when I had the energy and self-confidence of a worm. So I forced myself to put on a skirt, apply makeup, wear jewelry, and style my hair for the first time since the memorial. I still felt lousy, but was amazed at how many people assumed that I was doing better just because my exterior was polished.

Claire, Bennett, and I had our picture taken in front of the flowered Easter cross in the church courtyard, as was our tradition. Standing five feet tall, the wooden cross was covered with chicken wire. Every Easter, people brought flowers to tuck into the wire, and by second service, the cross was covered with a glorious array of blooms. We stood in front of the cross, a family of three, right where our family of four had posed the previous year. Claire wore her Disneyland souvenir necklace, a dolphin on a black cord. Her flowy, light blue, tie-dyed blouse was a definite contrast to her pink track pants and tennis shoes. Bennett, still in his dress-up phase of age six, proudly wore his thrift shop black tux with white dress shirt. I leaned in to hug them, as we all put on our half smiles to continue our annual Easter picture tradition.

After church we returned home for our annual family Easter egg hunt. I dreaded the event, remembering all the times the four of us had enjoyed this special family time in our backyard. I feared choking up at missing Lee, but I knew it was important for me to continue family traditions for the kids' sake. As usual, my anticipation and dread were worse than the actual event. The kids squealed and had a great time searching for candy, chocolate eggs, chocolate rabbits, toys, and a few small gifts. I realized, but did not care, that I was futilely trying to compensate for the pain by spoiling them with a lot of material items. The proportion of parental time spent purchasing and hiding the stuff as compared to kid time searching it out was obscenely unbalanced—a typical irony of parenting that I could no longer share and laugh at with my husband.

Another change we faced as a family was selling our high-mileage, older car and buying a different one. When the dreaded day came to sell our twelve-year-old station wagon, Bennett and I washed the outside of the car after I had cleaned up the inside. The three of us prayed together before I drove the car over to the Wheels and Deals lot in Santa Clara.

"We still have all the memories. It's just the car we are selling," I told the kids, well knowing that, of the three of us, I would have the hardest time letting it go. So many memories. So much love and care represented by all the time Lee had poured into that car. Or, I should say, he poured into his family by providing such reliable transportation for us.

Lee and I had planned to run that car into the ground before buying another vehicle. I agonized over going against the plan we had established.

"You are making decisions with Lee on your shoulder. What would he want you to do now?" My counselor Carol urged me to think in the here and now.

"Well, he would want me to have reliable transportation. But I feel guilty spending so much money."

"Given your current circumstances, what would he want you to do?" Carol had a gentle way of pulling me into the present, even as I tried to stay mired in my past.

"I know it's different now. It is so different. I need to sell the old car and get something newer and safer for the kids." As always, Carol let me vent and explore what and why I was thinking. Sure, budgeting with a dead guy, based on a family that no longer existed in that form, sounded crazy, but that was not unusual for a widow in the throes of grief.

After some review and Carol's gentle prodding for me to be objective in my plans, I decided to buy a new car. I decided to go with the "widow car broker," as we called the salesperson who brokered cars for several widows in our hospice group. I ended up with a gold-colored Honda Pilot. It seemed only fitting: once upon a time, I had a golden pilot—then I had the car.

Carol told me that my life would start to be doable, then manageable, then even worthwhile to live. As my mother told me, "The change is so slow as to be imperceptible."

I felt as if I had to relearn how to do everyday things on my own; but as the everyday tasks became more manageable, I started to tackle additional responsibilities. From there, I took on extra challenges, like fixing things on my own. One of the first things to break down was my vacuum cleaner. I wanted to call someone or just buy a new vacuum cleaner, but then I remembered Lee's words. He was the master fixer of all, and I would ask him in amazement, "How do you know how to fix that?!"

Lee's standard answer was, "You just *look* at it."

In remembering Lee's words, I mustered the energy to look at the vacuum cleaner. Sure enough, I recognized what the problem was—the beater brush was wrapped in wads of golden retriever fur. I cut out the fur balls and the vacuum cleaner worked. I felt like such a handywoman. "Just *look* at it!" became my home-repair motto for success, helping me tackle everything from screen doors to toilets.

Our family of three began to venture on outings together in the new car. Jen, my co-leader for our Bible study small group, invited us over for dinner one night. My kids had a great time holding five-month-old Keefe. When that novelty quickly wore off, they hung out with Jen's husband Kevin, while Jen and I visited.

"Jen, this is so nice. Thank you. It feels so good to be invited out, almost as if we were a family again." What I found interesting was that we had met Jen and her family after Lee died. Unlike most of our other friends, these new friends spent time with us without missing Lee.

"You *are* a complete family to us—a family of three." Jen's words were such a gift to me; they marked the first time that I thought our family of three could ever be normal.

[23]

The Sadiversary

MY FIRST SADIVERSARY

The long-awaited day: one full year of widowhood.
This is truly a mile marker in my journey of grief—
A point I never thought I would reach.
A seeming lifetime from my onset into grief hell.
I turn around from the mountaintop
To look back down the precipice of this past
  interminable year.
I remember how I toiled up this climb:
Mincing steps, marked by shooting pains,
Knife-like wounds into my heart as I stopped to wail
  in agony,
Gasping air as I reminded myself to breathe,
Surviving just minutes at a time when the path was
  unbearably rocky.
Steep, steep portions that reduced me to a sobbing,
  imperceptible crawl.
How did I survive this fated climb?!

So much of my journey enshrouded in fog,
Held up and urged on by a loving God.
Stretches of agonizing trail where God carried me.
A year of excruciating pain stretches behind me.
An incredible goal reached by my puny efforts and
God's amazing power.
After commemorating my traumatic first year,
I turn my head to face the future.
I inch my way to the top of the mountain ridge.
I look ahead, and what awaits me?
Unending ridges of an entire mountain range!
Oh sweet Jesus, please lead me on.

Shortly before the one-year mark of Lee's death, or the first "sadiversary," as it was known in my online widow community's parlance, my tear faucets once again became uncontrollable. As self-absorbed in my grief as I was, I was also tentatively poking my scrawny neck out beyond the end of my marriage to consider what would come next. I was suddenly sole parent of Claire and Bennett, who were only eight and six years old. Sole parent, sole provider, single mom—so many *alone* words. Alone words in a lonely life in a world where I was out of sync.

Before Lee died, I knew my role, had my place, and did my job as wife, mother, and homemaker. Years ago, I had transitioned from my career world—nurse, researcher, teacher—to mom and homemaker. That was a monumentous adjustment: a sacrificial, life-altering, role change. Trading my professional world for mommy life had put me into a tailspin at the time. God's grace and Daphne's friendship pulled me through that transition. After Lee's death, both God and

Daphne were at it again, helping me cope with a different and much more challenging transition.

A new habit I started at the beginning and end of every day was to step out my back patio door and look up at the stars. It grounded me, thinking that Abraham had looked at the stars from this same earth. The constellations have remained the same over thousands of years. That sense of closeness to God and continuity on earth was reassuring to me. Life would go on for me, as it had for all those who had looked up at the stars in previous years, decades, and centuries. I was assured that God had nature under his control, even though my life felt out of control.

One aspect of my transition, another big grief hurdle for me to conquer, was planning for the first sadiversary. My friend Dori, a women's Bible study friend whose daughters babysat for us, came up with a great idea. After much persistence, she received permission to plant a tree in Lee's honor at a nearby park. Dori and I met with the park supervisor and the ranger, who likely feared that we wanted some gaudy memorial. Convinced that we wanted nothing more than to add a native tree to the park in an inconspicuous manner, the two men showed us several options for tree placement. My responsibility was to water and fertilize the tree for three full years until it was established.

My sister, parents, and I enjoyed the scenic drive to the park-recommended nursery, Yerba Buena. Located in Woodside, California, they specialized in native plants and disease-resistant species. The nursery's tree expert gave us advice for our *Quercus lobata,* or valley oak. We learned that fertilizing and drip irrigation were not necessary for these drought-resistant, native California trees; instead, watering once or twice per week during the driest summer season was recommended.

After guidance from the ranger on where to plant the tree, we planned a family gathering to commemorate the event. Sentimental to me was the fact that the tree was planted near the park location where Lee and I always parted with a kiss when we ran together. Then he would begin his *real* workout and run the trail, while I would plod my tired legs back home.

On January 7, 2006, one year after Lee died, we gathered a small group of family and friends to plant the tree in Lee's honor. Dori's husband Bruce and Kelly's husband Jim dug the hole at the park before the rest of us arrived with the tree.

Several days before we planted the tree, I had discussed Bible verses with my children. Genesis 2:7. God formed man from the dust of the ground. Genesis 3:19. Dust we are and to dust we will return. Ecclesiastes 3:20. All come from dust and to dust all return. Psalm 103:14, 17. We are dust, but the Lord's love is with those who fear him.

As Bennett saw the clear plastic bag of Lee's ashes, he pleaded, "Don't use all of Daddy's ashes!"

"I won't," I assured him.

Bennett's contribution was crushed eggshells to use as soil amendments around the tree, as he had seen me do with my flowers. He also saved coffee grounds "because Daddy loved eggs and coffee." After Bennett dumped his compost into the hole for the tree, the kids and I used our fingers and added some of Daddy's ashes. Then Lee's sister Chris and her family, my parents, and my sister sprinkled more ashes into the hole, using either their fingers or the plastic spoon.

"Do the twins understand?" Claire asked with a poignant concern that tore at my heart. *Seven- and nine-year-olds should not have to spread their father's cremated ashes. It is not fair that they are forced to comprehend such a horrific fact of life.* I acknowledged Claire's recognition that her three-year-old cousins could not really understand what was happening, but then wondered to myself how the rest of us could comprehend the connection between these ashes and Lee's vibrant life.

Taking pictures took longer than the actual tree planting. While the tree was only a twig about as tall as Claire, we hoped that it would grow to stand sentry over the park for decades to come. The pictures show the three of us smiling, my arms firmly around my children, in an imprint of our survival one year after Lee's death. My smile appeared forced, my grasp around my children fiercely protective, and my frame no longer emaciated. Nine-year-old Claire had already passed my shoulders in height. Her hair, then grown to the middle of her back, was a windblown testament to her refusal to comb it. Yet Claire's cheetah-print pants, bright pink tennis shoes, and jaunty stance gave her a look more preteen than young schoolgirl. At seven years old, Ben stood tucked into my armpit, looking like a typical second grader with sweatpants, long-sleeved t-shirt, and toothless grin.

After planting Daddy's tree, we enjoyed my dinner of roast beef, potatoes, carrots, leeks, and salad. I love celebrating the way my family did that day: openly and honestly, albeit with pangs of grief, with our usual festive, holiday-type dinner, as we gathered around the dining room table.

We toasted champagne to Lee's life, with the kids lifting their glasses of milk to our crystal wine glasses (a wedding gift from Dennis, the fighter-pilot colleague who had eulogized Lee during the memorial service).

Talking with my children individually at bedtime that night, I was reassured that they were happy with how the events of the day had transpired.

"We honored his life," Bennett acknowledged with satisfaction. Both kids expressed the desire to go back regularly to picnic and take pictures. Bennett specified that he wanted only the three of us to go back together. When I asked if we could invite Grandpa and Grandma Carson for Daddy's birthday picnic at the tree, since they were on a trip and could not be there for the planting, Bennett liked the idea.

Previously, vandals at the park had destroyed other newly planted trees, leaving the sawed-off trunks behind. Malicious mischief, it was termed. I was concerned about vandalism to Lee's tree (that is, our twig), but my parents came up with a plan. Mom decided to pray for the tree, and Samuel suggested that Lee's guardian angel, now out of a job, could guard the tree. Not that I understood guardian angels, but I liked the idea.

After facing the sadiversary, my focus turned to the task of rebuilding my life. In an attempt to move beyond my tiny circle of kids and grief, I decided to take a community education class to learn Arabic. After taking the Perspectives on the World Christian Movement class at my church in 2003, I had wanted to become a missionary to women in Afghanistan. Studying the language would either fuel the dream or discourage it. Plus, I needed to get out of the house.

The class met at the high school near my house. There were several retirees in the class, but one of them took my breath away. He sat two rows up and two rows over from me, an average-looking man. In my grief-focused state, I noticed an uncanny similarity to Lee. On side profile, he had a strong jawline and rounded chin. A tanned face. An oh-so-worn wedding ring that looked as if it had been on his finger for half of a century. A head of graying hair that was beginning to turn white. Little glasses. Yes, I thought, Lee would eventually have had gray hair and glasses. This guy was such a type of what Lee would have—*should* have—been as he aged, that I had to look away. My eyes welled with tears, and I choked back sobs. As my tears dripped onto the desk, I debated running out of the room. *Breathe. . . . Just breathe,* I reminded myself. Slowly, I fought the urge to let the anger and grief swallow me once again. I committed to staying seated and facing my pain; I had to grieve the loss of my Lee as he would have aged.

Thankfully, when the man turned toward my side of the room, his eyes looked nothing like Lee's. Yet his neat, trim appearance, average build, conservative dress, and 1970s military-style haircut were consistent with my missing man.

After every grief hurdle I faced, there was always another one to deal with. In March of 2006, I faced the milestone of what should have been my twentieth wedding anniversary. I wanted to commemorate the significance of the event, yet I knew it would be a painful reminder of what had died with Lee. I wanted to push past the grief hurdle of vacationing alone with my children for the first time. I decided on a Caribbean vacation, something similar to what Lee and I might have done. I tried to prepare myself, though, for how different this kid-vacation would be from Lee's and my usual scuba-diving-in-paradise trips. This trip was definitely different, but also fun.

In the format of the popular MasterCard commercial, I summarized the ups and downs of our vacation:

IXTAPA 2006

An all-inclusive resort on the Mexican Riviera
  during spring-break season:
Mucho dineros.
Forgetting the birth certificates, missing the plane,
  and having to start our travel one day later:
Extra dineros.
First family vacation for just the three of us:
Precious.
Crying every day—on the balcony, at the beach, by
  the pool, in the restaurants, at the buffet:
Catharsis.
Sunburn, tan, and small, white hand patterns on my
  back, as sunscreened by a nine-year-old:
Hilarious.
Mole, chilaquiles, ceviche, seafood galore:
Delicious.
Siblings who actually played together without
  fighting:
Delirious.
Enjoying life with our sweet, joyful children on what
should have been our 20th wedding anniversary:
Priceless.

[24]

The River

IN MY EARLY MONTHS of widowhood, I felt as if I had died with Lee. The first year after Lee died forced my recognition that he was indeed *dead.* The truth of the loss had to penetrate every aspect of my life. Every layer of my physical and emotional being needed to be peeled away to identify what had been lost. During the second year, I realized that Lee *stayed* dead. He would never come back. I was alone and at times, oh so lonely. The third year after Lee's death, I focused on the fact that *I was still alive.* I did not die with Lee. I needed to allow God to rebuild purpose and joy into my life.

The treadmill of my life kept rotating, but I could barely keep up without tripping over my little rectangle of responsibilities. Looking ahead beyond my footsteps seemed impossible back then. Although I continued to heal, I still could not foresee the promises of Jeremiah 29:11, "'For I know the plans I have for you,' declares the Lord, 'plans to prosper you and not to harm you, plans to give you hope and a future.'" The future seemed painful to consider; I did not want to plan or even think about what was ahead for my family. As I focused on God's help for my everyday survival, I trusted that God held the hope and plans for my future, even though I did not.

Several months into widowhood, while meditating on David's cry in Psalm 22, I thought about how I would express my own cry to God.

CRY OF MY BROKEN HEART

Oh my God, how can this be?!
There was so much of me
Poured into partnership with Lee.
The depth of what became "we"
Grew grounded in the Trinity.

"Until death do us part"
I vowed with all my heart.
It was a God-ordained start.
So Lord, how do I peel apart
This union, your work of art?

I lost my backpacking guide,
The one who skied by my side.
All those double-diamond runs yet to be tried.
One flesh ripped open wide—
Oh my Jesus, the tears I have cried!

He is gone, my precious husband.
No more companion, lover, friend.
All too soon it came to an end.
And from all this, how can I mend?!
What is to be, oh God, my Sovereign?

Oh, how I miss my Lee!
No more of you and me.
I am now successor, trustee,
Representative payee.
Oh my God, what are you making of me?

Jesus, what becomes of me now?
And dare I even ask—how?!
Let me forget myself just now,
And reflect on the blood, sweat from your brow.
At the cross, I surrender and I bow.

Oh my Savior, what good can come
From heartfelt pain that makes me numb?
I want my loss to be undone,
Yet over and over you lead me on.
Oh my Savior, lead me home!

I was so lost that I felt hopeless; heaven seemed my only escape. Grief books do not specify time frames because the grief journey is so unique for each individual. In my experience, it took years before my energy returned. When the suffocating, circulation-stopping, life-ending, quick-sand sense of loss eventually eased, I applied my newfound energy to making changes. Grief therapy helped me to process my priority of parenting while grieving and to move on while providing stability for my children. Two-and-a-half years after Lee died, after much prayer and counseling to explore the *what now?!* phase of my grief, I decided to move back to my hometown in Minnesota.

Before any move, a lot of work needed to be done to sell my house in California. After a total of twenty-plus years of use and enjoyment by two families, the house needed to be rejuvenated. My first course of action was to spend over seventy miserable hours steaming and scraping the 1980s wallpaper from the ceilings and walls of most rooms in my house. Wallpaper removal was a project that Lee and I had intended to accomplish together, but never did. Other preparations required hiring extra help, sometimes multiple crews per day. Landscapers removed rotted garden boxes, cut down dying trees, and created new perennial flower beds. Interior walls were demolished, resurfaced, repaired, and/or painted. Flooring throughout the house was replaced. Thanks to God's incredible timing, the house sold after two offers and just eleven days on the market.

My team again helped me to accomplish what I could not have finished on my own. Katie, a friend from my old church, spent hours packing up my kitchen breakables. The only thing that broke was a crystal bowl I had wrapped by myself.

When several women from my Bible study group heard that I was swamped with household tasks, they asked how they could help. Seven women swooped into my house one morning. Each woman took a room, and I circulated with tape, boxes, and markers (and tears) as they packed up the rest of the household goods. Their packing assistance saved me days of work and allowed me to prepare my Bible study teaching for the following week.

As the seven women packed, I went into my son's room and apologized for the mess; but Susie had it all under control. "Don't worry about it. I have an eleven-year-old, and I know what it's like. I combined all the spy stuff and put it in this box. The foil ball is carefully packed in there. The Legos ended up here, and I put the toy cars all together in that box." Susie was a boy's room packing professional! I was so relieved. Dreams of breaking the world-record foil ball may be typical among young boys, but I did not want my kids to lose aluminum foil or anything else during this move. My team again cared for us, as they had before, beginning from the time of Kelly's help that first night, and faithfully continuing all the way to the move two-and-a-half years after Lee died.

After decades of living in many different cities, I returned to my hometown of Red Wing, Minnesota. Sold a house. Bought a house. Got rid of almost half of the household contents. Moved two kids and a dog two thousand miles across the country. Started life over with a few extra challenges along the way.

My "new" house did not have memories of Lee. The home was a fresh, neutral place that did not cause me to experience any flashbacks or pangs of remembered times with Lee. Being in a different community was also a fresh start. The fact that Lee was not in our Minnesota home was both the best thing (no painful memories) as well as the worst thing (new people could not reminisce with me).

The process of rebuilding my life continued. When I moved beyond functioning in survival mode, I finally paid attention to medical issues that I had previously postponed. A root canal and crown replacement cured my tooth pain. A lesion on my lower eyelid, possibly cancerous, proved to be benign upon biopsy. My surgery to remove two baseball-sized tumors produced quite a cancer scare, but thankfully they also were benign. After I recovered from surgery, I resumed working out with my YMCA buddies and skiing with my book-club friends. I bought a snow blower and learned how to use it. In my former days of lap-swimming with Lee, he had refused to teach me flip turns, fearing that I would crack my heel against the side of the pool. Resolved to learn new things in my new life, I took lessons from a swim coach and learned how to do flip turns. I worked on raising my children alone, making new friends, settling into the community, and discovering myself as a single woman.

As a single—or only—parent, my responsibilities had increased significantly, and, without my parenting partner, the fun times in parenting seemed much less exciting. Rich Ballo (2004), widowed author of *Life without Lisa,* gave me excellent advice on parenting while grieving. During his book signing, Rich advised me to join my kids. Despite my sense of overwhelming sadness, he suggested that I play with my kids, as they were able to disconnect from grief and enjoy life. That advice enabled me to join my children in times of fun and distraction.

When he autographed my copy of his book, Rich wrote the phrase "Never give up!" This became my rallying cry. Claire and Bennett were God's main reasons for me to continue on, and God used their lives repeatedly to encourage me and give me hope. Their growth and change became milestones that I learned to savor, knowing that Lee would also be so proud of them. He would have been proud of all of us as we transitioned to a different life in a new place.

The mighty Mississippi River anchors my hometown of Red Wing, Minnesota. For over 150 years, the river has provided stability in commerce and recreation to this town nestled into the bluffs. The Mississippi flows in an overall north-to-south direction throughout the midsection of the United States. However, just before the river courses past our town, it makes a sharp curve, the sharpest corner on the navigable portion of the river. From there the river wends its way, briefly northeast and then southeast, past Red Wing where limestone bluffs, carved by centuries of weather, overlook the town.

That river bend continues as a metaphor for my journey. After the big zigzag of changed direction in my life, I settled into the routine flow of raising my children in a small Midwestern town. I returned to my family, the "grief colony" of widowed people (grandmother, mother, stepfather) who loved me and had themselves navigated widowhood. Comparing loved ones to weathered limestone seems harsh, but that was how I viewed them. Constant and strong like the stable bluffs in our community, my family members' rock-solid faith in God inspired and comforted me.

Living near my extended family was a nice change from the separation of time zones and thousands of miles. Instead of being airline flights removed, I could be present during family emergencies, like the time my ninety-eight-year-old paternal grandmother was again hospitalized for chest pain. My Aunt Carolyn coordinated myriad logistics as Grandma transferred from her apartment to the hospital, and later from an assisted-living facility to a nursing home. At the end of Grandma's life, our family kept a bedside vigil as she waxed and waned, and then waxed again with strength that surprised us. After living through almost a century of joy and loss, Grandma remained an amazing example of faith and fortitude. She rallied several times in her typical bursts of energy, despite the fact that her organs were failing and medical care could offer her nothing more.

"We don't know how to do slow deaths," Mom quipped, "because our family has had only sudden deaths." Comfortable with our morbid humor, we laughed at the irony that several weeks was slow in our collective experiences.

Grandma slipped in and out of lucidity during her final days. Her last words to me were delivered with a faint twinkle in those ever-bright blue eyes as she weakly grasped my arm and held me close to her. "I really liked your husband, you know." The understatement of the phrase was obvious from her wry smile.

"I liked him too, you know, Grandma. I loved him."

"I did too."

"Grandma, please say hi to Lee and tell him that I love him." The squeeze she gave my hand was soft but definite. I knew Grandma understood.

After several weeks in the nursing home, Grandma died in June of 2008. At her funeral service, Pastor Stehr's words gave a profound summary of Grandma's life, "Behind every great woman, there is a great God."

What a legacy Grandma left for our family.

As He did for my grandmother, God has given me contentment and joy after loss. I am grateful for the innumerable blessings God has showered on my children and me. I try to slow down to appreciate God's handiwork, whether to savor a multi-hued, orange-red, full-sky sunset, or to wonder how cirrus clouds sketched on a cerulean sky puff like a windblown dusting of powdery snow. The sensational but fleeting beauty with which God paints the sky—present for just a short time—is to be appreciated and remembered, but not mourned forever.

Lee's role in my life now is memory, not relationship. A shirt I bought at a thrift shop—in my size and favorite color, no less—had these words on it: "For that which is boundless in you abides in the mansion of the sky." Lee is my life lesson of love and partnership that I hold close to my heart.

As I mentioned in his eulogy, I used to call Lee the "captain of my heart," but now God is my Captain, as Steve Fry's (1986) song "I'm Abandoned" proclaims. What I have, I give in honor to the Captain with a capital *C*. He is my God, and His perspective extends far beyond this earth.

So many tears and so much grief—the river of my sorrow coursed through my mind, my heart, and my life, changing me forever. As often as the tears flowed, so too did God's love, comfort, and support, sent through His precious servants to keep me afloat in the swirling current that had threatened to pull me under. The Father to the fatherless and defender of widows, as Psalm 68:5 describes God, has journeyed with me through every aspect of my grief. I am so very grateful.

Someday my life will transition to another river, in the heavenly city, described as "the river of the water of life, as clear as crystal, flowing from the throne of God and of the Lamb" (Revelation 22:1). As Psalm 46:4 proclaims, "There is a river whose streams make glad the city of God, the holy place where the Most High dwells."

Meet you at the river, Lee.

ACKNOWLEDGMENTS

Real names. Real people. Real actions of those who gave of themselves and of God's love. I cannot adequately express my gratitude for the love, service, and support showered on my children and me throughout our grief journey. Thank you so very much to everyone who helped us—those mentioned by name, as well as those who remain anonymous. May God reward you and bless you for all that you have done, as only He can.

REFERENCES

Ballo, R. (2004). *Life Without Lisa: A Widowed Father's Compelling Journey Through the Rough Seas of Grief.* Naples: Quality of Life Publishing Co.

Curtis Chapman, S., & Hall, M. (2004). "Voice of Truth" [Recorded by Casting Crowns]. On *Casting Crowns* [CD]. Beach Street Records.

Eldredge, J. (2003). *Waking the Dead: The Glory of a Heart Fully Alive.* Nashville: Thomas Nelson Inc.

Fry, S. (1986). "I'm Abandoned." Sparrow/Birdwing Music. Capitol CMG Publishing.

Glover, B. (2004). "You Were There" [Recorded by Avalon]. On *The Creed* [CD]. Sparrow Records.

Husband, E. (2003). *High Calling: The Courageous Life and Faith of Space Shuttle* Columbia *Commander Rick Husband.* Nashville: Thomas Nelson Inc.

Lewis, C.S. (1950). *The Lion, the Witch and the Wardrobe.* United Kingdom: Geoffrey Bles.

Moore, B. (1995). *A Woman's Heart: God's Dwelling Place.* Nashville: LifeWay Press.

Rice, C. (2003). "Untitled Hymn (Come to Jesus)." On *Run the Earth, Watch the Sky* [CD]. Rocketown Records.

Sharkey, S., Lesser, J., and M. Barry. (2011). Takotsubo (Stress) Cardiomyopathy. *Circulation, 124,* e460-462. Retrieved July 20, 2015, from http://circ.ahajournals.org/content/124/18/e460.full.

Smith, E. (2008). *What is Theophostic Prayer Ministry?* Retrieved June 8, 2015, from Theophostic Prayer Ministry: Celebrating the Presence of Christ at http://www.theophostic.com/page12414933.aspx.

Smith, M. W. (2004). *Healing Rain* [CD]. Reunion Records.

Stevens-Pino, M. (1971). "For Those Tears I Died (Come to the Water)" [Recorded by Children of the Day]. On *Come to the Water* [Vinyl]. Maranatha! Music.

Three to One (2004). On *Three to One* [CD]. Milpitas, CA: C3 Studios.

Made in the USA
Lexington, KY
10 March 2016